AIRPOWER OVER GALLIPOLI 1915–1916

Titles in the Series

Airpower Reborn: The Strategic Concepts of John Warden and John Boyd

The Bridge to Airpower: Logistics Support for Royal Flying Corps Operations on the Western Front, 1914–18

Airpower Applied: U.S., NATO, and Israeli Combat Experience

The Origins of American Strategic Bombing Theory

Beyond the Beach: The Allied Air War against France

"The Man Who Took the Rap": Sir Robert Brooke-Popham and the Fall of Singapore

Flight Risk: The Coalition's Air Advisory Mission in Afghanistan, 2005–2015

Winning Armageddon: Curtis LeMay and Strategic Air Command, 1948–1957

Rear Admiral Herbert V. Wiley: A Career in Airships and Battleships

From Kites to Cold War: The Evolution of Manned Airborne Reconnaissance

The History of Military Aviation

Paul J. Springer, editor

This series is designed to explore previously ignored facets of the history of airpower. It includes a wide variety of disciplinary approaches, scholarly perspectives, and argumentative styles. Its fundamental goal is to analyze the past, present, and potential future utility of airpower and to enhance our understanding of the changing roles played by aerial assets in the formulation and execution of national military strategies. It encompasses the incredibly diverse roles played by airpower, which include but are not limited to efforts to achieve air superiority; strategic attack; intelligence, surveillance, and reconnaissance missions; airlift operations; close-air support; and more. Of course, airpower does not exist in a vacuum. There are myriad terrestrial support operations required to make airpower functional, and examinations of these missions is also a goal of this series.

In less than a century, airpower developed from flights measured in minutes to the ability to circumnavigate the globe without landing. Airpower has become the military tool of choice for rapid responses to enemy activity, the primary deterrent to aggression by peer competitors, and a key enabler to military missions on the land and sea. This series provides an opportunity to examine many of the key issues associated with its usage in the past and present, and to influence its development for the future.

Drawn by Chris Robinson

AIRPOWER OVER GALLIPOLI 1915–1916

STERLING MICHAEL PAVELEC

NAVAL INSTITUTE PRESS
Annapolis, Maryland

Naval Institute Press
291 Wood Road
Annapolis, MD 21402

Library of Congress Cataloging-in-Publication Data

Names: Pavelec, Sterling Michael, author.
Title: Airpower over Gallipoli, 1915–1916 / Sterling Michael Pavelec.
Description: Annapolis, Maryland : Naval Institute Press, [2020] | Series: History of military aviation | Includes bibliographical references and index.
Identifiers: LCCN 2020016785 (print) | LCCN 2020016786 (ebook) | ISBN 9781612510231 (hardback) | ISBN 9781682475454 (ebook) | ISBN 9781682475454 (epub)
Subjects: LCSH: World War, 1914–1918—Campaigns—Turkey—Gallipoli Peninsula. | World War, 1914–1918—Turkey—Gallipoli Peninsula—Aerial operations. | Allied and Associated Powers (1914–1920)—Armed Forces—Turkey—Gallipoli Peninsula. | Great Britain. Royal Air Force. Squadron, No. 3 (Fighter) | World War, 1914–1918—Aerial operations. | Combined operations (Military science)
Classification: LCC D568.3 .P385 2020 (print) | LCC D568.3 (ebook) | DDC 940.4/26—dc23
LC record available at https://lccn.loc.gov/2020016785
LC ebook record available at https://lccn.loc.gov/2020016786

♾ Print editions meet the requirements of ANSI/NISO z39.48-1992 (Permanence of Paper).
Printed in the United States of America.

28 27 26 25 24 23 22 21 20   9 8 7 6 5 4 3 2 1
First printing

Book design: Alcorn Publication Design

Contents

ACKNOWLEDGMENTS

Any project of this scale comes with a debt of gratitude to a number of people. First and foremost, I want to thank Dr. Tim Travers for sparking my interest in this topic a number of years ago, when I was one of his grad students at the University of Calgary. He was working on *Gallipoli 1915* (Stroud, Glocestershire, UK: Tempus, 2001) and gave his graduate class access to the primary documents he had discovered. As an avid airpower historian, I was intrigued that there was nothing written about the air war, even though it was only a very small part of the bigger story. In a graduate course in 1997 I took up the cause, researched to the extent I could, and caused a panic for my advisor when I submitted a sixty-five-page paper for a thirty-page assignment. Without batting an eye, Dr. Travers said that I should either cut it down and make it into an article or expand it into a book. I received an A minus.

Fast-forward a number of years. I graduated from The Ohio State University with my PhD in 2004, after completing a dissertation on WWII airpower and the birth of the jet programs in Germany, Britain, and the United States. But I always wanted to return to my Gallipoli research and write the story. Dr. Jeffrey Grey at the Australian Defence Force Academy Canberra asked me to come down under to help them with an online master's program, and he gave me a few extra days in the Australian War Memorial archives, where I found some fantastic resources for my Gallipoli project. With renewed vigor, I was excited about resurrecting the idea and getting back to writing on the obscure topic.

By 2010 I had an idea, some resources, and some free writing time. I met with Adam Kane, now the director of the Naval Institute Press (NIP), and pitched the idea over a couple of beers. Three weeks later I had a book contract. I received some funding from my employer for further research, and was off to the races. The staff at the National Archives (Kew Gardens) was very helpful, as were the archivists at the Imperial War Museum in

London. I had further assistance from Ms. Than Ngyen, who helped guide me through the archives at Chateau de Vincennes, and who supplied more resources after my very brief visit. Dr. Emre Sencer at Knox College set me up with some grad students in Ankara at the Turkish Archives. After moving to Norfolk, Virginia, to teach at the Joint Advanced Warfighting School (JAWS), I was assisted by three Old Dominion University graduate students who helped me with translations and editing; in this regard, I offer my special thanks to April Eads, Robyn Headley, and Ilker Egri.

After a difficult three years at JAWS, where the leadership put little stock in the value of scholarly publications (although my faculty colleagues Dr. Greg Miller, Dr. Byron Greenwald, and Dr. Keith Dickson were very supportive), I returned to Air Command and Staff College at Maxwell AFB, Alabama. I was given the freedom and some research money to complete this project. I offer special thanks to my close friends and bosses Dr. John Terino (chair, Department of Airpower) and Dr. Paul Springer (chair, Department of Research) for their continued support and flexibility.

I also want to thank Adam Kane for his understanding and patience while I was writing. He was willing to take a chance on this manuscript when it was still in planning stages. I appreciate the support and patience of Paul Merzlak, formerly with the Naval Institute Press. I am especially grateful to Dr. Paul Springer, my friend and series editor at NIP. I hope this adds in a small way to your excellent series on military airpower.

Most importantly, I want to thank my family and friends for their support while I was teaching and writing, often at the far corners of the earth.

I visited Gallipoli with Dr. James Tucci, Dr. Kevin Holzimmer, and Dr. Richard Muller of the School of Advanced Air and Space Studies; we were able to walk the battlefields of Gallipoli. I cherish the times we had there.

I am grateful to all of you for your input, assistance, and patience; I could not have done this without you.

Dr. S. Mike Pavelec
Hope Hull, Alabama

AIRPOWER
OVER GALLIPOLI
1915–1916

Introduction

One hundred years have passed since the Gallipoli campaign in World War I. The bulk of the story has been written and re-written a number of times. This project is not an attempt to recount the broad outlines of the campaign, but to supplement them. In the many volumes written about Gallipoli, there is little reference to the audacity of the few airmen and fragile machines that plied the air in the contest; *Airpower over Gallipoli* adds the fascinating story of the airmen and their machines to the Gallipoli corpus.

During and immediately after the campaign, official documents recorded the struggles of the Royal Navy and ANZACS at Gallipoli and their ill-fated attempts to knock the Turks out of the war. The immediate analysis showed a lack of coordination and poor leadership, as well as insufficient supply resulting from an impossible logistics chain. The commanders were rebuffed and reassigned; a few were called to task over the failure at the Dardanelles. But in all the records, airpower only gets passing reference if at all.

In the years since, a number of outstanding works analyzed the campaign, the sacrifice, and the ultimate failure of the Allies at Gallipoli. The latest, and still the best, is Tim Travers' epic tome *Gallipoli 1915*, which devotes more than three hundred pages to a detailed account of the campaign on the sea and on land. But even Travers discounts the role of airpower in the campaign—he does not even mention any of the air commanders or their exploits. My quest is to address this oversight by shedding light on the first significant air battle of the war; indeed, the first in military history. I am fascinated by the role of airpower and the enabling function of the aerial weapon. This book demonstrates that airpower was important, interesting, and innovative, and that the record of the airmen and their aircraft at Gallipoli deserves its own record.

Based heavily on official documents and published government records, the legacy of airpower at Gallipoli is important for a number of reasons.

First, the basic chronology reveals that airpower played a significant role in the campaign, even if it was not enough to turn the tide. Second, the story follows a number of dynamic and influential leaders as they struggled to realize the promise of airpower in modern warfare. Finally, the employment of airpower over Gallipoli marked the expansion of joint operations, adding the third dimension of air combat to the tactical mix, even if they did not realize it at the time. Joint land, sea, and air operations during the Gallipoli campaign ushered in a new era of warfare, leadership, and planning that had (and continues to have) an important role in modern warfare.

Airpower over Gallipoli tells the neglected story of the aviators and flying machines that opened a new domain of warfare. The dashing, adventurous, and frequently insouciant air commanders were misunderstood, misused, and disregarded at the time, but they played an important role in the campaign and set the stage for joint military operations going into the future. Their courageous efforts paved the way for modern military airpower.

CHAPTER ONE

The Birth of Airpower

The idea of airpower was born in the first decade of the twentieth century. Between 1903 and 1909, aviation evolved from defensive observation to offensive maneuver. Balloons had been used for military purposes since the mid-eighteenth century; Napoleon had a balloon corps early in his military career.[1] Lighter-than-air craft—balloons, blimps, and zeppelins— evolved and were adapted for military purposes throughout the wars of the nineteenth century. Balloons were used in the American Civil War[2] and the Franco-Prussian War, and German zeppelins wrought havoc in Britain and on the Continent in the early stages of World War I.[3] But it was the advent of controllable, heavier-than-air aircraft that fundamentally changed the character of war.

On a sunny, windy day on Kill Devil Hills at Kitty Hawk, North Carolina, two unassuming American bicycle makers lifted off from the ground in an airplane of their own design. The Wright brothers were the first to harness controlled heavier-than-air flight on 17 December 1903.[4] The Wright Flyer was a unique prototype, built for the 1903 winter flight tests. The Wrights had tested earlier unpowered gliders, and even built a small wind tunnel to test aerodynamic theories. In the lead-up to the 1903 tests, they constructed their own gasoline-powered engine, finding none that suited their purpose on the open market. The engine, a four-cylinder inline power plant of their own design, produced 12 horsepower, and weighed 180 pounds. The engine powered a chain-drive system that rotated two hand-carved propellers in opposite directions to prevent instability. The fabric-covered wood-frame wings could be "warped" for directional control. The Wrights incorporated a rudder in the back and a canard elevator in the front for additional control. The prototype was only powerful enough to raise one of the brothers off the ground; Wilbur crashed the plane on 14 December, so it was Orville who flew the historic 120-foot flight. Although mankind was a long way from conquering the air, the first steps had been taken in powered heavier-than-air flight.

A number of aeronauts had attempted to master flight, but in 1903 the time was right for a convergence of the technologies that led to the successful Wright test. In Germany, Count Ferdinand von Zeppelin earned government contracts and poured vast amounts of his own wealth into lighter-than-air dirigible designs, his eponymous zeppelin airships.[5] Another German, Otto Lilienthal made significant progress in heavier-than-air gliding, but had not managed powered flight before his untimely demise in an accident in 1896.[6] In France and Britain experimentation began and continued on both lighter- and heavier-than-air aircraft with varied success. Industrialized nations, with their advanced technology, bred innovation in the air, but there remained a number of fundamental barriers for success. For lighter-than-air platforms (including both dirigibles and blimps) national efforts organized the vast sums of funding, aluminum metalworking for materials lighter than steel, and chemical manufacturing for the hydrogen that sent the ships aloft—to say nothing of the massive, heavy engines that powered the machines in the air. For realization of heavier-than-air controlled flight, innovators had to tap into the highest technologies of the time: light internal combustion engines, woodworking and fabric skills, as well as the nascent field of aerodynamics in order to construct air-worthy machines. Thus, while there were a number of adventurers working toward conquest of the air, the Wright Brothers achieved it first, and led the world with the first successful controlled heavier-than-air flight at the start of the new century.

Progress followed quickly. Aviation was and remains very expensive; early aviation companies depended on important government contracts or very wealthy investors—sometimes the experimenters themselves—for survival. The Wrights ran into difficulty when they could not secure much-needed government contracts in the United States. There was more interest in Europe and money flowed from national sources as well as wealthy entrepreneurs who funded experiments. Louis Blériot in France was one wealthy designer who combined a personal fortune with government contracts to eventually surpass the Wrights' accomplishments.[7] A successful engineer, he had made a fortune designing accessories for the growing French automobile market, including an improved headlight designed for the French automakers Renault and Panhard. Between 1905 and 1909, Blériot and another French aircraft designer, Gabriel Voisin, worked on a number of designs. Most were abject failures, but the men persisted. By 1909, Blériot had three flying prototypes: the Blériot IX, X, and XI planes. The Blériot XI became his most successful and significant design. The Blériot XI was a monoplane tractor design (engine in front), constructed predominantly out of wood and fabric. Like the Wright brothers, Blériot was unhappy with existing engines, but instead of building his own he turned to an Italian motorcycle engine designer. Alessandro Anzani fabricated a three-cylinder air-cooled piston engine that produced twenty-five horsepower. Another aviation contact built a laminated walnut wood propeller for the machine, contributing to its stability and success. The Blériot XI flew at an astonishing forty-seven miles per hour (more than seventy-five km/h). In July 1909, Blériot won the *Daily Mail* (London newspaper) prize of £1,000 for flying across the English Channel from France to England; it took only thirty-six minutes, thirty seconds.[8] He flew his Blériot XI into history. Later that summer, Blériot was joined by designers from France, Germany, America, Britain, and other countries in exhibiting their wares at the inaugural Paris Air Show. More than three hundred designers participated in the show, attracting thousands of visitors, including many national military representatives.[9] During the two-week exhibition, a number of aeronauts piloted their aircraft for the watching crowds. European military leaders began to contemplate the importance of airpower for future military operations. In the shadows of the Great Naval Arms Race that was brewing between Germany and Britain, another arms race was taking shape over airpower.

With the conquest of the previously insurmountable geographical barrier, the English Channel, and overwhelming civilian and governmental interest in aviation, the European nations took notice of aviation and airpower for a number of reasons. In Britain, the Committee of Imperial Defense (CID) established a subcommittee for Aerial Navigation, which investigated the military applications of aviation. In a 1909 report the subcommittee argued that given the technology of the time, dirigibles were the most advanced and promising, and that airplanes were simply too new and fragile.[10] The CID recommended substantial financial support for dirigibles and balloons, including £35,000 for a zeppelin-type dirigible, and that the government allow private companies to continue development of airplanes.[11] The British government expanded the CID's research and development facilities at South Farnborough, to include balloon and dirigible construction as well as airplanes. In 1912, the Army Balloon Factory was renamed the Royal Aircraft Factory. That same year, the British organized the Royal Flying Corps as the overall organization for military aviation. The Navy argued for their own flying service;[12] the Royal Naval Air Service was officially formed on 1 July 1914.

In France, the military took an earlier interest in aviation. The Service Aéronautique was established in 1909, the same year that Blériot crossed the channel and the air show premiered. The French had the largest number of designers and manufacturers at the time; the best aircraft were being built there. The French military aviation arm benefited from the highest technology and the best designs, as well as pilot designers, such as Blériot and Henri Farman—both opened instructional schools for French military pilots. In an ironic twist of fate, the first French military pilot was trained at the school set up by the Wright brothers in Pau, France. While the Americans were still deciding whether aviation was important at all, the French—based on their history and proximity to real and perceived enemies—were working to establish military dominance in any way possible.[13] Aviation presented that opportunity.

In Germany, a heated argument continued between existing successful lighter-than-air designs, including but not limited to the zeppelins, and their heavier-than-air competitors. By 1910 the zeppelin was a proven technology, flying scheduled service and offering enormous potential. The German zeppelin fleet flew passengers and mail between established hubs, capitalizing on the (relative) speed, luxury, and comfort of the technology. Military thinkers and planners considered the stability and efficiency of the zeppelin as they contemplated future military scenarios. Substituting bombs for passengers in wartime meant that the zeppelins could serve as stable, useful bombing platforms if the need arose. The Germans were not the only ones to realize the potential—British author H. G. Wells predicted aerial warfare, including the use of zeppelins, in his prophetic 1908 book, *The War in the Air*.[14] The Germans also had a very robust engine manufacturing industry and were on the cutting edge of high-technology engines. Designers like Daimler, Benz, and Mercedes were already transitioning from steel and iron engine blocks to aluminum, saving weight while increasing efficiency. The Germans were concerned that the airplane was not nearly as efficient or effective as the zeppelin, but they were willing to continue experimentation to explore options. German (and Austrian) companies like Rumpler, Albatros, and Gotha manufactured aircraft with government support and funding.

But not all nations were able to compete. Nations without an industrial base fell behind. Imperial Russia, while covetous of European airpower, had the resources but did not have the industry to build their own fleet. They began to buy European models to try to copy the technology but realized that they would have to industrialize further before they could develop indigenous aviation manufacturing capabilities.[15] The Ottoman Empire took an early interest in aviation, but had neither the resources nor the industry to build homegrown aircraft. They too turned to European manufacturers for aviation technology. In the United States, aviation languished not because of lack of industry, but because of government and military neglect. The first aircraft purchased from the Wrights by the U.S. Army was the 1910 Military Model B. In the United States, the sentiment remained that the Atlantic and Pacific Oceans were still large enough to protect the nation from adversaries, thus less spending and interest focused on aviation in the earliest years. But conflict leads to consideration for novel weapons, and the Europeans soon turned their attention to increasing military capabilities, including the idea of airpower.

* * *

Military aviation was years in the making. In France, Louis Blériot and his company convinced the French government to fund prototypes. After his successful channel crossing, the French grew increasingly interested in military aviation, including both heavier- and lighter-than-air craft.[16] By 1910, two private companies, Blériot and Farman, were producing aircraft with another half-dozen companies entering the fray into the new decade. Combining early successes along with a high-technology industrial base, the French led the world in aircraft manufacturing. In Britain, the government began manufacturing balloons as early as 1904, and later ventured into aircraft production.[17] In addition to the government facility, which was privatized in 1909, a number of independent companies emerged to bolster British military aviation, among them the most recognized names in aircraft manufacturing—Avro, Short, and Sopwith. The Germans were torn between lighter- and heavier-than-air craft, but made excellent strides with both. In addition to zeppelin production, German manufacturing excelled at lighter engine designs and airplane construction, and a number of airplane manufacturers sprung up. The Rumpler company began early manufacture of military aircraft, followed quickly by Albatros, Aviatik, and the Dutch designer Fokker. Across the southern border in Austria-Hungary, Lohner and Etrich produced complementary designs. Like the French and the British, the Germans also ventured into engine manufacturing and drafted excellent designs to construct competitive military aircraft.[18]

In December 1909, Louis Blériot flew a demonstration flight in Istanbul[19] with a Type XI, and the outcome was immediate and substantial. Without indigenous manufacturing capabilities, Minister of War Mahmud Sevket Pasha sent Turkish officers to France and Germany to learn how to fly; he also contracted with both countries for aircraft.[20] The Turks began building an air force to modernize their military when they saw the importance of the new technology. Lieutenant Colonel Süreyya Bey was put in charge of forming an aviation school and an airbase and given a budget of two thousand gold livres to put it together and buy some aircraft. The Tayyare Komisyonu (Aircraft Committee) selected Yeşilköy, just south of Istanbul, for the base.[21]

Events in war, when the Italians used airpower in 1911 in Libya against the Ottoman Empire, confirmed Turkish intentions to procure a modern air force. That year the Italians attacked Ottoman forces in Libya, sparking the Italo-Turkish War.[22] While important for the political ramifications—the Turks lost Tripoli and Libya to Italy—an important event occurred during the fighting over the far-flung Ottoman province. On 23 October 1911 Italian captain Carlo Piazza flew a French-built Blériot XI over the Turkish troops to gather information on their location. The aerial reconnaissance mission ushered in a new era of warfare and the birth of military airpower.[23] Nine days later, another Italian pilot, Second Lieutenant Giolio Gavotti dropped a small bomb—in fact a hand grenade—from his Austrian-built Etrich Taube, the first instance of aerial bombing.[24]

Military aviation was born in the skies over North Africa. The Turks were able to capture a French-built Nieuport from the Italians, and quickly pressed it into service. Facing a desperate need, the Turks advertised for foreign pilots and machines to come to their aid at the same time that they sent additional officer pilot candidates abroad for training. The Turkish government offered contracts for men and aircraft to bolster their lack of airpower. With little money in the treasury, the Turks asked wealthy citizens to provide funds for foreign equipment, which was gladly offered. In March 1912, the Ottoman Empire bought two Deperdussin aircraft from France. Simultaneously, the French agreed to supply airframes to the empire and to train pilots and mechanics in France. Ottoman Turks were sent to France and machines were sent to Turkey. By the end of the summer, four airplanes arrived in addition to two balloons for observation. To bolster their forces the Turks hired German pilots to fly against the Italians; the French were reluctant to act as mercenaries for fear of the political implications of French pilots fighting against the Italians. Indifferent to such distinctions, two German pilots with two German planes and a handful of mechanics traveled to the empire for the price of DM 60,000.[25] England was the next contract customer; the Ottomans paid for two English planes and pilots, and training for five more Turkish pilots in England.

In August 1912 a change in government brought disaster for the fledgling Turkish Air Force. The new minister of war, Nasim Paşa, was not a fan of aviation; he canceled all outstanding international contracts and disbanded the service.[26] Buildings under construction at Yeşilköy went unfinished and the few aircraft that were available were left outdoors, unprotected from the elements. When the First Balkan War (1912–13)[27] erupted in October, only one plane was available for operations at Yeşilköy and only five were flight-worthy in the rest of the empire. The Ottomans faced enemy airpower again, but by that time they only had six operational aircraft, all of which were rendered useless (through overuse and neglect) during the conflict. Official government disinterest meant that the Ottoman air arm withered.

Eventually Nasim Paşa was replaced as the result of a coup, and the new government recognized that they needed additional pilots and aircraft for military operations. They renewed earlier training and procurement plans. Pilot students were dispatched to France, Britain, and Germany, and additional orders were cut for more aircraft.[28] But it was not enough for the government to send pilots away for instruction, and Turkish officials asked the European powers for advice on how to modernize their aviation arm.

By the end of the Balkan Wars (July 1913) the Ottomans could only cobble together three serviceable aircraft by cannibalizing the entire fleet.[29] After a severe storm in August that collapsed an aircraft hangar, only one plane remained. When that single aircraft crash-landed at the end of September due to a faulty engine, they were left without any planes.[30]

The Ottomans sought military assistance to rebuild their forces. They contracted with the British for two warships, which were paid for but not delivered.[31] Rebuffed by the British, they turned to the Germans for assistance with army organization and training; General Liman von Sanders was appointed the chief of the German military mission and ordered to report to Istanbul in June 1913.[32] As the French were recognized leaders in aviation technology, they sent a mission to Istanbul to advise on military airpower. In April 1914, French general Goÿs de Mèzeyrac was named as the chief of the French military mission to Turkey to organize Ottoman aviation.[33] Mèzeyrac outlined what the Turks would need to be able to establish a viable air force and even provided comments and suggestions for defending the Gallipoli Peninsula. In his correspondence, he outlined that he had instructed the Turks on how to defend the Dardanelles and how aviation could assist the mission. Interestingly, in the months before the war, he also opined that airpower would be useful in forcing the straits and could potentially knock the Turks out of a future war if airpower could be brought to bear on the city of Istanbul.[34] As a bomber pilot, he was one of the first to speculate on the potential of strategic bombing in war. It is not clear whether his reports were read outside official French circles, but it can be surmised that as a pilot familiar with bombing he had important ideas about the efficacy of airpower, especially as it pertained to an unprepared Ottoman Empire. Mèzeyrac returned to France in August as Europe prepared for war.

The German military mission to the Ottoman Empire was led by Liman von Sanders.[35] In his own recollection, supported by documents from the German archives, Sanders and forty-one other officers were ordered to Istanbul.[36] The penultimate name on the list, directly above Veterinary Doctor Thieme, was the name of the junior officer who was tasked with advising on all matters having to do with airpower, Oberleutnant Erich Serno.[37] Serno was asked to join the mission to advise the Ottomans on building an aviation arm for their military; his advice became increasingly important after the French exit. Serno, an important figure in the later Gallipoli Campaign, began his pilot training in Germany in 1911, and became an accomplished pilot, distinguishing himself in the air against the French on the Western Front in the opening days of the war. He was a Kriegsakademie graduate and was selected early for command roles.[38] Sanders arrived in Istanbul on 14 December 1913 to begin the process of modernizing the Turkish military, especially the army; Serno followed in January 1915, and began his role as aviation advisor.

Serno, then a German army captain, was given a commission in the Ottoman army as a major, complete with a new uniform. He was named the consultant for the Turkish High Commission on Aviation,[39] and later commander of the Ottoman Fliegertruppe No. 1.[40] In his first series of reports, Serno offered that the Turks had no aviation capabilities at all as of October 1914, and he began his mission in earnest to build their capacity.[41] He was given all authorities—and money—to build an air force, without much oversight or constraint. He faithfully submitted reports and requests, but for the most part they were approved without counter. With money and authority, in early spring 1915, Serno set out to build an Ottoman air force.

His first task was to procure planes and pilots. He ordered contracts for German planes and German "civilian" pilots—military aviators who would shed their uniforms and travel as civilians to the empire. At the same time, he advised that the Ottomans send officers to Germany for pilot instruction. At the start of the war in Europe (August 1914), there were a handful of Turks in pilot schools in Germany and France. The officers were expelled from France when the Ottoman Empire joined the Central Powers in October, and the remaining pilot trainees in Germany had not yet completed their programs. Serno advised that more should be sent immediately to flight school in Germany. In addition, German aircraft and pilots would be ferried from Germany to Istanbul to build an air force.[42]

Problems arose immediately. At the time, Bulgaria and Romania were neutral, and were unwilling to allow military hardware to cross their borders from Germany to the Ottoman Empire. The pilots traveled on trains as civilian tourists using visas that identified them as medical professionals and circus workers. The latter visa designations were cover for the massive crates labeled "circus equipment" containing disassembled airplanes. In an audacious move, two planes were ferried by train to the Romanian border, assembled, and attempted flights across the three hundred kilometers of neutral frontier. In those early days of aviation, the distance was almost too great; both planes eventually arrived, but they were so beat up that they were useless—Serno had to find new ways to get aircraft to the empire.[43] His other task was to find suitable ground for an airfield. Serno chose a level patch of ground on the outskirts of Istanbul at San Stefano, locally known as Yeşilköy, as the site for the first airfield, resurrecting the site of the original Ottoman airpark. In spring 1915 he put local contractors to work clearing the field and rebuilding. By March Serno had three small hangars, two barracks, a balloon shed, and a suitable landing field for airplanes. In addition, Serno ordered the construction of a ramp to the waters of the Sea of Marmara for seaplanes.[44]

Thus, by the time the Allies decided their Mediterranean strategy, the Ottomans—with German help—had land and air forces in-theater, and were preparing for entry into the war. Liman von Sanders had rebuilt the land forces, and Major Serno had built up Ottoman airpower. Although he had few resources, the force was ready for operations. At their disposal, the Ottoman Empire boasted four airplanes, one balloon, and five seaplanes, all based at Yeşilköy. The pilots at that point were Germans—including Serno—but there were about a dozen Turkish officers at or headed to pilot training in Germany. The Ottoman buildup was fraught with difficulties, including a lack of indigenous manufacturing, but continued to operate with help from their German ally and advisors.

Politically, the Ottoman Empire was roundly disregarded as a minor power across Europe. It had not fared well in the Italo-Turkish conflict or the Balkan War and was perceived as unprepared by the Entente Powers. England rebuffed Ottoman naval aspirations; France considered their own aviation preparations insufficient and canceled all foreign contracts for machines at the outbreak of hostilities. Turkish pilot trainees were expelled from France before the fighting even started. Only the Germans, who were intent on keeping the Russian fleet penned in the Black Sea were interested in helping preserve Ottoman military strength. With the outbreak of war in August 1914, the Ottoman Empire was forced to take sides. It wanted an alliance with England, but England's alliance with Russia precluded Turkish friendship. It initially declared neutrality, but by October sided with the Central Powers. The Allies considered the Ottoman Empire the "sick man of

Europe" because of its political instability and lack of military capabilities. Turkey's lack of industry and manufacturing meant that all significant military hardware would have to come from outside, supplied by its German ally. But it did have manpower, determination, and traditional rivalries that it could count on to motivate Ottoman Turks to fight against the Greeks, the Russians, and any invasion of its dwindling empire.

The British had built up aviation before the war and were ready to fight with airpower when war broke out. Two British air services went to war in August 1914: the Royal Flying Corps (RFC) and the Royal Naval Air Service (RNAS). The RFC was subordinate to the army, and the RNAS was a component of the Royal Navy. The RNAS in particular became important to the Gallipoli story, predominantly because Lord Kitchener, British secretary of state for war, was unwilling to allocate RFC assets to the far-flung adventure. He commented that the war in France was too significant to release any assets, especially the preciously small RFC, for any foreign campaigns.[45]

Even before the Gallipoli Campaign, the RNAS was active in the war. The Royal Navy had built up an air arm for the fleet, including balloon ships and seaplane tenders. The balloon ships included four merchant ships under conversion at the start of the war, the HMS *Canning*, HMS *Hector*, HMS *Manica*, and HMS *Menelaus*.[46] The balloon ships carried tethered kite balloons (28,000 cubic feet capacity, Type H) in a hold. They were inflated on the deck and sent aloft, offering observers (called "pilots") an oblique view of the battlefield from 1,000 to 1,500 feet in the air. A telephone cable wrapped around the winch line provided communications from the pilots to the ship, which then relayed messages to naval or land artillery units. The drawback was that the early balloons were filled with explosive hydrogen and made large, appealing stationary targets. They were also very susceptible to weather conditions and could only be used in permissive environments when the winds were light.

One other ship type was useful in the later campaign, the seaplane tender HMS *Ark Royal*. It was a converted merchant ship that carried seaplanes in its hold. Using cranes on either side of the ship, the planes were lifted from the hold and onto the water, where they took off from the sea for missions. When the planes returned from missions, they were hoisted from the sea onto the ship for repairs and storage. It was not the modern conception of an aircraft carrier, but instead a seaplane tender. The *Ark Royal* and later the HMS *Ben-my-Chree* were the two seaplane tenders that played roles in the Gallipoli Campaign. The *Ark Royal* carried six seaplanes for operations: two Wight Type A1 Navyplanes, three Sopwith 807s, and a single Short Admiralty Type No. 135. It also had two Sopwith Tabloid aircraft in storage, planes that needed a land base for use. They were later used when a suitable airfield was constructed.[47] Commander Robert Clark-Hall was the *Ark Royal's* ship captain and concurrently the RNAS seaplane squadron commander. The planes were useful but limited by sea conditions. They could not fly if the sea was either too choppy or too still, as the early machines did not have the power to fight large waves or to "unstick" from still water. Clark-Hall commented (in official documents as well as post-war analyses) that the Short Admiralty Type No. 135 was the most valuable plane and the only one that could fly in less than ideal conditions, primarily because it had the most powerful engine, rated at two hundred horsepower.[48] The *Ark Royal* and its small complement of floatplanes was dispatched to the Mediterranean in February 1915 with the rest of the fleet.

The final British air contingent to be sent to Gallipoli was 3 Squadron RNAS, converted from the Eastchurch Squadron. Led by charismatic Commander Charles Rumney Samson (RNAS), the band of pilots flying a variety of aircraft had already made their mark on the Western Front with bravado and daring.[49] Samson joined the Royal Navy in 1898 and served aboard ships until 1911. That year, he was chosen to be one of the first four Royal Navy officers to learn to fly and was awarded his wings after only seventy-one minutes of flight time. He trained at Eastchurch, and after graduating from the course became the base and squadron commander.[50] The men who were assigned to Eastchurch for training and flying were eventually mobilized as Royal Naval Air Service 3 Squadron.

Samson was an exceptional pilot and became famous in his own time. He was the first British pilot to take off from a ship when on 12 January 1912 he took to the skies from a wooden ramp affixed to the HMS *Africa*, which lay at anchor for stability. He is credited as the first pilot to take off from a ship underway when he repeated the experiment in May from the HMS *Hibernia*. He was instrumental in the development of radios for planes, bombsights and bombing tests, and navigation lights for aircraft. His inquisitive nature led him to try new things with aircraft and he in turn encouraged this in his men.

Another Eastchurch trainee, Commander Eugene Gerrard, was one of the other four originally chosen to learn to fly. He was an alternate, but when one of the other trainees declined the posting, Gerrard went to Eastchurch. Upon graduation, he was assigned as the commander of the Central Flying School and chose to join the RNAS when it split from the army in 1914. He was also an aviation innovator; he is credited with two of the earliest high-altitude records. His first record was ten thousand feet, with then-major Hugh Trenchard as a passenger. Gerrard went on to command RNAS 2 Squadron.

When war broke out in Europe, 3 Squadron was first tasked with coastal patrols, flying over the English coast and watching for German aircraft that never arrived. At the end of August 1914, the squadron was relocated to the continent, to begin offensive operations against the Germans around Ostend.[51] Once there, Samson and his men—twenty pilots and another forty in support (mechanics, clerks, drivers, a doctor, and a vet), along with sixteen airplanes and a number of vehicles—secured a suitable airfield, and began operations against German targets. Interestingly, Samson and his pilots used "motorcars" as well as their aircraft for reconnaissance duties in the opening stages of the war. Samson declared that he was the first to put machine guns and light artillery on cars and trucks for offensive armed reconnaissance missions early in the war.[52] The squadron's exploits were stuff of legend; 3 Squadron RNAS pilots carried out aerial reconnaissance missions against enemy forces, which evolved into minor bombing raids in support of ground troops. When cameras were procured, 3 Squadron began photography missions to take pictures of enemy formations. In addition to reconnaissance and tactical bombing, the squadron began strategic operations against distant zeppelin sheds in December, flying long sorties to bomb the sheds at Brussels and Antwerp, even flying a few missions at night.[53] When the squadron was recalled from the front in February 1915 and replaced with another squadron, Samson was disconcerted. He did not understand why, given all their successes, 3 Squadron was being recalled.[54] But the Admiralty, and Churchill in particular, had another assignment waiting for the vaunted aviators: the Dardanelles. On 27 February, Samson was called to the Admiralty office and informed that the squadron was going to the Mediterranean. Apprehension was replaced with joy and the squadron "had a great celebration that night."[55] They were headed to the Dardanelles to fight against the Ottoman Empire.

The French added the final piece to the Allied airpower puzzle. General Albert d'Amade was put in charge of the land forces, which included a number of North African colonial troops,[56] while Vice-Admiral Boué de Lapeyère, the commander of the French Mediterranean Fleet sortied the naval support.[57] Accompanying the fleet was the *Foudre*, the first ever seaplane tender.[58] The *Foudre* was originally a torpedo boat tender, converted in 1910 to carry the world's first seaplanes, the French-built Voisin Le Canard floatplane. By the start of the Gallipoli Campaign, the *Foudre* carried four Caudron Type J seaplanes to fly in support of the fleet. In addition to the seaplanes on the *Foudre*, a squadron of land-based planes were shipped by sea to the Dardanelles, accompanied by their newly promoted *capitaine*, Antoine Césari.[59] He was another daring pilot in the long list of extraordinary World War I pilots. He had served in France at the outbreak of war and was recognized for his innovation and adaptation. He pioneered bombing techniques and was involved in some of the earliest attacks on German airship hangars.[60] He earned his wings in 1912 and after the start of the war was promoted quickly for exceptional gallantry in the face of the enemy. His organizational skills were exceptional, and he moved from 1st Group to 2nd Group; he was eventually promoted to capitaine and commander of the expeditionary squadron.[61] Not content to sit behind a desk, he flew nearly every day and led the squadron in flight time and missions as its commander.

Césari's squadron, No. MF. 98(T) comprised eight Farman eighty-horsepower HF.20s, a reconnaissance biplane.[62] The squadron was labeled MF for the Maurice Farman aircraft it flew, and had the postscript (T) for the island where it was based. Césari traveled with his squadron by sea, and they set up a working aerodrome on Tenedos. The French land-based squadron, once operational, began missions over the French lines on the Asian side of the Dardanelles in support of the French efforts. But at the same time, Césari and Samson cooperated in combined French and British air operations.[63] It is interesting to note that there was little guidance from the campaign commanders (admirals and generals), and a British RNAS commander and a French army (aviation) capitaine planned and executed aerial operations for the entire campaign.

As the war clouds gathered over the Dardanelles, aircraft arrived in support for both sides of the fight. Capitaines, majors, and navy commanders would lead the high-tech air war for control of the skies over Gallipoli and the Dardanelles. By February 1915, there were a total of four German land planes and five seaplanes for the Turkish-German contingent, flown initially by German pilots, flying against ten seaplanes for the Allies, six British and four French attached to their seaplane tenders. More planes were to be added, as the Ottomans bolstered numbers with more aviation assets, while the British and French both added individual squadrons of land-based aircraft. The fight for the Dardanelles focused initially on the sea power that the British and French brought to the campaign, but aircraft played an increasingly important role in the effort as the Allies sought ways to overcome Turkish obstacles. Concurrently, the Ottomans (who were being advised by the Germans) added airpower to their approach to countering the Allies and fortifying their defenses. The air war for Gallipoli was about to begin.

CHAPTER TWO

Preparation for War in the Mediterranean

Winston Churchill sat at his desk surveying the map of Europe. The first lord of the admiralty wondered how the Royal Navy could be put to best use in the war. The Germans invaded Belgium and France the previous August; the war on the Western Front had mired into a stalemate. The Allies repelled the Germans closing in on Paris at the "Miracle of the Marne," and French and British troops held the line. By November 1914, a series of trenches ran from Switzerland to the English Channel.

The Royal Navy was assigned to the "distant blockade," barring access to the English Channel and the North Sea and thus preventing military supplies from reaching the Central Powers by sea; Germany and Austria-Hungary were penned in.[1] But Churchill wanted to find a way to use the navy in a more active role in the war. When the Ottoman Turks attacked the Russian Black Sea Fleet and the port of Sevastopol on 28 October 1914, and declared war in support of the Central Powers on 1 November, an opportunity presented itself to the British. The Ottoman action was in violation of the Triple Alliance, signed in August, and the entente reciprocated with a declaration of war on the Ottoman Empire on 5 November.

Churchill suggested two options for the use of the Royal Navy. While the bulk of the fleet was engaged in the distant naval blockade, a sizable force remained for an offensive.[2] Churchill proposed that an attack could be launched against Germany from the Baltic in a direct assault on the northern German coast; alternatively, an attack could be launched against the Ottomans in the Mediterranean.[3] Both courses of action had benefits and drawbacks. If the Royal Navy attacked Germany directly, it would have to contend with the German High Seas Fleet (*Hochseeflotte*) in the Baltic. The proposed offensive envisioned a naval attack followed by a landing force that would circumvent the bulk of the German army in the west and march directly on Berlin.[4] Jackie Fisher, the new first sea lord,[5] supported the plan. But Fisher argued that the German fleet operating in the North Sea and the Baltic and anchored at Kiel, would have to first be neutralized. The Royal Navy was up to the task, but it would likely be a bloodbath. Further, the landing force would have to come from somewhere; the Royal Marines were too small a force to attempt a landing and march to Berlin. Attempts to garner French assistance came to naught. When Lord Kitchener got word of the plan, he spoke out against it.[6] By January, Secretary of State for War Kitchener had convinced Fisher that the proposed plan was unworkable.[7]

That left the second option: A naval attack on the Ottoman Empire. The Mediterranean plan had its benefits. The Royal Navy, with help from the French, could attack the Ottoman Empire, force them out of the war, and open the Dardanelles for the Russians. It would not only encircle the Central Powers, but would also provide access to the Black Sea for the Russians to get supplies into and out of Sevastopol, bringing war material in and shipping food supplies—primarily wheat—out. Finally, Churchill could circumvent Kitchener's opposition and call on colonial and Commonwealth forces if need be. Kitchener was adamant that no British forces would be taken away from the "main fight" on the Western Front, but there were plenty of Commonwealth forces that Churchill could use; he was thinking specifically of the Australians and New Zealanders, already in Egypt.

The Ottoman Empire joined the Central Powers for a number of reasons. First and foremost, the historical enmity between the Ottomans and the Russians helped shape their decision. Further, they were angry with the British, who had promised to build warships for the Ottomans then kept the money and the ships, which were still under construction at the start of the war. The Germans took advantage of the rift with Britain by providing the Ottomans with the battlecruiser *Goeben* and the cruiser *Breslau*. The Germans fabricated doctored documents that indicated the Ottomans had purchased the warships, which were still serviced by German crews. When the Ottomans joined the Central Powers, this transaction gave the Allies the opportunity to launch attacks against the Ottoman fleet.

On 3 November, just after the Ottoman declaration of war and in anticipation of the official British declaration, the British admiral in charge of the Mediterranean Fleet Sackville Carden received orders to attack the Ottoman forts at the mouth of the Dardanelles, but to retire if there was risk to the ships.[8] Two British battlecruisers, the HMS *Indefatigable* and HMS *Indomitable*, with the assistance of two French battleships, the *Suffren* and *Vérité* fired on the forts guarding the entrance to the Dardanelles. A direct hit on the powder magazine destroyed the Sedd El Bahr fortress.[9] The attack produced mixed results. One of the forts was put out of action, but it was also an indication to the Ottomans that the British and French would attempt offensives in and around the Dardanelles.

By January 1915, Churchill was ready to put his plan into motion. The strategy was too simple by half; he asked Carden if the fleet could sail up the Dardanelles, fire on Istanbul, and force the Ottomans out of the war.[10] The initial plan was for the navy alone to force the straits, sail up to the Sea of Marmara, fire on Istanbul, force the Ottomans to quit, and open the Dardanelles for a passage to Russia. Carden's reply was that he needed time and equipment (more ships), but indicated that the proposed plan was achievable. Churchill began planning for a March offensive.[11] The strategy was to attack the Ottoman capital directly to force them out of the war. Unfortunately, the focus strayed very quickly.

The French boasted the largest naval presence in the Mediterranean. Before the war, the French and British had discussed naval operations in the Mediterranean if war came. They both considered the Italians the greatest threat, followed by the Austrians (who in 1914 had a significant naval presence in the Mediterranean). When the Italians chose neutrality at the start of the war, they were removed from the equation. The French focused on the Adriatic but were amenable to British plans in the Aegean.[12] In short, there was no significant hesitation by the French for a planned attack on the Ottoman Empire.

The French fleet in the Aegean, under the command of Rear Admiral Émile Paul Amable Guépratte, was substantial. Guépratte commanded four battleships, as well as a number of destroyers, submarines, and minesweepers. Additionally, Guépratte had a seaplane tender, the *Foudre*.[13] Even though the French had the stronger naval force in the Mediterranean, Guépratte was willing to let the British take the lead on any attacks on the Ottoman Empire. The Mediterranean was quickly divided by areas of influence; the French took responsibility for a naval blockade of the Austrian fleet in the Adriatic and continued to patrol the coast of the Levant. Britain insisted on control off the coast of Egypt and requested operational control of the Dardanelles front. The French allowed the British lead; Guépratte was ordered to follow Carden's commands when convenient to and not in conflict with other French Mediterranean naval operations.[14] At the same time, Guépratte was more excited about action than blockade and was willing to commit to the proposed plan.[15] For the duration of the campaign, the French based at Mudros Harbor, on the island of Lemnos.[16] The protected port in a natural harbor was approximately sixty miles from the tip of the Gallipoli Peninsula. The French built up a port, as well as a staging area at Mudros; just fewer than 18,000 men—with 5,300 horses—camped there awaiting orders.

The Ottoman strategy was to defend. They began a build up on the Gallipoli Peninsula after the first Allied naval attacks convinced them that the British and French would launch follow-on attacks. Although unsure of the Allied intentions, they were confident that they could defend the Dardanelles. The Ottomans had a close relationship with the Germans; Liman von Sanders was the chief of the German military mission to Turkey.[17] A consummate professional, he worked effectively with Enver Paşa (the Ottoman minister of war) and Lieutenant Colonel Mustafa Kemal—later an important Ottoman commander in the defense of Gallipoli. Under German command, the Ottomans built up the existing forts guarding the straits and incorporated new technology into their defense scheme, including heavy artillery and mobile artillery, as well as defensive fortifications and trenches.

At the mouth of the straits stood the fortress at Sedd El Bahr. Although the fort itself suffered tremendous damage in the 3 November attacks, the guns were serviceable. This exposed a serious weakness of the Allied naval gunnery. The naval guns fired horizontally, and caused significant structural damage, but what was really needed was plunging fire to hit interior fortifications. Further, fortress guns were very hard to destroy; naval gunfire did not incapacitate the guns themselves. The best the Allies could hope for was to destroy the forts and drive off the gunners.

In addition to Sedd El Bahr, the Ottomans had three more substantial fortifications guarding the straits, Kum Kale on the Asian side of the Dardanelles, the fort at Çanakkale (Asian side), and Kilid Bahr (European side) facing each other at the Narrows. Added to this were other hastily prepared defensive fortifications, equipped with howitzers, flat-trajectory cannon, and torpedo tubes. In all, the Ottomans had around 35 forts and defensive fortifications guarding the Dardanelles between the tip and the Narrows. In total, 87 guns defended the Dardanelles, 47 on the northern European shore, 40 on the southern Asian shore. After the first Allied naval attacks, the Ottomans began laying lines of sea mines, to deter ships entering the straits. By February, the Ottomans had laid 271 mines, in 9 belts, across the straits.[18]

The Gallipoli Peninsula presented a number of operational challenges to the impending confrontation. The Dardanelles flows out to the Aegean Sea, where a number of islands stand guard. Some of the important islands include Imbros, a large island only twelve miles from the Gallipoli Peninsula shore, Rabbit Island and Tenedos, to the south of Gallipoli, and the larger, but more distant Samothrace, and Lemnos.[19]

Sailing against the current, ships traveled from the Aegean up the Dardanelles. The currents are at least three knots on the surface, but can get up to five knots, causing problems for ships in both directions. The Dardanelles Straits is 38 miles long from the Aegean to the Sea of Marmara, 3.7 miles wide at its widest, but only 0.75 mile at the Narrows. Between Çanakkale and the point at the Narrows (about 2 miles north) the current is faster because of the bottleneck. The Dardanelles opens to the north into the Sea of Marmara, where the waterway becomes a larger, slower, more placid body of water, where today ships are staged for their place in line to deliver goods to Istanbul. At the far north of the Sea of Marmara is the Bosporus, the very narrow channel that separates Europe from Asia. The Bosporus is 19.25 miles long, and only 0.5 mile at its narrowest to 2.1 miles at its widest. The city of Istanbul, the cultural, political, and religious center of the Ottoman Empire, sits astride the Bosporus. To the north, the Bosporus empties into the Black Sea, where the Russian Black Sea Fleet was stationed at Sevastopol. With control of the Bosporus at the north end, and the Dardanelles at the south, the Ottomans bottled up the Russian Black Sea Fleet and controlled the vital sea-lane.

The military geography at the time also presented unique challenges. At the mouth of the Dardanelles, the Asian side was dotted with fortresses as well as historical sites. Overshadowing the ancient city of Troy was the massive fortification of Kum Kale. The hardscrabble land on the Asian shore was not the desired battleground, there was little to be gained from this area, and the Asian side presented a number of difficulties including few roads and a dearth of water. In addition to the lack of port facilities and logistical obstacles, there were few supply lines on that side of the Dardanelles (which was later the case on the Gallipoli Peninsula as well). Further, the Turks could more easily reinforce from the medium-sized town Çanakkale, only thirty miles to the north. The fort at Kum Kale, however, was an issue; the largest fort on the Asian side of the Dardanelles, with guns and a garrison protecting the waterway.

The Gallipoli Peninsula guards the European side of The Dardanelles.[20] The fortress Sedd El Bahr[21] sat at the Cape Helles point, guarding the water approaches. Another substantial fort on the European side (Kilid Bahr), two more forts on the Asian side, and multiple mobile artillery batteries made up the Dardanelles defenses. The Gallipoli Peninsula terrain is a mix of agricultural plain and rough, broken, hilly regions, ideal for the defense. From the point of the peninsula to the small town of Krithia, the ground sloped gently upward and was dotted with olive and almond orchards, and other agriculture. Otherwise, the geography is quite daunting. Except for the plain, moving north, the rest of the peninsula is marked by steep hills and deep ravines covered with thorny bushes. A ridge of high ground runs along the Aegean side of the peninsula, north to a dry salt lake at Suvla Bay. The highest point on the peninsula is dominated by Hill 971. This eminence overlooks the entire peninsula from the tip to the north, and more importantly overlooks the water on both sides of the peninsula including the Narrows.[22] Lesser hills included heights on the Chunuk Bair ridge, such as Achi Baba (730 feet), overlooking Krithia to the south; it was not high enough to see the Narrows. Unfortunately, few maps existed for the peninsula, the Dardanelles, or the area in general.[23]

The Gallipoli side presented other issues and benefits. There was some fresh water, some agriculture, and a few roads. Not enough of any of these, but less desolate than the Asian side. Further, there was not a close garrison on the European side; the nearest town of significant size was Gallipoli, forty-three miles north of Cape Helles.[24] In 1915, there was only one, single-track dirt road from the town of Gallipoli to Sedd El Bahr. Supply came by water down the Dardanelles from Gallipoli to either Çanakkale on the Asian shore or the port at Ak Bashi Liman on the European shore. Thus, even though the terrain was more difficult, Turkish logistics were equally hampered.

At the strategic level, Gallipoli is about three thousand miles from England by sea. In 1915, this was at least a two-week sea voyage under the best conditions. Factor in the threat of enemy submarines and weather, and a military campaign was a Herculean task. Lessons learned from the Crimean War (1853–56) were useful and important, but the British decided to mount a similar logistical campaign sixty years later. The technology had improved, but the challenges were comparable. British outposts in Egypt were closer to Gallipoli and were used extensively, but it is not an overstatement to suggest that logistics were a constant issue in the Allied camp. For the Ottoman Turks, logistics were local, but still complicated. The Turks maintained the supply route from Germany and central Europe throughout, but were hamstrung by a lack of technology compounded by difficult local transportation. In addition, at the beginning of the Gallipoli Campaign, Romania and Bulgaria were neutral and were reluctant to allow war material to cross their borders between central Europe and the Ottoman Empire. This hampered the transport of aircraft, usually shipped in large crates; there was no easy way to transport aircraft from Europe for the fight. Matériel headed for the Gallipoli Peninsula was ferried by sea from Istanbul to Çanakkale or Ak Bashi Liman where it was dispersed to needed areas, but men and beasts marched from the ports to the front lines. With few exceptions, machines were unknown in the Turkish lines; the Turkish army traveled on foot. As the Allies gathered seapower in the Aegean, the German-Ottoman team began reinforcing the Gallipoli Peninsula. By 1915, the aforementioned forts and artillery emplacements guarded the Dardanelles. There were mines in the water, laid in lines to prevent seaborne incursion. And there were about 65,000 men available for the defense of the Dardanelles, but they were woefully unorganized and ill equipped.[25] After the initial naval attacks, Liman von Sanders reorganized the Ottoman forces into six divisions of around 10,000 men each and consolidated headquarters for ease of command.[26]

In this, the first mechanized industrial war, the employment of aircraft in the Gallipoli Campaign changed the character of war forever. The introduction of the new technology had a fundamental effect on planning, warfighting, and the inchoate idea of joint operations in three dimensions.[27]

For aviation, the new technology in the upcoming conflict, Gallipoli presented unforeseen difficulties. The heat was problematic in the summer, causing overheating and loss of compression in the early engines. Hot summer air also hindered the lift of the severely underpowered machines. Choppy seas prevented seaplanes from flying. They had trouble getting off the surface of the sea, again due to the limitations of their engines. The dust and wind combined to ravage the fragile planes on unprotected airfields; all of the air commanders faced issues with getting enough materials to construct suitable hangar facilities. With a lack of wood, there was little to build revetments. Both the British and French used the planes' packing crates to build facilities. But with a lack of resources, it was often more important to build housing for the men than protection for the planes. Finally, the closest airfield for the Allied campaign was Tenedos, approximately fifteen miles across the Aegean from Cape Helles. Flying over water presented additional issues: the salt air conspired against the primitive machines; the fragile parts corroded and wore out even more frequently than their counterparts on the Western Front. In addition to the problems with metal parts, laminated propellers would often delaminate because of the heat and salt air—sometimes in flight. The British began operations from the sea on the *Ark Royal*, while 3 Squadron set up a land base at Tenedos. The French staged from Tenedos for their efforts in the campaign. The Ottomans had an established land and seaplane base at Yeşilköy, just south of Istanbul, but more than two hundred miles north of the beaches at Gallipoli. They later built an additional aerodrome closer to the front at Galata, as well as a seaplane base at Çanakkale and later a small landing field for land-based planes just outside the town.

For the British, the Royal Naval Air Service supported the naval expedition. Kitchener wanted to keep the army's Royal Flying Corps on the Western Front; Churchill was limited to the forces under his command and dispatched Royal Navy assets instead. The air component for Carden's fleet came in three types: kite balloons tethered to ships, the navy seaplane tender HMS *Ark Royal*, and a squadron of land-based planes (RNAS 3 Squadron, led by Commander Charles Rumney Samson). Samson's 3 Squadron was not on station until March 1915, so the air war began at the start of the year with the seaplanes and balloons.

In February 1915, the Royal Navy sent the HMS *Ark Royal* to the Mediterranean. The *Ark Royal* was the first ship designed as a seaplane carrier.[28] The *Ark Royal* carried eight aircraft: six seaplanes and two land-based Sopwith Tabloids. The Tabloid was a single-seat reconnaissance aircraft, but the two on the *Ark Royal* were not equipped with floats for use from the sea. They carried Lewis guns mounted to the top wing that fired over the propeller arc, but their most common use was for scouting. Their nine-cylinder Gnome rotary engine provided one hundred horsepower (hp), giving them a top speed of eighty-seven mph. The *Ark Royal* had a small platform on the deck for the aircraft to take off, but it was too short for recovery. Thus, until a landing site was found and constructed or the planes were equipped with floats, the two Tabloids sat dormant in the *Ark Royal* hangar space. The six other planes were equipped with floats and could be used. The contingent included three Sopwith Admiralty Type 807 seaplanes, with the same Gnome engines as the Tabloids. There were also two Wight Type A.1 Navyplanes equipped with two hundred hp Salmson-built Canton-Unne engines and one Short Admiralty Type 135 seaplane with that same engine.[29] Using the ship's cranes, the aircraft were lowered to the sea from the decks and took off from the water. When they returned, they landed close to the ship and were hoisted back on board. The three 807s had a more difficult time with the weather and sea conditions than the other three aircraft; they were severely underpowered for their size and had trouble taking off from the water. If it was too choppy, they could not be used. If the water was too calm, they had trouble "unsticking" from the surface. The more powerful aircraft had an easier time with the erratic weather conditions, but also faced the same problems. Frequently, weather prevented any flights.

In the initial phases of the campaign, the aircraft could be equipped with small bombs or fléchettes, but their primary role was observation with a secondary mission of mapping. The pilots—and observers in the two-seaters—flew over the targets, drawing rudimentary maps of the enemy locations, encampments, and gun emplacements.[30] The maps drawn by the pilots and observers contributed to the operational planning for both the naval attacks as well as later landings at Gallipoli. Frequent reports confirmed that the aircraft were underpowered and insufficient for the tasks that they were expected to complete.[31] As the pilots became more proficient with the machines, they were asked to provide aerial spotting for naval gunfire. The pilots aloft observed naval artillery fire and provided corrections to the navy gunners. However, only the Short seaplane was equipped with a one-way wireless radio transmitter; the equipment was both too bulky and heavy for the other aircraft. When the radio worked it was beneficial for artillery spotting. When it did not—or when other aircraft were spotting—naval artillery had to rely on after-action reports when the pilots returned to the fleet.

One other aircraft made its debut in the initial phases of the campaign. The HMS *Manica* was a kite-balloon tender, arriving on station mid-April with its complement of six observers. The steamer carried a 28,000 cubic foot tethered balloon, along with hydrogen in cylinders to inflate it. With the ship anchored 4,000 yards off the coast, the balloon was filled with gas, and then winched to a height of up to 1,500 feet. The balloon's tether cable was entwined with a telephone wire so that the observer could communicate with the ship below, and the ship radioman could relay messages to other ships. When aloft, the observer could spot for other ships' guns, improving accuracy.[32] The benefits of the kite balloon on the *Manica* were that the balloon could stay aloft for hours, allowing the observer to make lengthy reports on ships' fire and draft detailed maps of the battlefield. The balloons were relatively stable—at least compared to the airplanes—and did not have to be "flown"; the observer was simply a passenger. The drawbacks were numerous, but acceptable because of the benefits. The balloon was filled with hydrogen and extremely flammable. Fortunately, during the entire campaign, there were no accidents or fires on either the *Manica* or sister ship, the *Hector*. And the observation was not perfect; whereas the airplane pilots could fly directly over targets and bomb or photograph them, the balloon ship observers were defenseless, had no offensive weapons, and saw the battlefield at an oblique angle. The distinctive terrain at the Gallipoli Peninsula prevented balloon observers from seeing many of the Ottoman encampments and depots.

The day after arrival, on 10 April, Squadron Commander John Mac-worth (the only fully trained balloon observer in the RNAS) in the first ship in the fleet fitted with a kite balloon, soared aloft and reported that the technology was absolutely useful for the campaign. His report back to London spurred the Royal Navy to commission six further ships of the type.[33] In the official history, Sir Walter Raleigh reported that "the kite balloon is the ugliest thing that man has ever seen when he looks up at the sky, but it serves its purpose."[34]

In addition to the kite balloon ship, a full RNAS squadron was dispatched to the Dardanelles. On 26 February, Commander Charles Rumney Samson was ordered to report to the offices of the Admiralty from his base in France. The leader of 3 Squadron RNAS was a contentious figure but known for his ability to inspire his men and get jobs done. His 3 Squadron had been very productive in the first few months of the war, perfecting bombing techniques, harassing the enemy in the air and on the ground, and making the first night flights. The Eastchurch Squadron—as they were known—had been together for years, training before the war, then flying and fighting together since the start of the war. The close-knit group was daring and dashing, setting a good example for conduct in the air war, but they were not such shining examples of military decorum or regulation. The squadron flouted rigid military discipline and regulations in their daily lives and in the air. Samson was an interesting character and uniquely qualified for the position. First and foremost he was RNAS and not Royal Flying Corps, so it did not bother Kitchener that he and his squadron were sent to the Dardanelles—away from the Western Front.[35] Furthermore, Samson and his pilots had a reputation for daring and bravado and were perfectly suited for work in a dangerous and distant theater. While in Belgium, the Eastchurch Squadron pioneered bombing tactics against German targets. One of the squadron pilots, Flight Lieutenant Reggie Marix, was already famous for a bombing raid on a German airship hangar at Düsseldorf and the destruction of both the hangar and an airship.[36] The Eastchurch squadron innovated aerial tactics, to include bombing from the air, as well as providing close air support against Germans on the ground in addition to their required observation roles. Samson had even introduced a type of armed car; he put machine guns on the squadron's Rolls Royce and the pilots took turns driving up and down the front lines shooting at German troops.[37] While in Belgium, they tried different weapons on different platforms, including heavier 3-pound guns on the back of trucks, and machine guns on motorcycles. Innovative on the ground and in the air, Samson and his squadron were always thinking of ways to attack the enemy. They were all very excited when ordered to travel to Gallipoli.[38] The first naval aviation squadron to be sent overseas, 3 Squadron RNAS was initially posted to Belgium at the start of the war, and in February 1915 they were sent to the Mediterranean.[39]

On 27 February Samson got his orders: 3 Squadron was recalled from Calais (where it was based at the time) and returned to London for refit and repair. It was then ordered to sail for the Mediterranean as soon as practicable. With four other pilots[40] and twenty-seven men, 3 Squadron loaded one airplane, Samson's favorite Royal Aircraft Factory BE2a with tail number 50,[41] two trucks, two Rolls Royce touring cars, and two light tenders in train cars to the south of France. Samson had flown No. 50 for three years and considered it to be his most reliable airplane. The rest of the squadron—pilots, men, and airplanes, along with stores and ammunition—were sent by ship to catch up to the advance party in Marseilles. They took all the aircraft then available in England and contracted for more from the French, which they picked up along the way. After a few days in Marseilles, the advance party squadron loaded up on the steamer *Abda* and sailed for the eastern Mediterranean. The rest of the squadron followed from Plymouth on the ships *Inkosi* and *Moorgate*.[42]

On 3 March, Samson and the first part of 3 Squadron arrived at the port facilities at Imbros—an island 12 miles from the mouth of the Dardanelles—without incident. They were ordered to set up an aerodrome farther south on Tenedos, some distance from the Gallipoli Peninsula. After weathering a frightful storm, they were ready for flights from Tenedos on the 27th. The first complement of aircraft included the BE2a No. 50, two Maurice Farman MF.11 Shorthorns, and eight Henri Farman HF.20s.[43]

The BE2a was a two-seat observation plane, powered by an air-cooled V-8 engine producing one hundred hp. Its top speed was seventy-two mph, but it could carry a radio and stay aloft for more than three hours. No. 50 was obsolete by 1914, but this plane was Samson's favorite and he continued to fly it in combat throughout the campaign. The Shorthorn was a French two-seat pusher aircraft; the engine was placed behind the pilot. The observer sat in the front of the plane and had an unrestricted view forward. The Shorthorn was powered by a one hundred horsepower air-cooled V-8 Renault engine. Its top speed was only sixty-six mph, but it had an endurance of nearly four hours. The HF.20 was also a two-seat pusher, powered by an eighty hp Gnome rotary engine. Samson thought the HF.20 was underpowered and "practically useless for war work."[44]

In the first week of April, the rest of the squadron finally arrived by sea and brought another eleven aircraft. This hodgepodge provided additional resources and expanded the mission set, but also compounded supply, logistics, and maintenance requirements. The contingent included a handful of improved BE2s, C models. There were also two Sopwith Tabloids (the land planes transferred from the *Ark Royal*), a Breguet Bre.4 two-seat bomber—assigned personally to Flight Lieutenant Reginald Marix—and what is listed as a Canton Unné Maurice Farman (probably another Shorthorn), a mainstay of the squadron, with the tail number 1241.[45] Samson had twenty-two total aircraft, but only five were operational, the BE2s and the Breguet. The rest were hampered by lack of power, lack of parts, or terrible flying characteristics. There were 102 men and 18 officers; at least one horse, Samson's personal mount; and 6 mules included in 3 Squadron at Tenedos. This eclectic group (excluding the equine) flew the bulk of the missions in support of the Allied effort at Gallipoli.

At the beginning of hostilities, the French seaplane tender *Foudre* was with the Mediterranean fleet. In the first decade of the 1900s, the ship began service as a torpedo boat tender; it carried small torpedo boats into action, lifted them from the decks onto the water, and sent them into action. After the first French seaplanes were invented in 1911, the *Foudre* was converted into a seaplane tender. It lowered aircraft from the decks to the water, where they took off and landed. Later, a small takeoff deck was added to the front of the ship, but the planes still had to be recovered from the water by cranes. In 1915, the *Foudre* employed four Caudron Type J biplane seaplanes.

In addition to the four floatplanes, the French dispatched a land-based squadron. Designated MF. 98(T), this squadron was diverted through Marseilles and Egypt to its final base at Tenedos, was ready for operations by April. Tenedos was a small island fifteen miles off the tip of the Gallipoli Peninsula, but only two miles off the Asian coast of Turkey, near the ancient site of Troy. Commanded by the newly minted flight captain, Antoine Césari,[46] the French escadrille played a significant role in the battle for Gallipoli.[47] MF. 98(T) included eight pilots with their own planes, a contingent of eight Maurice Farman HF.20s. The HF.20 was a two-seat pusher biplane, powered by a Gnome Lambda rotary engine that produced eighty horsepower.

Already obsolete on the Western Front, the plane and the squadron were relegated to the secondary theater at Gallipoli.

The eighty-man squadron was ordered to map, photograph, and observe for the French fleet, in preparation for the impending naval battle.[48] The French focused on the southern Asian side of the straits, targeting the fortress at Kum Kale up the coast to Çanakkale. With his small contingent of aircraft, and only a few men, Césari worked to provide aerial intelligence for the French fleet. Because the British and French were colocated at Tenedos, Césari and Samson chatted frequently, building the bond between aviators that is common in wartime. Samson recounted that the British and French coordinated frequently on raids, but that the British often had to supply their French brethren with bombs as they did not have an adequate supply. Each team helped the other out with maintenance and spares, and even traded aircraft—unofficially—exchanging equipment for operational effectiveness.[49] Césari commanded a smaller contingent than Samson, but had between twelve and sixteen airplanes and eighty men in total, including a dozen pilots. With little guidance from French high command or the admiral, Césari set to work to make his small squadron useful to the Allied effort.

The enemy was equally interested in aviation and aircraft. The Germans sent aviation experts at the same time and in addition to army officers to complement the Ottoman forces. As one of the most easily recognized aviation specialists in the Prussian Army, Oberleutenant Erich Serno traveled to Istanbul, and received a promotion: major in the Ottoman army and organizer of the revived Osmanli Hava Kuvvettleri (Ottoman Air Force). He was disappointed with what he found at the primitive aerodrome at Yeşilköy, so in the first week of February 1915 he began to build a viable Ottoman air force starting with twelve German civilian pilots and another dozen mechanics and riggers.[50] One thing the Ottomans lacked was the industry to manufacture their own machines. All of the aircraft and most of the spare parts had to be brought in from outside the empire.

The German mission quickly ordered procurement of additional resources to build up the fighting force. At the time of the Ottoman declaration of war, the Ottomans had the promise of a number of aircraft from Germany and the Austro-Hungarians, thirty-six in total for all of their fronts including the Caucasus, Palestine, and the eventual Gallipoli front. However, they had trouble getting aircraft from central Europe to the Empire, and in March 1915, they only had eleven aircraft available for the Gallipoli front—five Albatros B.1s and a single Etrich *Taube*, in addition to the five seaplanes at Çanakkale.[51]

Thus, at the beginning of the year 1915, the two sides were ready for a fight. The strategies were straightforward: attack versus defend. The Allies prepared battle plans to attack the Dardanelles, defeat the "sick man of Europe," and open sea-lanes for the Russians. But the Ottomans were prepared to defend their homeland vigorously, and to defeat the Allied strategy.

CHAPTER THREE

The Dardanelles Naval Campaign

The Royal Navy was the centerpiece of the operational plan to force the Ottoman Empire out of the war. When Churchill shifted focus to the Mediterranean, he called on the commander in the theater to offer an estimation of the Royal Navy's ability to force the Dardanelles and sail on to Istanbul, where it would shell the city and force Ottoman capitulation.

Vice Admiral Sackville Carden offered his professional military opinion. In a series of telegrams between 3 and 13 January, Carden argued that given a large enough fleet, the Dardanelles could be forced in an extended operation concluding with an attack on the capital directly.[1] Given the go-ahead, Carden prepared the fleet for the first attacks on the Ottoman positions at the Dardanelles. He envisioned the operation in four phases: first, the destruction of the defenses at the mouth of the Dardanelles, on both the European and Asian sides of the strait; second, a drive on the straits to destroy gun emplacements up to the Narrows; third, the destruction of the fortresses guarding the Narrows; and fourth, minesweeping in the straits, elimination of any residual resistance, and restaging in the Sea of Marmara.[2] Carden believed the operation would take up to a month.[3] On 28 January, Prime Minister Herbert Asquith, Chancellor of the Exchequer David Lloyd George, and Churchill approved the plan, although the military demurred. Both Lord Kitchener, secretary of state for war, and Jackie Fisher, the first sea lord, had their reservations about the plan. Kitchener deferred; he did not object strenuously because no ground troops were proposed in the initial operational plan. Fisher conceded, and the plan went into action.[4]

Interestingly, the French had concocted a plan before the war to force a Turkish surrender with airpower alone. In July 1914, Général Louis de Goÿs de Mèzeyrac, then commander of the French First Bombardment Group, proposed a bombing operation on Istanbul. He submitted that his group could fly from the French base being set up on the island of Tenedos to Istanbul where they would drop bombs on military targets and leaflets on the civilian population. The combination of shock and surprise would frighten the Ottoman government into capitulation and encourage what he considered a pro-French revolution in the city. Mèzeyrac had been stationed in Istanbul prior to the outbreak of war and had advised the Ottoman high command on various military matters, specifically airpower.[5] He was convinced that the population was more sympathetic to the French than the Germans, and simply needed a reason to break from Germany and join France. He thought an airstrike, with an attack and a propaganda mission, would convince the Ottomans to switch sides.[6] His plan was turned down for unknown reasons, but probably because French leadership thought that the bombers were better used on the Western Front.[7] In the early days of aviation, bomber pilots specifically thought that bombing from the air could disrupt a population and government completely, leading to a decisive strike and capitulation. But at the time the French did not have the ability to carry out such an attack, regardless of the potential strategic outcomes.

The British and French fleets sailed for the impending fight. Churchill thought it was important to begin naval operations immediately in order to catch the Ottomans off guard with a surprise attack.[8] If successful, the Allies would not have to land troops. If the initial naval attacks were not decisive, it would still prepare the battlefield for an amphibious invasion. Churchill thought that ground troops might be necessary, but he remained hopeful that the Royal Navy could accomplish the task alone.[9] By the end of January 1915, the Royal Navy and the French fleet were staging just outside the mouth of the Dardanelles. The complement included the HMS *Queen Elizabeth*, a *Dreadnought*-class battleship, and the HMS *Ark Royal*, the newest seaplane tender in the fleet. The *Ark Royal* arrived on 17 February, two days before the first bombardment of the forts at the mouth of the Dardanelles.

The HMS *Ark Royal*'s keel was laid in 1914 and was designed from the start to carry seaplanes. While not a modern aircraft carrier, it was designed to carry and house floatplanes, with a number of cranes to lower and recover the planes from the water.[10] Squadron Commander Robert Clarke-Hall, RNAS, was the ship's captain.[11] Clarke-Hall had risen through the ranks with the Royal Navy earning awards and promotions at a steady pace. After graduating the Britannia Naval College in 1897, he was assigned to the China squadron. He served in the Royal Navy during the Boxer Rebellion and returned to England, where he was attached to the Central Air Office in the seaplane design section. His follow-on assignment was with Eastchurch Squadron, working for Squadron Commander Charles Samson, who he eventually succeeded when Samson was named No. 3 RNAS commander. When the *Ark Royal* sailed for the Mediterranean, Clarke-Hall was acting commander of the ship as well as the squadron commander for the seaplanes. He was thirty-one years old.

The six planes on board *Ark Royal* could be lifted from the deck and lowered to the sea, where they would take off on missions. Upon return, they landed on the water close to the ship, then the cranes lifted them back on to the deck for repair, refit, or storage. That February, the *Ark Royal* carried two Sopwith Tabloid land-based aircraft as cargo; they could not be used until a suitable airfield was set up. The ship's contingent of seaplanes included three Sopwith Type 807 seaplanes equipped with one hundred horsepower Gnome Monosoupape engines, another two 1914 Wight Type A.1 pusher biplanes with two hundred horsepower Salmson-built Canton-Unne engines, and a single Short Admiralty Type 135 seaplane with the same engine as the Wights.[12] The weather conditions had to be ideal for all but the Short to perform. Only the Short Type 135, with its two hundred hp Salmson engine, was trustworthy in questionable weather conditions. Even at its largest, the force never had more than six aircraft; more often, due to inhospitable weather, there were none available for operations. One lasting concern was that the Type 807s could not climb high enough to fly above menacing Turkish rifle fire.

The arrival of the *Ark Royal* on 17 February signaled the beginning of aerial operations over the Dardanelles. In the adverse weather of late winter, the machines were severely constrained. Of the four scheduled flights, two were canceled due to engine difficulties and one pilot could not get his underpowered craft to lift off the water, thus only one mission was actually flown.[13] The successful Wight pusher gathered valuable information on the defensive fortifications guarding the straits and came under enemy rifle fire for its troubles. The plane returned to the *Ark Royal* with seven bullet holes.[14] Concurrently, teams were sent to reconnoiter Tenedos and Imbros for suitable locations for airfields for land-based operations.

The Ottomans had issues of their own. The German delegation to aid and assist the Turks, headed by General Liman von Sanders and accompanied by his aide-de-camp Major Carl Mühlmann (the official historian) and Major Erich Serno (German liaison to the Turkish air contingent) were also very short of supplies and manpower. The Ottoman air force could only rely on the use of one obsolete Blériot monoplane during the initial Allied naval attacks. In fact, in March there were only four German aircraft total in the empire.[15] In an interesting side note, the German aircraft were intermittently flown and shipped by rail—labeled as "medical supplies" or as part of a circus train—on their journey through neutral Bulgarian territory. According to Serno's report, the first German replacements did not arrive before the beginning of March.[16] Thus, during the initial naval attacks on the straits, the Allies could boast air supremacy in the theatre. Unfortunately, the weather was a constant problem for the primitive, temperamental machines. Ultimately it was the weather, not the opposition, which was the limiting factor on Allied aerial operations.

But there were concerted efforts to make the nascent technology as viable as possible. The fact that the Allied planes were sent at all is an indication of the willingness to experiment with the new technology. After all, aircraft were making great strides on the Western Front, and seemed an obvious addition to the force in the Mediterranean. Considering this, it is surprising that so few resources were dispatched. There were complimentary technologies that could have been influential. First, a number of new weapons associated with aircraft technology were sent for use. The planes employed offensive weapons such as bombs and fléchettes, and other improved equipment already in use on the Western Front. Defensive weapons included pistols, carbines, shotguns, and light machine guns (in the two-seat aircraft), which were frequently put to use in low-level observation flights. Finally, new tests were conducted with the two wireless telegraphy (or w/t) radio devices—airborne radio—that were brought along with the planes on the *Ark Royal*. Unfortunately, both radio sets malfunctioned on the first day of the naval attacks: the lone pilot able to operate that day was limited to after-action reports following his return to the fleet.[17] Further, the early radios were one-way transmitters. The observers in the air sent messages to the fleet, but could not confirm transmission. Frequently, the fleet did not get messages or chose to ignore them, which was not apparent until the planes returned. This lack of effective communication and trust hampered air-to-surface communication throughout the campaign.

The first Royal Navy and French naval bombardment of the Ottoman forts on the shores of the Dardenelles began on 19 February 1915. The Allied naval contingent comprised 274 medium and heavy naval guns, including eight 15-inch guns on the HMS *Queen Elizabeth*. The Ottoman forts were equipped with an estimated nineteen guns, only four of which were modern, long-range pieces.[18] Remembering the ease that the Germans had destroying Belgian forts at the outset of the war, the fleet prepared to demolish the Turkish strongholds. The difference was that the Germans in Belgium had had more observation planes for spotting and had employed high-angle firing howitzer guns whereas the Allied fleet only had low-angle, although very destructive, naval artillery. The comparison, according to H. A. Jones, was that, "shells from guns knock at the front door, which may be made infinitely thick, whereas howitzer shells come in at the roof."[19] The naval bombardment would have to be very precise and powerful to knock out the Ottoman fortress defenses that guarded the Dardanelles.

The morning of 19 February dawned bright and full of promise for the Allied fleet. Only one of the *Ark Royal*'s Shorts was able to get off the sea in the morning; Flight Commander Kilner and his observer, Sub-Lieutenant Park, took off for their first flight at around 0730 hours. They observed and reported the position of the barracks and fort at Helles, as well as the position of guns at Cape Tekke on their return to a position near Mavro Island, where the *Ark Royal* had anchored. The first flight was successful, but problems had already developed; the w/t radio was not functioning.[20] Thus, even with aerial observation, the fleet did not have a good idea about the effectiveness of the naval fire, and the airmen were impotent to help direct fire. The observers' contributions were limited to after-action reports upon landing.

Another pilot/observer team (Williamson and Bromet) carried out the second flight of the day at 1120 in one of the Wights. The officers were ordered to spot artillery for the HMS *Cornwallis*, which was firing on the fort at Orkanie. Although the observer tapped out messages on the w/t, the *Cornwallis* did not correct fire according to the information from the observers. In the after-action report the flyers were confident that they could have successfully aided in the destruction of the fort had it not been for a broken w/t transmitter. When Williamson realized that communications had broken down, he decided to put his time to good use, and spent the rest of his flight time and fuel observing the accuracy of the morning's naval bombardment. He returned to report that the guns were still in operation at Orkanie, Kum Kale, and Sedd el Bahr.[21]

By mid-afternoon, Admiral Carden decided that the bombardment had been successful, and ordered closer naval operations against the forts. When his ships were fired upon, he realized that his naval artillery had not been nearly as successful as hoped.

That afternoon, another two sorties were launched. The two planes flew artillery-spotting flights, this time for the HMS *Inflexible*, firing on Helles. But once again technology failed, both w/t radios malfunctioned and were useless. In the end, observers reported that it did not matter. There were apparently so many ships firing on Helles that spotting for one ship, the *Inflexible*, was an impossible task.[22] The fleet retired for the day; the seaplanes were hoisted onto the *Ark Royal* and reassessment of the situation began.

Thanks to Mother Nature, there was plenty of time. For the next five days, bad weather precluded operations in the air or on the sea. Socked in by poor February weather, the fleet sat and waited. In context, there were severe constraints on the technology. Although the aircraft offered an important component to the attacks, they were limited by the weather and ability to transmit data back to the fleet. Better communication was needed between the aerial observers and the fleet. Naval artillery faced limitations of its own; the fleets needed a way to be able to destroy the fortresses guarding the straits and silence the Ottoman guns. Each of the components added to the whole, but the tactics had to be revised for better success. The operational pause gave time to reconsider the Allied effort to break the stalemate.

Back in London, the British began proceedings on 20 February that would inextricably involve the Allied forces in a land campaign on Gallipoli. Kitchener ordered General John Maxwell, the British military commander in Gallipoli, to inform General William Birdwood, commander of the Australia and New Zealand Army Corps (ANZAC) troops training in Egypt, of proposed landings on the peninsula to be coordinated with future naval attacks. General Maxwell was ordered to contact Admiral Carden and coordinate the transportation of the troops to the theatre, as well as find out how best to assist the Allied naval expedition.[23] The early reports of the naval attacks had not yet reached Britain; this provides further support for the contention that Kitchener had already considered deploying land forces on Gallipoli regardless of the outcomes of the naval attacks.[24] But although he was considering the use of land forces, he was still unwilling to commit troops fighting on the Western Front. The ANZACs were not yet in combat, and they were in the area and available.

The weather cleared for renewed operations on 25 February. A change in naval tactics promised better naval artillery results against the Turkish forts. The plan was to keep the ships at anchor for stability and precision. The *Queen Elizabeth* and the *Agamemnon* pounded the forts from long range. The attacks were somewhat successful; Ottoman gunners were forced to abandon the coastal forts because of Allied naval artillery. The naval artillery performed well against the fortifications but found it difficult to destroy the Turkish guns. The forts were temporarily evacuated, but to the chagrin of the Allies, when the forts were reoccupied the guns once again began to fire.

For the flyers, the weather continued to cause problems. On 25 February the sea was too choppy for the planes to take off, and there were no flights. Artillery spotting came from other ships anchored at right angles to the *Queen Elizabeth* and *Agamemnon*; it was not entirely effective but was the best the Allied force could do under the circumstances.

By 26 February the weather cleared sufficiently for aerial operations. Only one flight was recorded that day, but it yielded a wealth of information for the fleet. On return, the observer reported that there were guns along the inside of the Dardanelles Straits, but there were no troops. The bad news was that the observer spotted transports and naval ships above the Narrows, en route to Çanakkale; most likely reinforcements headed to the peninsula.[25] With the Royal Navy and French fleets sitting at the mouth of the Dardanelles, the Ottomans were building up forces in the area.

The next day began a new phase in the Dardanelles campaign. Although the planes were again grounded due to poor weather conditions, the success of British Royal Marines deserves mention. Landing parties had been planned but called off on account of the bad weather. But when the naval commanders learned that some of the forts had been abandoned, they decided landings were worth the risk. Two small detachments of Royal Marines were landed, one from the *Vengeance* and one from the *Irresistible*, and were quite successful in reconnoitering the area. They destroyed a number of untouched field pieces and antiaircraft guns. These successes were enhanced by the fact that only one marine was killed and two wounded out of the first force of fifty, with no casualties in the second force of forty-five. The next day more forces were sent ashore, and they returned at the end of the day without loss.[26]

The marines' attacks continued sporadically over the next few weeks and succeeded in destroying most of the outer defenses to the straits. The landing parties observed two important things. First, they could not reach the Turks' inland forts and defenses; and second, the Allied naval artillery was not very effective against the guns themselves. The forts could be destroyed and the gunners often retreated in the face of naval bombardment, but the guns were very hard to put out of commission with naval artillery. Thus the inland forts and defenses, as well as the Turkish mobile units, were still operational and effective against the Allies, and in particular the Allied minesweepers. The minesweepers had been trying to clear the straits for an all-out naval attack but had been constantly harassed by Turkish guns. The only solution at that point was to coordinate close support from destroyers while the plodding minesweepers continued their hazardous duties. However, the civilian-contracted minesweepers were unable (and often unwilling) to face the weather, the mines, the currents, and hostile fire in their duties—the straits remained mined.

One solution considered was the use of aircraft. In the role of observers to direct naval fire or as bombers to deliver bombs directly, the aircraft might have been more effective against the stubborn Turkish defenses. But the weather continued to work against the Allies; the planes simply could not be used. And while the Allied fleet waited on favorable weather, the Turks continued their preparation for the perceived impending assault.

Royal Marine armed reconnaissance missions continued in March but met with stiffening resistance, to the point where a large concerted landing was considered and planned. The planning also coincided with increased aerial operations as the weather cleared. Admiral Carden was still optimistic that he could sail his fleet up the straits, and when he wrote to Kitchener on 4 March, it was decided that the troops in the theatre (40,000 British, French, and ANZAC) should be assembled at Mudros Island off the Gallipoli Peninsula. Further, it was assumed that the number would be enough for a landing on Gallipoli if needed; otherwise they would be delivered directly to Istanbul if the Dardanelles could be cleared.[27] The onus was on Carden to force the straits using whatever means necessary, then the land forces would come and solidify any gains made by the naval forces. The plan was set in motion for a renewed naval attack directly on the Dardanelles.

After the poor weather during February, the air contingent of the *Ark Royal* looked for a break in March. On the 1st, a single plane was able to fly; two other flights failed when the planes broke down. One plane lost its float on takeoff and was nearly lost completely. Another plane's engine was overheating dangerously and had to return to the ship for repairs.[28] The one plane that was able to fly came back with important information from the observer: the temporary field emplacements along the waterway did not yet have guns, while the forts had artillery, but few troops. Further, he noticed minefields in the water, and reported strings of mines blocking the Dardanelles.[29] This was confirmation to the Allies of the exact location of the Ottoman mines in the strait.

On 3 March, everything seemed to be working correctly, even the malfunctioning w/t radio was finally ready for service. Two flights left for duties: one to observe for enemy troops and guns, and another to spot for naval artillery fire from the HMS *Prince George*. The first gathered significant information on the Ottoman preparations and reported that there was noticeable, but not yet significant, enemy buildup in the area. The other arrived on station just as the *Prince George* steamed away, the admiral had not coordinated the timing for the team.[30]

On 5 March, disaster struck twice. The first seaplane set out at 0914 to spot for the *Queen Elizabeth* and was climbing through three thousand feet when the propeller burst. It spiraled out of control and crashed into the sea. The pilot, Flight Lieutenant W. H. S. Garnett, suffered cuts and was in shock. The observer, Flight Commander Hugh Williamson, dislocated his shoulder and was also in shock, but both survived. The plane was a loss, further limiting the operational availability of the squadron.[31] A second plane was sent out to complete the mission of the first but returned after the pilot was shot in the leg. Flight Lieutenant N. S. Douglas was hit by a very lucky shot fired by a soldier on the ground.[32] On the airplane's return, a new pilot jumped in and resumed the mission. The third flight, with working w/t, spotted for the *Queen Elizabeth* until the end of the day. Unfortunately, in one day a valuable plane was destroyed and two pilots and one observer were lost to the effort. The operational pace was beginning to take a toll on the pilots and machines; more of both were needed.[33]

The British were in the process of sending an entire squadron to the Dardanelles; No. 3 Squadron, Royal Naval Air Service, was ordered to report to the Dardanelles on 27 February.[34] It is significant that the unit attached to the operation was not part of the Royal Flying Corps; the RNAS unit was perceived as more appropriate for the mission, as well as slightly less necessary on the Western Front. For the same reasons that Kitchener did not want to send his British ground troops from the Western Front to the Dardanelles, the decision was made to send an RNAS squadron rather than an RFC squadron. In addition, the French were preparing a squadron for the Dardanelles. Antoine Césari was promoted to captain on 5 March, put in charge of the newly created MF. 98(T) Squadron headed for Tenedos, and they too began packing for the Mediterranean.[35]

In the meantime, the remaining planes on the *Ark Royal* flew missions in support of the fleet. A combined attack was planned to force the straits with the assembled naval power. The idea was to sail up the Dardanelles with the battleships, destroying the forts and clearing a path to Istanbul. Carden realized that it was dangerous as he would have to deal with both gunfire from the shores as well as mines in the water. He needed to silence the forts' guns to sweep the mines but needed to sweep the mines to get the ships in close enough to destroy the forts. He turned to the airmen to spot the mines so that they could be neutralized or avoided.

The fliers were tasked to find the mines during the day and the civilian minesweepers, pressed into service, would sweep the channel by night. The training for the novel aerial mission was not very complicated. The British placed a number of dummy mines around the *Ark Royal*, so that the observers could determine the best altitude and time off day to attempt reconnaissance. Flying at one thousand, fifteen hundred, and three thousand feet, the observers could spot mines placed around the *Ark Royal* at depths of five, ten, and eighteen feet under water.[36] The observation was done in ideal conditions and with foreknowledge of the mines placement, making it easy to spot the mines. Fortunately, the practice paid off and almost all of the mines in the Dardanelles Straits were spotted and mapped, and attempts were made to clear them.

Between 13 and 17 March the *Ark Royal* aviators attempted to spot and map the mines for the fleet. By the 17th all of the mines laid by that point had been mapped on the master charts, and the fleet prepared for the naval attack, slated for 17 March. However, several events coincided that threw off the plan for the naval attack. Vice Admiral Carden fell ill as the fleet prepared for the naval attack on the Dardanelles. On the advice of his doctor, he returned to England; his successor was Vice Admiral John de Robeck. De Robeck was still committed to the plan, but pushed it off until 18 March when he thought the weather would be better.[37] The plan called for sixteen battleships in three waves to sail up the Dardanelles, firing on the Ottoman forts while minesweepers cleared the way to the Narrows.[38] But the delay of a day allowed the Ottomans to lay a new string of mines in Eren Keui Bay, parallel to the Asian shore. All of the mines across the Dardanelles had been spotted and mapped, but the fateful string of twenty-six mines in Eren Keui Bay was laid on the night of 17/18 March.[39] The observation flights had not even been looking in the area where the new mines were laid.

On the morning of 18 March, as the fleet sailed into the Dardanelles, guns blazing, aircraft launched to spot for the fleet. Their task was to observe artillery fire as well as report any dangers. The naval attack began at 0830, but the first plane did not get off the water until 1035 hours, well after the initial attacks had already commenced. Flight Lieutenant R. Whitehead and Lieutenant L. Strain saw the vicious fighting between the ships and land batteries, reporting a number of the forts were abandoned due to the heavy naval shelling. The observer spotted a number of minelayers adding to the defenses north of the Narrows. It seemed that the Ottomans were worried that the Allies would break out past that point very early in the battle. Fortunately, that day the w/t radio was working, and Strain related messages throughout the flight. At noon the plane developed engine trouble and was forced to return.[40] The second flight of the day took off immediately to provide aerial observation for the battle. They were also able to use the w/t radio, and conveyed information back to the fleet on the progress. Flight

Lieutenant N. Douglas and Petty Officer B. Brady reported successful shelling of the forts as well as a direct hit on a barracks, but noted no decrease in shelling coming from the shore batteries.[41] They returned just before 1400. By that point the Allied fleet was taking heavy fire from the shore batteries, both the mobile emplacements and the forts. As the French battleship *Bouvet* advanced up the right flank, it hit one of the mines in the new minefield, with disastrous consequences. The *Bouvet* capsized and sank, with 660 men of the 710-strong complement lost in a matter of minutes.[42] Shortly after 1600, the HMS *Irresistible* was forced to retreat from the line under heavy Ottoman fire and turned directly into the unseen mine field. In sequence, the *Inflexible* and the *Ocean* also hit mines—four battleships were lost within the space of a few hours.[43] At nightfall, the attack was called off. The Allies had lost a quarter of their battleship power, and did not know the toll on the enemy, who had continued to fire until the Allied ships were out of range. The Allied fleet returned to the safety of their island base and weighed the costs of the day's actions.

The Ottoman/German contingent also flew that day. Serno had dispatched a single seaplane to Çanakkale, which arrived on 17 March. After assembly, Serno took it up on its first test flight.[44] As the sun came up the next morning, Serno took to the skies again, with a man named Schneider—one of Admiral Guido von Usedom's staff officers—in the observer's cockpit. As they climbed to 5,280 feet, they spotted the Allied fleet, preparing for the attack on the forts.[45] Without weapons, Serno and Schneider could only watch the events below them unfold. As the naval attack began, Serno turned back to the seaplane base at Çanakkale, flying as fast as the machine would carry them. They mounted horses, raced to Admiral Usedom's headquarters, and alerted the defenses that an attack was imminent. It is unclear whether they returned before the start of the attack, but Serno suggests that their information was instrumental in waking up the defenses and repelling the attack.[46]

The Allied air contingent can be absolved of culpability for the failed naval attack for three reasons. First, the initial mission did not take off until 1030 hours, two hours into the operation. A combination of calm seas and no wind—a beautiful day, but conditions that hampered launching seaplanes—kept the planes on the sea. Second, the mines in Eren Keui Bay were outside of their observation area: the observers were simply not looking for them there. Third, according to the official Turkish history, the mines were fortuitously laid on the night before the Allied naval attack, 17–18 March. Therefore, the observers would not have seen them prior to the day of the attack even if they had been looking for them. The pilots and observers were not at fault; it was a deeply flawed plan to begin with.

In fact, the aerial operations can be applauded for the successes that they did have. The radios were working, and the two flights that day did provide good intelligence for the fleet. They were able to spot for the naval artillery successfully. And even though the Ottoman guns were not silenced, the planes were able to direct fire to drive off the defenders from the forts and guns in various locations. The weather continued to hamper aerial operations, and mechanical issues troubled the fragile planes, but overall the addition of airpower to the naval attack was a beneficial component to the operational plan. However, there were still too few planes, not enough radios, and poor coordination for the planes to add a substantial advantage.

The failure of the naval raid cemented the Allied response. In London, Churchill agreed with Fisher that the attacks must continue.[47] But instead of additional naval attacks, the Allies began to investigate a way to disable the Ottoman guns with ground power, aided by airpower, and overcome the Ottoman defenses with an amphibious assault. The plan called for a substantial ground force landed on the shores of the Gallipoli Peninsula to gain the high ground and destroy the Ottoman defenses. Then the minesweepers could sweep the Dardanelles at their leisure, clearing the path for a renewed naval attack up the straits to Istanbul. The planned naval attack on the Ottoman capital was not completely discarded, it was merely modified to include an amphibious assault. In the interim, the air component would be bolstered, improved, and strengthened to include more planes, pilots, and arms, to provide a more effective fighting force from the air. A pair of dashing commanders and two audacious squadrons—one British, one French—were called on to provide aerial support for a new Gallipoli operational plan.

CHAPTER FOUR

The Landings

The Allies escalated at Gallipoli. The naval plan—aided by airpower—was not successful; de Robeck called for ground troops to assault the peninsula and gain a foothold at Gallipoli.[1] On the Allied side, the expansion of the joint operation meant more planning, preparation, and buildup in order to launch a successful amphibious attack. On 23 March de Robeck speculated that an invasion might be possible one month hence.[2]

The defenders set to work as well. There had been two substantial but ultimately unsuccessful attacks on the forts guarding the straits, yet the British and French navies lingered. Had they left, the Ottomans may have turned their attention to other fronts. There were other concerns around the Ottoman Empire, but the presence of the Allied fleet at the mouth of the Dardanelles was the wolf at the door. Ottoman Minister of War Enver Paşa turned to his German military advisor Liman von Sanders and asked him to lead the defense of the Dardanelles.[3] Sanders took command of the hastily assembled Fifth Army, tasked with the defense of the Gallipoli Peninsula. He had 60,000 men at his disposal, but realized he faced a monumental task to prepare for the impending assault. In his memoirs Sanders commented, "the British gave me four full weeks before their great landing."[4] The Fifth Army included five divisions, all of which had to be placed for best strategic result. Sanders could count on a reserve division on its way from Istanbul, but also had an entire peninsula to defend. He was not certain where the Allies would land and had to make calculated tactical decisions. He knew that the Allies would attempt to gain the highest ground, so he placed his divisions to defend Achi Baba near the southern beachhead and more around Chunuk Bair, farther north up the peninsula. Sanders realized that the Allied naval artillery was superior; his only hope was to defend against the amphibious assault and prevent the Allies from gaining a foothold and the high ground. He continued to lament that he had no airpower under his command and that harassment by Allied aircraft was frequent and disconcerting.[5] By that point the Ottomans only had four land aircraft in the entire theater (with only another three seaplanes at Çanakkale), which were only recently arrived from Germany. The land planes were flown across Serbia by German contractors and then crated up and shipped across neutral Bulgaria. After various bribes were paid to the Bulgarians, the crates were sent on by rail to Turkey where they were reassembled at the airfield at Yeşilköy. The shipment included a Rumpler B.1 and three Albatros B.1s. Another seven aircraft were held in Bulgaria after the government there declined to help the Ottomans.[6] By the end of March, one plane was sent to a hastily prepared airfield at Çanakkale where it began operations for the Ottoman forces in support of the Chunuk fort (but not under Sanders' command). The land plane and three seaplanes there were under the command of the local naval commander. Sanders only had jurisdiction over one land plane at the Galata airfield on the Gallipoli Peninsula. Interestingly, German pilots flew the planes; they had been quickly pressed into Ottoman service and given Turkish uniforms and ranks.[7] The planes were even more obsolete than the Allied models. The German land plane squadron commander at Galata, Erich Serno, accepted a commission in the Turkish army as a major and was joined by twelve German pilots and thirty-two mechanics. The pilots were all given commissions while the mechanics worked under contract to the Ottoman government (and wore Turkish uniforms). The two squadrons, located at Galata and Çanakkale, immediately added Turkish mechanics and hastily trained pilots to their ranks.[8]

There was substantial confusion in the Ottoman camp regarding command and control of the aviation assets. The land planes (in March only one) were assigned to the army high command with Serno in charge. The seaplanes (three of which were sent to the Çanakkale base) were under the strategic command of Admiral Usedom, as the Oberkommando der Meerengen (High Command of the Straits). Leutnant Pruessner was the pilot officer in direct command of the seaplanes in March; the Abteilung (German for "department," loosely translated as "group") included Kapitan Leutnant Hussein, the most experienced Ottoman naval observer.[9] But as events unfolded, there was no clear command and control over the aviation assets: land-based planes fell under the Army command whereas seaplanes were under the jurisdiction of the Dardanelles naval commanders. Issues with command and control complicated coordination and effectiveness of the Ottoman aerial assets.

After arriving on station in the middle of March, Commander Charles Samson's 3 Squadron RNAS advance party took to the air in their serviceable planes at the end of the month on the 27th, instructed to gather intelligence for the planned troop landings. Samson initially commanded 11 aircraft, a dozen pilots, half a dozen observers, and another 40 men, including maintainers, mechanics, and air operations clerks. By the first week of April, the rest of the squadron arrived by ship, bringing another dozen aircraft (for a total of 22—including the two Sopwith Tabloids from the *Ark Royal*) and the remaining manpower: a total of 18 officers and 102 men.

Over the next three weeks, No. 3 Squadron RNAS planes flew over the peninsula on a regular basis, mapping and photographing potential landing sites for the navy and army. One of the officers in particular was quite adept at photography. Flight Lieutenant C. H. Butler exposed nearly all of the seven hundred plates used by the army and navy to map the peninsula.[10] In an interesting twist of history, the pre-landing photographs taken by 3 Squadron were all made with a German-made camera.[11] Furthermore, the Allied flyers observed and recorded Turkish strongholds and depots. They successfully mapped trenches, machine gun emplacements, and heavy artillery, as well as encampments and supply depots. In the stages before the Allied landings, the British resorted to using "chiefly light-weight midshipmen" to augment the lack of trained aerial observers.[12] Under Samson's orders, pilots took as many bombs as they could into the air for every mission.[13] The pilots dropped bombs on any targets of opportunity during their flights. Although the small 20-pound bombs were ineffective against hardened targets, they did serve to harass troops on the ground.

An important discovery was made on 15 April. The Turkish land-plane aerodrome at Çanakkale was sighted from the air. On the 18th, a German pilot "had the cheek" to fly over the British squadron's Tenedos airfield, dropping three 16-pound bombs, none of which exploded.[14] In retaliation, Samson and two of his pilots—Richard Bell Davies and Charles Herbert Collet—flew to reciprocate against the newly discovered Çanakkale airfield. Samson recounts, "I always made it a rule, whenever possible, that if anybody bombed my aerodrome, we always returned the visit immediately, and gave them worse than they gave us."[15] He continues, "I certainly found it paid us, as they generally treated my aerodrome as holy ground. Every now and then, when some new Austrian or German arrived, they had a go; but they found it an unpopular pastime."[16] The three British planes dropped six 100-pound bombs on the main Turkish hangar and destroyed the plane housed inside. The operations they had carried out against the zeppelin sheds on the Western Front were useful experience for their missions at Gallipoli. The British achieved effective air supremacy over the peninsula with the bombing raid. The Turkish-German air contingent, specifically the plane at Çanakkale, was put out of action and did not resume air activity "of much account" before July.[17] Samson's squadron had complete freedom in the air, even though the Turks continued air operations with their unarmed seaplanes. During the spring and early summer the few remining Turkish aircraft were spotted in the air, but they were limited to unarmed observation flights against the Allied squadrons and the fleet. Samson's squadron continued their task of mapping the peninsula for upcoming operations.

Meanwhile, on the Aegean side of the peninsula, the *Ark Royal*'s seaplanes continued their work as well. Between the naval attacks on 18 March and the landings, the *Ark Royal*'s seaplanes launched sixteen flights, all to either spot for gunfire against coastal fortifications or reconnoiter enemy positions. On 28 March, Clark-Hall reported that an enemy aircraft attacked the *Ark Royal* with two bombs, neither of which hit. But the nervous captain sailed the ship from where it was anchored near Rabbit Island back to Tenedos for protection. It was a more distant base, but it was more protected from curious enemy planes.[18] Up to the landings, the remainder of the flights focused on observing for naval fire and spotting troop movements on the peninsula. Unfortunately for the British pilots, the weather was always a concern and the reports indicate that on a number of days it was simply too nasty to fly the fragile machines. On 15 April, two of the *Ark Royal*'s seaplanes attempted to bomb the Turkish battleship *Torgud Reis*, anchored off the town of Gallipoli in the northern area of the straits. No damage was reported, but it is interesting that the seaplanes could range that far and actually attack ships afloat.[19] The best results were reported on 16

April, when a seaplane directed naval fire against a large Turkish ammunition magazine. It scored a direct hit, destroying the enclosure and "causing a considerable volume of white smoke."[20]

All of the British records from both Samson and Clark-Hall confirm the problems faced by the early aviators. The planes were vulnerable to a variety of issues, from weather to mechanical. Both commanders sent frequent requests for more machines and men, but continually complained about the environment at Gallipoli. It was amazing that with the constraints of the early technology the commanders were able to maintain the operational pace with the restrictions that they faced. On a regular basis both men mention lack of parts, from broken propellers to misfiring magnetos. They also suffered from a lack of lubricants, fuel, bombs, machine parts, and tools. The seaplanes' problems were compounded by the saltwater and consequent operations from the sea as well as the high humidity and increasing temperatures. Furthermore, the lack of adequate radios meant that communications between the planes and the ships were problematic at best. This was less of a problem for Samson, who operated almost entirely independently from the fleet, but it remained an issue for Clark-Hall's fliers. Nonetheless, the pilots flew, observed, and continued their outstanding work as best they could for the planned amphibious invasion of the Gallipoli Peninsula.

Two days before the landings, 3 Squadron mounted its biggest raid to date. A motley collection of five aircraft took off at around noon to bomb the Turk encampment at Maidos. Samson flew in No. 50 alone, Collet was in a BE2c, and Davies, Marix, and Richard Edmund Charles Peirse were in Maurice Farmans; Marix was accompanied by Bill Wilson, his observer.[21] Combined they carried seven 100-pound bombs and another six 20-pound bombs and attacked the Turk camp "with fairly good effect."[22] The target was the 57th Regiment, which had been in training since the end of February, under the direct command of Colonel Mustafa Kemal. Kemal described the 57th as "his most solid regiment."[23] Although good, and highly trained, the Ottoman forces tended to be mixed ethnic Turks and Arabs (and others) and most were illiterate.[24] Samson recounts that in the attack, more than twenty of the enemy were killed and a larger number wounded, while the camp was set on fire.[25] The disorganized soldiers scattered and were forced to take refuge in the hills.

On the morning of 25 April, the Allies landed on the shores of Gallipoli. To the north, on the Aegean peninsula, the first wave of Australian and New Zealander (ANZAC) troops were quietly lowered into their landing boats from the HMS *Queen,* HMS *Prince of Wales*, and HMS *London*. The ANZACs aimed at the beach at Gaba Tepe. When they landed they found themselves more than a mile north of the intended landing spot, facing difficult terrain. They immediately tried to press up the imposing hills, but were rebuffed by rifle fire, artillery, and quick reinforcements from Kemal's division. Though the ANZACs landed 19,000 troops by the end of the day, they were pinned down at the place they designated ANZAC Cove.[26] Seven flights were made that day by the floatplanes from the *Ark Royal*. They were ordered to spot for naval artillery to cover the landing forces "until military observers [on shore] were in position themselves to control ship's fire."[27] Further, the pilots were ordered to observe and report enemy troop movement. Unfortunately, due to the rough terrain and inability to see the battlefield, "few results were obtained."[28] Thus, even though the floatplanes had their most active day, they did not add substantially to the offensive undertaken at ANZAC Cove. The first day's objective—to gain the high ground—was unsuccessful when lead elements were pushed back to the beaches after nightfall.

The balloon ship HMS *Manica* and No.1 Kite Balloon Section also starred in the opening act of the Gallipoli landings. The balloon spotted for naval artillery at ANZAC Cove, and witnessed the landings from an offshore perspective. Although the balloon observers could not see the inland features of the Gallipoli Peninsula in detail because of the steep terrain, they were high enough to observe the straits on the other side of the peninsula. The balloon observers were able to coordinate fire to drive a Turkish battleship—the *Torgud Reis*, which had been attacked by aircraft on 15 April—away with well-directed naval artillery from the HMS *Triumph*. The balloon observers had the benefit of communications, but they did not enjoy the clarity of vision of the planes. The balloon was important for observation of the Straits, but her view of the peninsula itself was oblique hence imprecise and ineffectual against land targets. However, the account of the balloon observers deserves mention. On 26 April, the *Manica*'s balloon spotted for the naval guns of the *Triumph* and the *Queen Elizabeth*. The balloon observed Turkish transports in the straits and directed naval artillery on them. The Turkish transports, bringing reinforcements to the area were prime, slow-moving targets for the Allied naval guns. As the balloon observers "put the *Queen Elizabeth*['s fire] on to the largest of them, signaling the first shot fifty yards short and the second fifty yards over. After the third shot, to the listening ears of Vice-Admiral de Robeck came the message 'O.K.' 'What do they mean by O.K.?' he shouted down the telephone. 'Have we hit her?' The question was signaled to the *Manica* and back came the reply: 'Yes, she's sinking by the stern and I am putting you on another.' "[29]

Interestingly, the Ottoman ship was a captured British steamer, formerly the *Scutari*. It was at that point that de Robeck telegraphed London for more balloons for the naval force. Eventually he received two more for observation and spotting duties in the Gallipoli Campaign.

At the tip of the peninsula, British troops landed at Cape Helles on beaches designated S, V, W, X, and Y. General Ian Hamilton, commanding the entire landing, sent the British 29th Division against the toe of Gallipoli. Troops waded ashore in the face of strong defensive positions. The invasion included the collier *River Clyde* intentionally grounded at V Beach with two thousand men aboard, who poured out of makeshift ramps when the ship beached. As the British attacked, they faced prepared defenses and strong resistance.[30]

Samson's squadron flew top cover for the Helles landings, recording sixteen flights that day. Samson was first in the air at 0515 with Lieutenant Osmond in the front seat of the Maurice Farman observing.[31] Although Samson was convinced that the landings would not be successful,[32] he recalled that it was a "splendid morning for air work."[33] His pilots tried to spot for the ships' guns, but with all of the firing and only one working radio, it was nearly impossible. They simply flew above the maelstrom and took notes for later reports. The pilots and observers also tried to bomb the Turkish positions, but to little effect. Samson had seven aircraft available for the landing operation, and all flew a number of times that day.[34] All of his pilots flew, even Bill Wilson, the "heaviest pilot"[35] who flew with Bill Samson (the squadron commander's brother) and returned to base with a number of bullet holes in the plane, the reward for flying low due to the combined weight of the two men. Samson lamented that "if my Squadron had been given a freer hand, and allowed to devote itself to low bombing, we might have been able to assist the landing to a greater extent than we did."[36] But with limited aircraft and primitive technology—to say nothing of accurate, effective, and unceasing Turkish rifle fire—it was unlikely that the squadron could have made much more of an impact than it did; it was constrained by numbers and equipment. The squadron's contribution was limited to spotting, reporting, and mapping duties, with an occasional lucky hit with small bombs dropped by the pilots and observers. Its actions were important before the amphibious invasion: the squadron flew to provide tactical intelligence for the sea and ground forces. Samson's efforts on the day of the landings showed both the abilities and the limitations of the technology at that time. Incidentally, in the margins of the squadron's flying log, Samson recorded that in sixteen flights they racked up 36 hours, 55 minutes of flight time and 2,362 miles on that fateful day.[37]

On the Asian side of the shore at Kum Kale, French troops landed without the benefit of air cover; no British planes could be spared for the French landings. It remains unclear as to where the five or six French floatplanes and the tender *Foudre* were located on the day of the landings. A few French ships sailed north on the Aegean side of the peninsula to deceive the Turks into believing that a landing might go ashore at Besika Bay.[38] As well, the French troops landed on the Asian shore of the Dardanelles were evacuated over the next few days; the ruse was simply to hold the Ottoman forces on that side of the waters to assist the Gallipoli landings. Because the French effort was diversionary, the records do not indicate the extent of their air operations on the day of the landings. In the end, the naval deception held two Turkish divisions in place to the north while the amphibious assault on the Asian shore held defenses in and around Çanakkale, but did not substantially change the successes of the landings at Helles. In other words, the French efforts did not help the British and ANZACs to achieve strategic victory.

The campaign commanders de Robeck and Hamilton failed to understand the potential of aircraft and aviation assets in the execution phase of the landings at Gallipoli. Both Clark-Hall and Samson led their missions as best they could, within the limitations of the technology, but did not have a significant effect on the operations on the peninsula. In the amphibious assault, there was little coordination between the sea, land, and air components; no one realized the potential benefits of combining the assets for a more effective outcome. For the primary mission—spotting for naval artillery—the planes could have been more useful if the communications technologies had been used more effectively with better coordination. Unfortunately, there was a lack of radios for communications, even though the technology was available. Furthermore, when the planes did try to communicate with the ships to control the fires more precisely, ships' gunners usually ignored the information. Thus, even though the pilots and observers had a bird's-eye view of the battlefield and could have assisted in placing shot more effectively for the benefit of the troops on the ground, miscommunication and poor coordination meant that the ships fired at what they thought was important rather than in direct support of the landings. Granted, ranging and fire were very primitive at the time and could have had disastrous results, but overall there could have been better coordination between the air and sea components. As well, there was no way for the troops on the ground in the invasion force to communicate with the aircraft or vice versa. Thus, there was a complete absence of communication between the troops on the ground and the aircraft flying overhead. Finally, even though the planes carried small bombs, neither the *Ark Royal* floatplanes nor 3 Squadron planes had any way to distinguish more important from less important targets in the melee of the invasion. They did not know the best ways to support troops on the ground, thus could not help effectively. And there were no guns on the early aircraft; the concept and execution of close air support was still in its infancy. The only viable mission for aircraft in April 1915 was to observe and report, giving Hamilton information on the progress of the invasion force at the end of each mission. It is unclear if the daily reports made it back to fleet or military headquarters at the end of each day. There is little mention in Samson's memoirs or squadron logs of communication to de Robeck or Hamilton other than weekly meetings to discuss the role of aircraft. Clark-Hall, on the other hand, had access to communications and a more-or-less direct line back to de Robeck. It can be assumed that he made more regular reports back to the fleet, although the written reports of the *Ark Royal* were submitted weekly. That said, it is unclear from the records to what extent these reports affected the progress of the campaign. Early in the Gallipoli campaign the air component was simply an additional technology that offered situational awareness, to say nothing of the adventure within the squadrons, but did little to directly influence the ground and naval campaign against the Turks.

On the ground, the Royal Naval Air Service did provide an interesting component to the invasion force. After the introduction of the armored car and armed motorcycles in Belgium (championed by Samson), the RNAS decided to pursue the technology. By the Gallipoli Campaign there were a number of "squadrons" built around cars, trucks, and motorcycles carrying guns. Two armored car squadrons, Number 3 and Number 4, as well as No. 10 Motor Cycle Machine Gun Squadron were sent to Gallipoli when it was determined that they could not be used on the Western Front, which had devolved into static trench warfare. Before the landings at Gallipoli, the machine guns were stripped from the vehicles and put on the landing ships for use in the amphibious invasion.[39] A week after the landings, the cars and motorcycles were transported to the peninsula, where they were refitted with their guns so they could resume their role as mobile gun platforms. During the campaign, they provided transport, conveyed messages, and (as designed) raced around shooting. Although officially attached to the RNAS, they functioned as a component of the ground war and fell under the direction of the ground commanders.

One important factor became painfully clear to the two British squadron commanders: the lack of logistics support. The fleet and the RNAS squadron were a long way from their home bases in England and faced long lines of communication and supply. With the fever pitch of operations, both Clark-Hall and Samson found it difficult to keep their squadrons operational. Both lamented the lack of spare parts, compounded by too few pilots; they voiced the need for additional aircraft in nearly every report back to London.[40] The long sea-lanes of communication hampered efforts across the board for the entire fleet and ground force, but delays were especially acute for the demands of aerial warfare.

In the week following the landings, the two squadrons were busy and continued their observation flights in support of the fleet and the ground forces. Concurrently, the *Ark Royal*'s seaplanes faced problems; there were few flights that lasted more than an hour in duration due to mechanical failures. The operational tempo was beginning to show on the overtaxed aircraft and crews.[41] Samson's squadron flew unceasingly, logging many hours in the air. On the 29th, Samson flew a Maurice Farman with Hogg acting as observer for the HMS *Prince George*.[42] On that day the ship heeded the aerial intelligence and was able to score a direct hit on a Turkish gun battery. Hogg "signaled 'up 200 yards shrapnel,' and the old *P.G.*, ever keen to respond to us, fired two salvos of 6-inch shrapnel, which blew half the crews to Allah."[43] The Turks started to realize that it was not safe to be spotted from the air, even if they could not bring down the Allied aircraft. British ground troops reported up through Hamilton that when aircraft were overhead the Turks did not fire their guns, for fear of being fired upon by the ships directed by the aircraft observers.[44] Aircraft began to prove their deterrent role; when the planes were in the air, the Turks were reluctant to expose their mobile artillery batteries. This encouraged the planners to incorporate the aviation arm into operational planning. If the Turks did not fire when the planes were up and active, the ground forces stood a better chance of successfully launching offensives on the ground. Hamilton was learning how to use airpower to his advantage.

Samson wanted to put an airfield on the Gallipoli peninsula. With aircraft at the front, he reasoned he could provide more and quicker air coverage for the ground troops. He went by ship to the Helles beaches and scouted a suitable place for a few aircraft. The ground troops at Helles had advanced three miles up the gently sloping ground towards Kirithia, still two miles distant. Samson thought it offered enough room to erect an airfield at the front. The site he chose, a half mile inland from the Lancashire landing at W Beach, was a small but flat area, suitable for a few planes.[45] He later bragged, "Well, we were some aviators that have been able to land and get off again from that little patch."[46] And he was correct—it was indeed a small landing area. Unbeknownst to him at the time, the small strip was also within range and in direct sightline of the Turkish guns on Achi Baba, the initial objective of the landing force. With only a few depressions, the ground from the Helles beach rises steadily to the heights at Achi Baba, where the Turks had ample artillery. They could see the aircraft and the Helles landing site. A hillock on the water side was used to hide the aircraft, but the airstrip was in full view of the Turks.[47] Samson planned to keep a couple of aircraft there, for immediate use against the Turks and to cut down on the travel time back-and-forth from Tenedos. The strip could also serve as an emergency field for damaged planes, so that they would not have to fly over water to return to base.

The Helles airfield was abandoned after only a short while. Samson was instructed by Hamilton to vacate the premises; the ground troops in the area took heavy fire whenever aircraft were there. Samson concurred; he lost five valuable aircraft to enemy fire at this exposed airfield. In his memoirs, Samson recounts a hilarious anecdote: when the squadron abandoned the Helles landing strip, they left a dummy airplane to see what the Turks would do. The Turks wasted 127 shells firing at the counterfeit aircraft on the first day without damaging it. Moorehead recounts that "the Army had the enjoyment of watching the Turks bombard it for a week on end. Some 500 shells exploded on the field before the machine was demolished."[48]

On 30 April a reconnaissance flight spotted a Turkish encampment north of Bulair.[49] At two and a half hours, it was one of the longest flights to date for the squadron. Upon return, when told of the seven thousand Turks at the location, Samson dispatched "as many planes as I could muster," including his own, to bomb the location.[50] The three (or possibly four) planes dropped six 100-pound and nine 20-pound bombs on the enemy with "excellent results."[51] From the documents, it is clear that there was little oversight from the commanders of the fleet or the ground forces on what the aviators were up to. Samson's squadron was able to attack targets of opportunity according to their own wishes restricted only by the weather and availability of machines. The *Ark Royal* floatplanes and kite balloons were tied more directly to the fleet, acting as observers for the navy. Samson and his squadron on Tenedos were completely isolated from the fleet and the ground forces, literally and figuratively, and had complete autonomy in planning and prosecuting operations.

At the start of May, two new forces entered the fray, one for each of the belligerents. On Sunday, 2 May, French land-based aviation arrived in theater. Captain Antoine Césari landed at Tenedos with his new squadron, Escadrille MF. 98(T).[52] He commanded eight officers and about forty men, and employed eight Maurice Farman HF.20s, with eighty-horsepower Gnome rotary engines. The two-seat pusher had the engine behind the pilot, and the observer in the nose of the aircraft. MF. 98(T) began operations at once, scouting the Asiatic side of the Dardanelles, and supporting the French troops that had been relocated to Helles after evacuating the Asian shore. As the French and RNAS were both at the same aerodrome, the interaction between the two was immediate and fortunately friendly. Samson and Césari got along famously, sharing drink, food, and company. The squadron leaders also shared parts and machines mounting impromptu raids together.[53] At one point, Samson gave Césari two Nieuports in exchange for a Maurice Farman adding, "Of course we did these things unofficially."[54]

The Turks, with German help, were rapidly trying to catch up in the air. After the devastating raid on their airfield at Çanakkale in April, they reconstituted quickly, and by the start of May had two replacement land-based machines for observation and scouting. Further north, the Turks organized a navy sea aircraft squadron, with three trainers:[55] two Nieuports—one with wheels and one with floats—and a single American-built Curtiss F flying boat. They were based at Yeşilköy airfield. The field was shared by the army aviation training squadron, which also had a ramp to the Sea of Marmara for seaplanes.[56] After the landings, at least one of the seaplanes—probably the Curtiss—was moved to a temporary base at the town of Gallipoli. On 2 May the Turkish seaplane flew toward the 3 Squadron base at Tenedos and Marix took off after it. Samson reports that Marix forced the seaplane to land near Kephez point, killing the observer, whether by a rough landing or action by Marix is unclear.[57] Although the substantiating evidence is lacking, if this incident is factual it marks the first loss of an aviator in the campaign. The next day an Ottoman airplane attacked the HMS *Manica* with two bombs, but both missed their mark.[58] From that day forward there was a marked increase in the mission notations for both the *Ark Royal* floatplanes and 3 Squadron flying logs for "Enemy Aircraft Patrol." The Allied airmen began searching in earnest for enemy aircraft in the theater.

According to the German records, the lack of aviation assets was a constant concern for the defenders.[59] Serno had ordered a number of aircraft from Germany, but continued to have issues actually getting them. Neutral Bulgaria and Romania persisted in complicating shipment of military goods from Germany to the Ottoman Empire. Thus, even though there were planes available, in crates and ready for transport, the Ottoman forces lacked airpower because of the tyranny of distance. The planes at Yeşilköy were unsuitable for combat operations and were needed for the ongoing training mission. The few planes at the front faced continual harassment by the Allies, who seemed to be gaining strength every day. Serno needed better airplanes quickly to even attempt to stem the Allied airpower capabilities. Although two squadrons were constituted on paper—one land-based and one seaplane—on the day of the landings, and into the early summer, both were "paper tigers." The land-based *Abteilung* (squadron) assigned to

Sander's forces only had one plane stationed at Galata, and the seaplane squadron had only two or three planes at Çanakkale. Ottoman-German airpower logistics and capabilities would not be resolved until July. In the meantime, the Allies enjoyed nearly complete air supremacy.

The landings at Gallipoli expanded the campaign exponentially. Both the Allies and the Central Powers raced to reinforce and expand their operations. As part of the increase, both sides bolstered their airpower. Men and machines were rushed to Gallipoli to strengthen respective forces. For Clark-Hall, Samson, and Césari, it meant additional airpower resources for the campaign. The Ottomans also worked to add machines and men for operations, although they faced more issues. But even with widespread excitement for the capability, there was little coordination as to the use. Clark-Hall, Samson, Césari, and Serno were able to mount more flights, but there was no strategic coordination to guide the use of airpower in how it could benefit ground or sea operations. Both sides began to look for ways for airpower to have strategic and operational effect in the campaign for Gallipoli.

CHAPTER FIVE

Summer over Gallipoli

After the landings, airpower played an increasingly important role in the Gallipoli Campaign. On both sides, airmen ratcheted up the tempo of operations to try to shift the balance of power on land. However, both sides were still plagued by a lack of coordination with their high commands, as airpower was not effectively integrated into operational planning. It was a heady time for the pilots and observers, who had absolute autonomy, but a nadir for strategic and operational planning as no one could figure out how to best employ the aerial weapon. Thus, operations continued as before; Allied and enemy pilots flew and fought as best they could in hopes of influencing the war on the ground and at sea.

Once the landing areas were consolidated, the Ottomans rushed reinforcements to drive the Allies back into the sea and off the peninsula. On 1 May, 18,000 Turks tried to push the ANZACs off their beach, but the ANZACs had superior naval fire and held. The ANZACs launched a counterattack the next day but could not drive the Turks out of their trenches. Because of the terrain, the HMS *Manica*'s kite balloon observers could not see the Ottoman positions to spot for naval artillery. The *Ark Royal* planes could not effectively guide the naval fire due to the lack of working radios. The Turks remained hidden in their trenches in ravines behind the high mountains. All of these factors combined to negate the flat trajectory of the British ships' fire.[1] At Helles, the Turks tried a night attack on 1–2 May, but the beach held.[2] Both sides reinforced and dug in; trench warfare became de rigueur at Gallipoli. The Allies could not advance in the face of the strengthening Turkish defenses, and the Turks could not force the Allies off the beaches because of Allied naval artillery. An opportunity arose for airpower to turn the tide of the war. For the German pilots attached to the Ottoman Army, the ability to drive the fleet away could affect the ground war. For the Allied pilots and observers, cutting Turkish logistics arteries to the lower peninsula presented an opportunity. Both sides ramped up operations to disrupt the others' strategic plans.

Fortunately for the Allies, they had more aircraft. Samson recounts the efforts that began early in the month to restructure the squadron's efforts against Turkish supply lines and logistics. In the first two weeks of May, the squadron logged a record 55 percent of the flights as bombing or spotting for naval artillery in support of the ground troops in the two battles for the town of Krithia.[3] Included in this number were attacks on the Turkish aircraft at the Çanakkale airfield, as well as several photographic missions. Samson wanted to attack deeper targets, such as roads and encampments, but did not have the necessary equipment for deep-penetration strikes until 17 May.

In London, there was a shakeup at the government level. Jackie Fisher stepped down as the first sea lord on 15 May, after heated arguments about the outcomes of the Dardanelles attacks and Gallipoli landings. He was replaced by Admiral Henry Jackson, who was much less sanguine about forcing the straits with naval power. Jackson declared that another attack on the Dardanelles with the Navy, considering the potential losses, was "a mad thing to do."[4] A few days later, Churchill was asked to step down from his position as the first lord of the admiralty and was replaced by former Prime Minister Arthur Balfour.[5] For the Gallipoli expedition, it was bad enough that Fisher was gone, but their true champion, Churchill, was also replaced by a leader who was not nearly as interested in what was happening in the campaign.

In the midst of all the political intrigue in London, the fleet faced new problems. The heavy fighting resulted in a dwindling supply of artillery shells for the fleet, and a lack of bombs for the airmen.[6] Long supply lines from England were tenuous at best, and the need for materials became acute. Fortunately for the Allies, the Turks also faced material shortages. The Turks suffered from dwindling supplies of ammunition for their guns and faced supply shortages for the troops.[7] Each side tried to exploit the other's vulnerabilities—the Allies through the air, the Turks with torpedo attacks on the Allied fleet. On the night of 12–13 May, the Turkish destroyer *Muvanet*, commanded by German Kapitänleutnant Firle, torpedoed and sank the British battleship HMS *Goliath*, at anchor in Morto Bay at Cape Helles.[8] Most of the crew was lost, including the captain, resulting in a number of decisions by de Robeck. The *Queen Elizabeth* was recalled to England, to remove her from harm's way. She was replaced by older, smaller battleships, including the *Exmouth* and the *Venerable*. An order went out to the fleet to be wary of Turkish torpedo boats and German submarines.

The Turks received more aircraft at the middle of the month. Three new Gotha WD.1 seaplanes arrived by train on or about 15 May. They were assembled at the seaplane base at Yeşilköy and began operations immediately.[9] Pilots were trained on the massive new machines, which began flights over the Sea of Marmara spotting for British submarines that were reported in the area. At the time, the British sub E.11 was lurking through the waters looking for targets.[10] As the pilots gained confidence in their machines and familiarity with operations, they were transferred farther south to face the rest of the Allied fleet. The new German commander (in Ottoman uniform) Kapitänleutnant Ernst Liebman was put in charge of the three seaplanes at Çanakkale. In addition to the seaplanes, a small land-plane squadron at Çanakkale was given an official designation as the First Aircraft Company (*Inci Tayyare Bölük*) and placed under the command of the German pilot Ludwig Pruessner. By the middle of the month it included three recently arrived Rumpler B.1s.[11] Pruessner no longer commanded the seaplanes, so instead focused his attention on the land-based aircraft missions. With these meager resources the German-Turkish team mounted frequent attacks against the Allied aircraft and bases.

The Turkish buildup continued on the peninsula. They planned for a massive offensive on the night of 18–19 May, to drive the ANZACs off the beaches. Airpower thwarted their plans. On 17 May, Marix's "Big Breguet" bomber was finally ready for operations. The Breguet Bre.4 bomber was a two-seat pusher, with a 200-horsepower engine, a formidable weapon of the time. It could lift two men in addition to a 660-pound bomb load and was considered the squadron's best bombing platform. Samson recounts that although it was highly capable, it was also finicky, and only Marix was willing to fly the temperamental machine.[12] One plan was to use the plane for bombing Istanbul directly. It was an audacious plan, and the machine had the range and power to bring ordnance to bear directly against the Ottoman capital. But first it had to be tested in shorter-range missions.

Before the war, the French commander of the military mission to Turkey, Goÿs de Mèzeyrac, theorized and wrote about a strategic attack with aircraft on Istanbul.[13] Although it is not clear if Samson ever saw this specific report, he also concluded that a bombing attack on Istanbul was realistic and showed strategic promise. The Breguet was prepped for the mission. The bomber flew for the first time on 17 May but was not immediately cleared for a mission all the way to (and back from) Istanbul. Instead, Marix and Samson decided to mount a shorter flight to certify the airworthiness of the craft. There were reports of a troop buildup near the port facilities of Ak Bashi Liman, on the Gallipoli side of the Dardanelles just north of Çanakkale. The reports had come in from the previous two days' observation flights.[14] Marix loaded the plane with one 100-pound and fourteen 20-pound bombs (380 pounds total) and Samson climbed into the observer seat, as an "infrequent passenger."[15] They took off from Tenedos and headed for the port, climbing as they went. When they arrived over the target, they spotted four transport ships and several smaller vessels "unloading stores and troops."[16] Samson unloaded all of the bombs, scattering stevedores and destroying stores. Fifty-seven men were killed or wounded.[17] Marix and Samson continued their three-and-a-half-hour flight, observing the troop buildup in the area.[18] Samson reported that captured Turks later told him that the bombing created such chaos and confusion that the port was out of commission for two days because of both the damage to the facilities and the reluctance of the stevedores to return to work.[19]

Samson reported his mission and outcomes to the admiral that evening, including intelligence on the Turk troop buildup. The admiral related the information to Birdwood and Hamilton. General Birdwood informed his subordinates of an imminent attack, and the ANZACs prepared for a Turkish offensive. On the night of 18 May, the Turks launched an attack, but because they had lost the element of surprise, it was stymied by the prepared ANZACs. The Turks pressed the ferocious attack for six days, but "the air had robbed the assault of surprise, the defenders could not be shaken."[20] On 24 May the Turks asked for a local armistice to collect their dead. Tactical airpower was beginning to have a strategic effect on the battlefield. There was still a lack of coordination between the fleet, ground, and air, but Samson began to realize that his planes could enable the ground troops through observation and bombing. He accelerated efforts to provide these missions for the campaign.

It was a good thing that Samson was an emerging strategic leader; his were the only British aircraft in operation at the end of the month. In the last week of May, German submarines snuck into the midst of the fleet and torpedoed the *Triumph* on the 25th and the *Majestic* on the 27th.[21] The effect solidified the stalemate on the peninsula, thereafter all ships were ordered to remain in harbor at Mudros unless actively shelling Gallipoli in support of the troops, and even then only with heavy escort. The *Ark Royal* was ordered to Mudros harbor, as she was too slow and subsequently vulnerable to German submarines. The *Ark Royal*, instead of patrolling off the coast, became a depot ship locked in harbor. In his final report, Clark-Hall recounted the contributions of the *Ark Royal* floatplanes for the month of May, including the two lent to the *Minerva* and *Doris*. He recorded twenty-six of thirty-one days suitable for flying, and twenty-one days of operational flying. His planes flew a total of sixty-three hours fifty-four minutes, averaging only three hours of flying per day. He reported that all of his aircraft needed repair—none were fit to fly by the end of the month. He had constant trouble with maintenance and operations; few of his aircraft were suitable except in the best weather conditions. He went on to report that there was a specific problem with operating floatplanes from monitors (*Minerva*) and cruisers (*Doris*): "The exposure [to the elements] and firing the ships' 6-inch guns has a very detrimental effect on the machines, and when they return from these ships they always require thorough overhaul."[22] The floatplanes continued to operate from the sheltered harbor at Mudros, flying spotting and observation missions. But relocating to Mudros mean that the *Ark Royal* pilots had to fly more than fifty miles just to get to the peninsula, reducing their loiter time over the beaches.[23]

At the end of May tragedy struck the French escadrille when a pilot was blown up by his own bomb. Bombing technology was in its earliest days, and the French tried to convert naval artillery shells to aerial bombs. One of the French pilots mounted a converted naval artillery shell for aerial operations, but the bomb got hung up while in flight. When he landed, the jarring loosed the shell, which exploded beneath him, killing him instantly and destroying the plane.[24]

Both Césari and Samson related similar stories, as each of the squadron commanders had experienced problems with the ersatz bombs. In Césari's case, he armed his plane with a bomb and headed to pick up his observer at Helles. At some point, he realized that the bomb's timing mechanism had been activated. Césari climbed back to the observer's seat, while the airplane was in flight, to release the bomb from the rack. He was successful and the bomb detonated only a few hundred feet below his machine in flight. Samson's escapade wasn't quite as dramatic. Although he did not have to climb around his aircraft while trying to fly it, he did have a tense moment when he thought he had a hanging bomb that had not released. He performed a very soft landing then ran for his life from the still-running aircraft after touchdown. Only after jumping out of the still running plane did he realize that the bomb had in fact released, just not exploded when it hit the ground. It turned out that the bomb had indeed released and he was in no danger. His squadron mates were curious about why their commander had acted so strangely.[25]

These events reveal the delicate nature of early aerial warfare and the ingenuity involved in incorporating offensive weapons with aviation technology. It was not an easy—or safe—thing to attach bombs to aircraft to be used against an enemy. The pilot or observer could drop 20-pound bombs from the cockpit, but larger, heavier bombs had to be mounted to the airplanes with hastily manufactured mechanisms that frequently malfunctioned. In hindsight, it is very impressive that the pilots and mechanics were able to adapt the early machines for offensive aerial operations.

At the end of May, Flight Commander Osmond of 3 Squadron took up one of the Voisins, loaded with two 100-pound bombs. He spotted a Turkish battleship, the *Barbarossa*, lying at anchor at Ak Bashi Liman and attacked it from the air. He dropped his payload and scored a direct hit on the ship, killing eight sailors and putting one of the turrets out of action. The *Barbarossa* retreated up the straits from the port and did not return.[26] The squadron's pilots were getting better at both observing significant troop concentrations as well as more accurate in their bombing attacks, especially against stationary targets.

Samson constantly asked London for more machines and men, and he was finally rewarded with two additional Voisons at the end of the month. The planes were "not half bad machines, . . . but they were not so good as the big Maurices [Farmans]."[27] The Voison IIIs were two-seat pushers, with 130-horspower Canton engines, capable of achieving 65 miles per hour and 4.5 hours endurance.

On 4 June, the Allies mounted renewed attacks across the line at Helles. The French and British planes were tasked with observing and spotting for naval artillery. Four 3 Squadron aircraft operated temporarily from the improvised airfield on Helles providing constant aerial coverage for the attack. Although the Allies had fire superiority, the Turks were dug in and the attacks were fruitless. During the day, armored RNAS cars made their debut in battle. The eight cars raced up and down the lines, firing into the Turkish positions with their machine guns. Unfortunately, the cars could not change the outcome of the attack as the Turks were adequately entrenched. When two of the vehicles were lost to enemy gunfire and the squadron commander, Lieutenant Commander Colmore, was wounded, the cars were withdrawn. General Hamilton decided that they were unfit for use in trench warfare and they retired for the day—and for the campaign.[28] Samson was more optimistic about his war wagons, arguing that had they been used at the landing they "might have turned the tide [of the battle]."[29]

That afternoon, Osmond returned to the squadron at Tenedos and reported to Samson that he had spotted a German submarine near Rabbit Island. Samson jumped into No. 50, armed with a single 100-pound bomb, and took off in chase. He spotted the submarine shortly; it was on course toward the French battleship *Henri IV*. Samson dropped down and let loose his bomb, which exploded on the surface. Although there was no apparent damage to the sub, it submerged, going under the French ship without attacking it. Samson lost sight of the sub and continued on his observation flight unarmed.[30] On his return flight from Helles, Samson spotted the sub sailing on the surface up the Dardanelles. He had no bombs but decided to dive and attack the sub with his rifle. It was a gallant gesture, but Samson wrote that he had missed the "chance of a lifetime" because he had no bombs to drop on the German sub.[31] A new chapter in aerial warfare had opened at Gallipoli: antisubmarine warfare. From that point forward, the squadron logs recount almost daily "submarine patrols."

At the start of June, 3 Squadron received the first substantial reinforcements of aircraft in months. Eight Henri Farmans were dispatched to Gallipoli in crates. The Henri Farmans were HF.20s, two-seat observation pusher biplanes. With their 80-horsepower Gnome rotary engines, they could only fly at seventy miles per hour for two-and-half hours. Samson recounts that they "were perfectly useless, of course."[32] These aircraft had already been pulled from the Western Front, as they were obsolete in the face of rapidly evolving technology. The Admiralty decided to send them to Gallipoli, regardless of their uselessness, to placate Samson's requests. He went to de Robeck to discuss the matter in person. Samson commented to the admiral, "If we keep them the Admiralty will credit me with eight new aeroplanes, and we won't get any good ones; therefore I would suggest, sir, you send them off home again somehow."[33] Samson refused the aircraft; de Robeck made efforts to return them, and somewhere in transit they were "lost" in the long supply lines. The Admiralty inquired as to where they went, but neither Samson nor de Robeck admitted that they were on station at Gallipoli; eventually they were written off and new, better aircraft were dispatched to 3 Squadron. In Samson's opinion, after numerous requests for clarity from the Admiralty and constant denials from his desk, he "supposed some accountant at the Admiralty still regards me with evil intent."[34] The supply of obsolete aircraft to Gallipoli suggests two things: first, the RNAS was getting cast-offs from the Royal Flying Corps, and Gallipoli was getting the worst of the mix; and second, Samson was able to muster enough courage to refuse scarce machines and force the Admiralty to send adequate equipment, even if it took longer. The final interesting point in the intricacies of logistics is that by 1915, aircraft technology was evolving at such a rapid pace that frontline machines lasted only six months before they were rendered obsolete. Aircraft companies like the Farman works were producing new models about every six months; new planes immediately made old versions obsolete.

Over the course of the first few weeks of June, Marix was busy with the Breguet, preparing the craft for the ultimate bombing run on Istanbul. The rest of the squadron was busy observing, photographing the lines, looking for submarines, and of course bombing. The weather turned ugly on 10 June, preventing flying operations for two days, with only two flights on the 12th. Over the following day or two, Marix piloted the Breguet with Samson as the observer and found a gathering of Turkish troops on the reverse slope of a hill near ANZAC Cove. They dropped a 100-pound bomb that fell directly in the midst of the men. The explosion killed a number of men and scattered the rest.[35]

By 22 June Marix and Samson were ready for their big adventure. They took off from Tenedos at 0130 armed with fourteen 20-pound bombs on a mission to bomb Istanbul.[36] The intent was to bomb the city directly, hopefully leading to the strategic outcome of knocking the Ottomans out of the war. Whether that was even possible was never considered, but Samson was willing to try. Unfortunately, the plane's engine began to misbehave and they turned back just north of ANZAC Cove. On the return flight, Samson recounts that they dropped bombs along the way on every campfire they saw, eventually making it back to Tenedos.[37] Samson's personal mechanic, Edmond Dessoussois,[38] was distraught. He had worked with Marix on the aircraft for weeks in preparation for the mission, but they had been defeated. Without a reliable engine for the big bomber, Samson decided to cancel the idea of bombing Istanbul. He wrote, "None of my other aeroplanes could carry sufficient fuel as well as bombs for this long journey."[39] But lost in the disappointment was a hidden benefit: the squadron had mounted its first night bombing raid over Gallipoli. Though forced to return to base, the Bregeut had flown at night and the pilot and observer had bombed Turkish camps in the dark. They had opened another new chapter in the history of aerial warfare and were successful in their attempt, even if it was not the intent of the mission.

Samson realized this immediately. Within a week, he began to send aircraft up at night to bomb enemy encampments, disrupt supply lines, and create havoc by denying Turks their sleep. The Turks, in turn, had to respond to the night aerial attacks, and began to suffer from the constant threat of Allied aerial opposition. With near complete aerial superiority, Samson's squadron harassed the Turks day and night, dropping bombs and bringing naval artillery to bear with regularity and increasing precision.

On 22 June Captain Collet and Major Hogg took off from Helles when they saw an incoming enemy aircraft. Collet raced after the enemy, who turned tail and ran, as was often the case. Major Hogg, in the front seat with a rifle, shot at the German plane in a twenty-minute running battle. He hit the engine and brought the plane down, close to the French front. The French turned their guns on the downed aircraft and fired on it with their artillery. The pilot escaped on foot, but the accurate French fire "reduced it [the plane] to matchwood" in a matter of minutes.[40] Neither side had aircraft fitted with machine guns for aerial fighting; such weaponry was not yet available in the theater. On the Western Front, the Allies and the Germans were working feverishly on perfecting a technique to allow machine guns to be fired through the propeller arc. One method, innovated by French pilot Rolland Garros, involved attaching metal wedges to the back side of the propeller, so that bullets would deflect off. His method was successful, if crude; he shot down a German aircraft on 18 April 1915. In Germany, Dutch aircraft designer Anthony Fokker created a synchronizer gear that interrupted the gun when the propeller was in front of the bullet's path. It was quickly put into production, and installed on existing aircraft, and became the technology associated with the Fokker *Scourge* in the spring and summer of 1915. For a brief time, the Germans on the Western Front had sole possession of the technology of a true fighter aircraft: small, fast, maneuverable aircraft that fired its machine guns through the propeller arc in a steady, stable stream. The Germans dominated aerial fighting until the Allies copied the mechanism. At Gallipoli, thousands of miles away, the technology was not available until the end of the year. In the meantime, Allied pilots at Gallipoli shot at enemy aircraft with revolvers and rifles in an effort to bring other planes down. There was a constant fear of ground fire, but if the planes flew high enough, they did not have to worry about fire from soldiers on the ground. More worrisome was inclement weather and being bombed in their aerodromes.

By the start of July, enlistments were running out for a number of the 3 Squadron pilots. Men who had been with Samson since the start of the war were rotated home to England. Flight Lieutenant Peirse returned to England with a promotion to be a pilot instructor. Flight Commander Osmond also left after his last observation flight on 4 July.[41] Flight Lieutenant Bill Wilson and Samson's younger brother, Lieutenant Bill Samson, were sent south to Mytilene with a single Henri Farman and a small crew to fly observation over Smyrna (now Izmir).[42] That left only six pilots for operations and between eight and ten aircraft available. Three new pilots arrived, Flight Lieutenant Dawson, Sub-Lieutenant Kirby, and Flight Lieutenant Barr, all of whom were flying by 15 July.[43] But the pace of operations was beginning to take a toll on the squadron. They had been flying combat operations with only a brief pause in transit to Gallipoli since the start of the war and all were exhausted. Samson was especially worried about Captain Collet, who had lost weight and was not sleeping. The admiral decided to send half of the squadron on leave to Egypt, including Samson and Collet, beginning on 24 July. Richard Bell Davies took over as squadron commander and had six other pilots for operations: the three new pilots in addition to Marix, Newton-Claire, and Thomson.[44] Between 24 July and 11 August, these seven carried the load for the Allies as they prepared their next phase in the campaign.

While Samson and Collet were away, the squadron transferred to their new aerodrome on Imbros, in order to be closer to the action at ANZAC Cove and farther north on the Aegean side of the peninsula.[45] The main impetus for the move came from a report by a special envoy sent from Britain arguing for the consolidation of British airpower in the campaign. Wing Captain Frederick Sykes had been dispatched to Gallipoli to observe the air campaign and report his findings, based on his extensive experience on the Western Front.[46] Sykes had reorganized the air war for the Royal Flying Corps and thus was selected as the person best able to assist in making the air campaign at Gallipoli more effective and efficient. His 9 July report suggested a reorganization and resupply for the beleaguered forces there.[47] He recommended the move to Imbros, for centralized control, coordination, and maintenance, which prompted the squadron's move. His opinion, after working closely with the Royal Flying Corps on the Western Front, was to supplement the forces in Gallipoli with land-based RFC planes.[48] This was an unintentional slight towards Samson, who thought that his RNAS planes and pilots were performing the work better than any RFC pilots could.[49] However, instead of sending an RFC squadron, an additional RNAS squadron was dispatched, and both 3 Squadron and newly arrived 2 Squadron were elevated to Wing status. Samson, as commander of 3 Wing related that Sykes' presence did not change his daily routine substantially other than adding another layer of bureaucracy to his chain of command; henceforth Samson had to file all reports through Sykes' office as well as the existing chain of command.[50] Other than reporting to Sykes, Samson was left to command his wing as he saw fit, "go[ing about] in my own routine as usual."[51] Further, the new designation as a wing did not increase Samson's operational output; he did not receive additional resources or pilots in the short term.

After a short sojourn back to London, Sykes reported back to Imbros on 6 August, just in time for the renewed offensives in the campaign. For Sykes, there were two big problems hampering the efficiency of aviation in the Gallipoli campaign. The first was the variety of non-standardized equipment in use by the RNAS. Sykes reiterated the supply problems already mentioned by Samson and Clark-Hall reporting that there were—at the time of the Sykes Report—eleven floatplanes of five different types, and thirteen aeroplanes (land planes) of five different types with six different engines.[52] Replacements, spares, and parts were a constant concern, the long supply lines from England to Mudros exacerbated the problem. Secondly, Sykes argued that there was a distinct lack of coordination between the Navy, the Army, and aerial operations in the campaign; he reiterated problems already confirmed by previous reports. Sykes was especially harsh with regards to the aviator Samson, who was chided for not working more closely with the Army.[53] Sykes thought 3 Wing was not working closely enough with the land forces and recommended closer coordination. He did not realize that it was a two-way miscommunication; few of the land force commanders communicated with the pilots either. There was a lack of coordination to be sure, part of it was due to the technological limitations of the time and the fact that there were too few radios to go around. Further, the pilots were not in close contact with the ground forces on Gallipoli because they flew from an island off the peninsula. Finally, the ground commanders rarely heeded pilot reports and did not understand how to take advantage of the aerial weapon to best support ground operations. Blame could be passed around; Sykes focused on the aviators.

To the first concern, Sykes recommended standardized aircraft, suitable for the difficult operations and the unique environmental conditions of the campaign. Unlike the flyers on the Western Front, the Gallipoli pilots had to fly over water to get to their operational stations. In addition, the harsh climate, sand, and operating conditions required sturdy aircraft and constant and consistent resupply for parts, supplies, and maintenance components. Sykes relented on sending an RFC squadron, but did request an additional RNAS squadron for support and expansion of aerial operations. RNAS 2 Wing was dispatched to Gallipoli, which arrived in August.

As for command and coordination, Sykes set up a new headquarters (HQ) at Imbros, to coordinate the air-land effort more effectively.[54] But the Royal Navy maintained its command at Mudros Harbor at Lemnos. Instead of operating independently, Samson was ordered to report to both General Headquarters (GHQ) and the fleet to coordinate the air effort for the campaign. On paper, Sykes advocated closer cooperation for observation, artillery spotting, mapping, photography, antiair and antisubmarine patrols, and bombing missions. He divided the theater into four areas of operation: (1) Helles, (2) ANZAC Cove and Suvla, (3) the Dardanelles and the Asiatic Shore, and (4) the Gulf of Xeros and farther north.[55]

In practice, Samson still selected the missions, based on the needs of the daily grind and taking the best operational use of the few planes he had into account. As the campaign continued it became clear that there was an ideal program for coordination of the air and land campaigns, which was in reality limited by the number of planes available, the environmental conditions of the theater, and the competing personalities in the far-off theater of the war. Sykes' observations and recommendations were correct, comprehensive, and worthy, but reality tempered his expectations for the use of the air asset at Gallipoli.

As July bled into August at Gallipoli, the Allies planned a new offensive. Efforts were being made to reorganize the air forces and enhance coordination with the naval and ground forces. But the realities of the campaign, the limited number of aircraft, and the harsh conditions forced reality on the aerial efforts. Sykes wanted the air support to be more effective, as did the flyers. But conditions forced reality. The newly designated 3 Wing prepared to support the summer offensives as best they could as the air war over Gallipoli continued.

CHAPTER SIX

The Suvla Bay Offensive and the End of the Summer

At the start of August, the British and ANZACs planned a massive offensive to take the high ground and defeat the Turks on Gallipoli once and for all. The strategic plan remained the capture of the heights on the Gallipoli Peninsula so that the naval attacks could press the original plan. The offensive included renewed attacks at all of the existing locations as well as a new front at Suvla Bay. As the plan took shape, 3 Wing pilots kept busy gathering vital information for the planning process.

In addition to the big move from Tenedos to Imbros, 3 Wing pilots flew up and down the Aegean coast of Gallipoli to map, photograph, and observe Turkish locations. The wing flew thirty-one flights during 1–5 August, but a third of those were to move the planes to the new airfield.[1] In retrospect, the transition was not planned at a good time; transferring the entire wing to a new island as the army and navy prepared for a massive offensive seems awkward at best. The planes were easy to move; they simply flew to the new aerodrome. But the men, supplies, and facilities all had to traverse the waters by boat to Imbros, then be transported across land from a makeshift port to the new site. And the new airfield was not ideal. The landing strip had to be leveled and cleared, the first site chosen was at the edge of a cliff over the sea. All of the pilots had to familiarize themselves with the field, the prevailing winds, and the new conditions at Imbros. As the wing set up, the pilots used aircraft packing crates as living spaces and workshops; most of the enlisted men lived in tents.

Temporary 3 Wing commander Davies—Samson was still on R&R in Egypt—and two flight lieutenants, Dawson and Thomson, flew six flights with the wing's camera, to take photos of the proposed landing site at Suvla.[2] The rest of the squadron was busy moving, and once at Imbros took turns on familiarization flights and performing additional reconnaissance flights for the men on the ground on Gallipoli. Only two flights on the afternoon of the 5th were specified bombing missions. However, even these missions were only piecemeal, and were not coordinated. The specifics of the aerial operations are indicative of the lack of joint planning. Not only were Samson and two of his best pilots still away on R&R, the wing was also transitioning to a new airfield. It is painfully clear that neither the temporary commander, Davies, nor his naval or army superiors were cognizant of the close cooperation needed between the ground, sea, and air forces. Even at this point in the campaign no one really understood the value of the air weapon or its importance to modern warfare. Davies tried to use his aircraft to achieve best results, but there was little guidance from above on how to exploit the airplanes for strategic advantage. Davies ordered his men to perform as they had been doing thus far in the campaign, the only directive he received from HQ was to photograph the landing areas and observe and map Turkish positions for the impending assault.

The offensive opened on 6 August. At Helles, British and French troops launched an attack in order to fix Liman von Sanders' attention on the toe of the peninsula. At ANZAC Cove, the Australians, New Zealanders, and newly arrived 13th Division and 29th Indian Brigade attacked at Lone Pine, precipitating an offensive toward Chunuk Bair, the high ground. On the evening of 6 August two British divisions, the 10th and 11th, waded ashore at Suvla Bay, aimed at gaining the high ground to the north of ANZAC Cove, specifically Hill 971.[3] To the south, the British seaplane tender *Ben-my-Chree*, which had arrived in early July, was put under the command of the French admiral, Guépratte, and staged a feint toward the port of Sighajik (or Sigacik) to the south of Smyrna.[4] Two of the *Ben-my-Chree* seaplanes made reconnaissance flights over the port facility.[5]

There were major offensives across the entire Gallipoli Peninsula, all of which needed aerial support from 3 Wing, the *Ark Royal* seaplanes, and the two kite balloon ships off ANZAC Cove, the *Manica* and the *Hector*, the latter of which had just arrived from England. The

Ark Royal seaplanes were nearly useless for the offensive, as only high-altitude flights were authorized to preserve secrecy.[6] Jones records that the two most important spotting flights leading up to the Suvla landings were conducted with (army) Captain Walser (on 4 August, piloted by Davies in a Maurice Farman) and (army) Second Lieutenant Knatchbull-Hugessen (flown by Flight Lieutenant Walter Shackfield Newton-Clare on the 5th).[7] Both of these army observers noted that there were a number of Turkish gun emplacements, but that most of the outposts were unmanned.[8] On 6 August, as the offensives commenced on the southern tip and the ANZACs staged a breakout from ANZAC Cove, 3 Wing mounted eight reconnaissance flights to observe Turkish troop movements. At least one of the flights over Suvla reported that Turkish troops were seen leaving the area to reinforce farther south.[9] That evening 20,000 British troops were landed as the sun set on Suvla Bay.

Temporary Wing Commander Davies was caught on the horns of a dilemma. For the Suvla offensive, he was ordered to report directly to General Hamilton to coordinate airpower with the ground troops. However, even though de Robeck wrote the order, he did not inform his Royal Navy subordinates of the plan, and Rear Admiral Nicholson ordered Davies and his pilots to be at the beck and call of the ships to spot for naval artillery. Davies had to shuttle back and forth from Military HQ to the admiral's flagship to clarify orders. Neither the army nor the navy would concede their authority on the use of aircraft, and Davies did not get a straight answer from either de Robeck or Hamilton. Davies went directly to de Robeck's ship, but the admiral was not there; Davies had to meet with de Robeck's chief of staff, Roger Keyes. Keyes was noncommittal and the situation was exacerbated by comments from Alexander Ramsey, flag commander of the Inshore Fleet, tasked with providing naval artillery support. Ramsey stated to Davies in no uncertain terms, "I don't see what you're making such a fuss about, your rotten old airplanes will be no bloody good anyway."[10] Davies was utterly frustrated. He had orders from the army to support the troops on the ground and conflicting orders from the navy to spot for naval artillery, but only had the men and machines for one or the other. Keyes was not much help. When asked if the planes should support the landings, Keyes said, "Of course." But when asked if 3 Wing should support the navy, Keyes stated, "Obviously." Davies hedged his bets. He queried Keyes, "Then, sir, am I to understand that

I am to give priority to the general's orders carrying them out in full, and if, after doing so, I have any aircraft available, I am to carry out as much of the Inshore Squadron's orders as I can?" Keyes responded with, "Yes, that's what you're to do." He continued, "Well, now you know, you'd best get ashore and do it."[11] Davies returned to the wing to relate the modified orders and instructed his pilots that they were to support the army before the fleet, and do the best that they could for both.

Davies went up at first light on 7 August, with Knatchbull-Hugessen in the observer's seat, to reconnoiter Suvla. Seeing no movement from the Turks, and few guarded positions, they raced back to army HQ to inform the general that the way was clear for an advance towards the objectives, Chocolate Hill and Hill 971.[12] But because of conflicting orders on the ground, indecision, and meager supplies, the advance faltered at Suvla. Even though there was no opposition, the British troops did not advance quickly or efficiently, regardless of the information from the observing aircraft. The one-day delay and indecision gave the Turkish forces time to respond to the British advance on Suvla.[13]

At Chunuk Bair, the ANZACs made better headway. They had advanced up the hill, and lead elements captured the heights in the face of heavy resistance. But there was a lack of coordination and communication there as well, and the Turkish defenses did not break. For a few hours on 7 August, it seemed as if the offensives would prove successful, but in the confusion the ANZACs were pushed off the heights by a determined Turkish counterattack.

On the Turkish side of the lines, there was no lack of efficiency. Liman von Sanders concentrated his attention on the Helles offensive, and turned the defense farther north over to Mustafa Kemal. Kemal informed Sanders that he thought it best to have one commander in charge of the defensive situation from ANZAC Cove north to Suvla, called the Anafarta Battles in Turkey.[14] Sanders put Kemal in charge of the defenses on the evening of the 8th.[15] Kemal and the Turks reinforced quickly, counterattacked immediately, and negated the Allied advances. Helpless to stem the Turkish tide from the air, 3 Wing pilots could only watch as the Allies were driven off the heights and stymied on the ground below. Davies' frustration is evident in his recollection of the Suvla offensive, "The only redeeming feature of that day [7 August] was that all the aircraft remained serviceable so that we were able to complete the full programme for the Army as well as meet most of the demands of the Inshore Squadron."[16]

Over the next few days, as the battles raged on the ground, the wing was able to mount a full slate of flights. The wing flew ten flights on 8 August and another six on 9 August, spotting for the army and dropping bombs on the Turks.[17] But the small 20-pound bombs did not have a great effect on the enemy troops below, and the Allied offensives stalled. Communication between the pilots, army HQ, and the ground commanders was strained at best, as the landed forces did not heed the pilot's reports. The airmen could have had a more significant strategic influence on the attacks had there been better communication and deeper trust. It was a missed opportunity that could have produced a much different set of outcomes.

The wing finally received new aircraft, after months of hounding the Admiralty in London. The new planes arrived on 8 and 9 August—two new Henri Farmans[18] and two Nieuports.[19] A Henri Farman, listed as an HF.24 in the logbook, was test flown on the 8th and in operation the next day. Davies took HF.24 to the skies on 10 August, with Jopp as an observer in the front seat, on a reconnaissance flight. They spotted a German Etrich *Taube* over ANZAC, and flew to intercept.[20] Davies flew up behind the German plane and Jopp started firing his rifle at the enemy. Jopp got off five rounds before the pilot noticed he was being fired on, and pushed his plane into a steep dive. Davies reports that the Australians on the ground started cheering, thinking they had shot the enemy plane down.[21] They did not; the enemy got away. But the incident raised the wing's awareness of enemy air activity, and they increased their counter-air operations. The Nieuports were converted to fighter aircraft as best that the wing could manage, given the materials constraints they faced. The front observer's seat was covered over with fabric, and a makeshift gun rack was fitted to the upper wing. It was hinged, so that the pilot could swing the gun down to change the magazine. A Lewis machine gun was fitted above the wing to fire outside of the propeller arc, so as not to damage the spinning propeller. The wing finally had airplanes that could potentially bring down the enemy planes with machine gun fire.

When Samson returned from two week's leave on 11 August, he was happy to see the new aircraft and the record of accomplishments of the wing in his absence. Davies was sent on fourteen days of leave and returned command to Samson. The latter was a bit shocked to find out that his mission set had expanded and that the Allies were by that point fighting on three fronts on Gallipoli. He got two new pilots in addition to the four airplanes, but also had to begin sending his men on leave to rest. Samson states that he had eleven pilots total, but could only count on seven, due to rotations, leave, and pilots returning to England.[22] With seven pilots the wing was responsible for five main missions: spotting for naval artillery; coordination with the ground forces at Helles, ANZAC, and Suvla; antisubmarine patrols; counter-air operations; and constant reconnaissance. For all of these missions, Samson ordered his pilots to carry bombs and drop them on targets of opportunity. He wrote, "Really, at least three Squadrons were required. The situation would have been improved if I had more aeroplanes, also of more suitable type for the work in hand. Another difficulty I always had was in our complete lack of spare parts. It was only due to Mr. Brownridge and my splendid men that we kept going at all."[23] Old Number 50 had not flown in weeks, the rest of the original squadron aircraft were in dire need of new fabric.[24] There was an acute lack of oil and other lubricants, and virtually no spares for the airplanes. The pilots flew the four new aircraft more frequently as the older models deteriorated. The environmental conditions worked against the men, the planes, and the aerodrome. In the heat of the summer, combined with the winds, sand, and salt air, the delicate machines simply broke down. Samson notes that the wooden propellers, laminated wood carved into shape, would become 'unglued' in the heat and shatter in mid-flight. As well, the constant dust, sand, heat, and use decreased engine performance as the tired engines lost compression. Faced with both wood and metal fatigue, the planes' performance decreased in the harsh environment at Gallipoli.

The mechanics worked tirelessly to keep the machines in operational status; it was a good thing that the wing had more planes than pilots. Added to the maintenance issues were the abysmal living conditions, including flies, mosquitoes, a lack of clean water and substandard food. At the new site, mule carts brought up water from the army camp, which was constructed around the only well for miles.

Samson was unhappy with the landing field. He found a field that he thought was better, but it was covered by rocks and scrub brush. He enlisted the help of local Greek workers, but needed more men for the task of clearing the field. He was given seventy Turkish prisoners by Military HQ, and put them to work on the new airstrip. The Turks seemed to like the conditions better than those of their prison camp, and the airmen fed them better as well. Samson recorded that "they considered themselves members of the squadron."[25] With the new workers, many of whom remained attached to the wing for the duration of the campaign, Samson had a reasonable force to build a proper aerodrome under the negative conditions. Conscripted Greeks, with the captured Turks, supervised by RNAS overseers, used the collected rocks to build structures and buildings for the aerodrome. In true airmen's fashion, the first building constructed was the officer's mess, which doubled as the pilots' lounge and bar.

The few British floatplanes remained active during the Suvla offensive and beyond. On 11 August floatplanes from the *Ben-my-Chree* reported significant activity in the port of Ak Bashi Liman, where more Turkish troops were unloading. The next day, Flight Commander Charles Edmonds made an historic flight. He took off in a Short floatplane from the Gulf of Xeros, flew across the peninsula, and made the first successful torpedo attack from an airplane. Skimming close to the water at only fifteen feet, he released his 14-inch torpedo[26] in line for a transport ship. It exploded, and sent the ship to its watery grave.[27] He recalled,

> Approaching Injeh Burnu, I glided down and fired my torpedo at the steamer from a range of some 800 yards, with the sun astern of me. I noticed some flashes from the tug previously mentioned, so presumed she was firing at me and therefore kept on a westerly course, climbing rapidly. Looking back, I observed the track of the torpedo, which struck the ship abreast of the mainmast, the starboard side. The explosion sent a column of water and large fragments of the ship almost as high as her masthead. The ship was about 8,000 tons displacement, painted black, with one funnel and four masts. She was lying close to the land, so cannot sink very far, but the force of the explosion was such that it is impossible for her to be of further use to the enemy. She appeared to have settled down a little by the stern when I ceased watching her.[28]

Five days later he repeated this feat, sinking another ship with a torpedo. Later he found out that the ship he sank was already foundering from a previous submarine torpedo, but it did not detract from his historic accomplishment. Concurrent with his attack on 17 August, another torpedo attack was launched from the *Ben-my-Chree* floatplanes. Flight Lieutenant George Dacre took off from the Gulf of Xeros in another Short. While Edmonds torpedoed and set fire to a steamer, which burned but did not sink, Dacre had to land on the water near Galata because of engine trouble. With a temperamental engine, he could not lift his machine and the 750-pound torpedo, and had to taxi on the water. He was spotted, but fortunately ignored by a Turkish hospital ship, and continued toward the port, on the water at half power. He loosed his torpedo at a tug, and successfully sank the craft. With the weight of the torpedo gone, Dacre was able to take off and return to his ship before his engine quit altogether.[29]

On 19 August Samson set off with Jopp in a Henri Farman for "spotting and recon"[30] over Suvla. Their engine was hit by a piece of shrapnel, and they were forced to land on a hill near the dry salt lake. The plane rolled backwards down the hill; it was in full view of the Turk guns, which commenced firing on the plane. Samson and Jopp ran for cover while the Turks blasted away at the plane. When the firing ended, Samson surveyed the damage, and saw that the engine was destroyed. The two were able to catch a mail trawler back to the aerodrome, but not before spending a night at sea in the ship. Both spent the night seasick below decks.[31]

On return to the aerodrome, Samson was greeted by more bad news. Flight Commander Collet had been killed in an accident. Collet's plane lost power immediately after takeoff, and in trying to return to the airfield had stalled and crashed. The plane caught fire, and Collet was killed in spite of the heroic efforts of his passenger, Chief Petty Officer Michael Sullivan Keogh, to save him. Keogh was burned badly as well; he was later awarded the Albert Medal (2nd Class) for his bravery.[32] Collet had been with the squadron since December 1914, and had recently been on leave with Samson in Egypt. His death was a blow to the wing and a personal loss for Samson, who was a close friend. Other pilots had come and gone over the course of the war to that point, but Collet's death was the first loss for the wing.

The French MF. 98(T) Squadron and 3 Wing combined to bomb the new Turk airfield at Galata, just south of the town of Gallipoli on the Dardanelles side of the peninsula. The "large formation of enemy aircraft" (written from the Turkish perspective), bombed the airfield and destroyed a number of the buildings, including the main hangar.[33] The German planes were out of their hangars, and none of them were destroyed, but the facilities were ravaged by the Allied flyers. With complete knowledge of the others' airfields, each side mounted raids on the enemy aerodromes. Galata was a frequent target for both the British and French pilots; German aircraft visited Imbros and Tenedos. Both sides began to receive more and better machines after numerous requests for more airpower. The Turks benefited from new planes and German pilots; both land and seaplanes made their way to the theater. The seaplane base at Naga boasted as many as five Gotha seaplanes, WD.1s and WD.2s.[34] The land-based planes at Galata included the *Taubes* that were moved from Çanakkale for their protection, as well as the addition of Rumpler B.1s, LVG B.1s, and Albatros C.1s, which began to arrive in August.[35] Thus, at about the same time, both sides upgraded to faster, more capable machines that mounted machine guns for aerial combat. However, the Turks suffered from the same logistical problems as the Allies, even though their supply lines seemed shorter. All of the planes and spare parts had to come from Germany; none of the needed equipment was available in Turkey. By the time of the Galata raid, there were only three seaplanes in operation, all Gotha WD.1s, and only four land-based Rumpler B.1s.[36] All of the other machines had been destroyed or lacked spare parts. The four Fokker Eindeckers were out of operation, and the Allies had put three Albatros B.1s out of commission in the early July raid. Long supply lines hampered the operational availability for both sides when it came to the high technology of aviation. The Allies had to wait for everything, at the end of their sea lines of communication; the Turks could count on low technology and manpower because of their internal lines, but aviation equipment had to come all the way from Germany. Each side attempted to gain air superiority by attacking the other's airfields and destroying aircraft on the ground simply because they did not have the capability to combat each other effectively in the air. For the Turks, counter-air became their primary mission. For the Allies, it was yet another task that was added to their growing list of concerns.

The summer heat took its toll on the 3 Wing machines and men in the last week of the month. Only three aircraft were able to fly: a single Maurice Farman and the two new Henri Farmans. Samson had one additional flight in No. 50, but it was only a short test flight to check out repairs.[37] On

24 August there were no flights at all. Due to the operational tempo, the engines in the oldest machines were wearing out, and losing compression. The hot air in the August summer made them all but useless. Nor could the propellers "bite" the air, a function of density altitude. When the air is hotter, it is less dense. The summer heat created a situation where the air was not dense enough for the early aircraft to produce enough lift or thrust to fly.[38] The delicate machines had troubles in all but the best weather conditions.

At the end of the month, 2 Wing joined the fighting at Gallipoli, commanded by Wing Commander Eugene Gerrard, an accomplished pilot. The new wing was equipped with BE2c aircraft and a few Morane-Saulnier Type L parsol-wing monoplanes.[39] The new wing set up across the harbor from 3 Wing using a different airfield; it was sent to Gallipoli to directly support the army. Samson complained that the new, young pilots were inept and his 3 Wing was frequently called to re-do the work of the 2 Wing pilots. He recorded that "after they got used to the job they did very well indeed, though of course my men still regarded them as amateurs."[40] The new wing added twenty-two airplanes to the fight: six Moranes, six BE2c types, six Caudron biplanes, and four Bristol Scouts. The Caudrons were all but useless, because of the lack of power and the prevailing environmental conditions; 2 Wing therefore only had sixteen aircraft for combat operations. Gerrard brought sixteen pilots, two hundred men, and a "good supply of hangars, workshop lorries, and spare engines."[41] Samson was thankful for the spares and equipment, but commented that the planes were virtually useless and not the kind he had asked for.[42] An additional kite balloon ship, the HMS *Canning*, was dispatched to Gallipoli, to replace the HMS *Manica*, which returned to England for a much-needed refurbishment. The *Canning* incorporated a number of advances, including an armored hold in the forecastle so that the kite balloon could be inflated and stowed in a small hangar on deck.[43]

Over time, 2 Wing was assigned to do all of the reconnaissance and spotting duties, relieving 3 Wing to concentrate on long-range bombing and strategic attack.[44] Both wings were still technically under the command of Sykes, who coordinated orders from army HQ and the fleet, although Samson was given relative autonomy in assigning 3 Wing missions. However, Davies commented that the 3 Wing pilots were miffed that Sykes superceded Samson, and they believed Samson should have been promoted to the commanding position.[45] But according to Samson's recollection, he did not seem to mind, as long as he was able to command his wing as he saw fit.[46]

On 30 August, Samson took off with Jopp in the observer's seat in one of the new Henri Farmans. They spotted transport ships at Ak Bashi Liman and coordinated indirect fire from Monitor No. 15, at anchor 18,000 yards away across the peninsula off ANZAC Cove. Although the ship could not see the target, which was obscured by the peninsula, Samson and Jopp directed the ship's fire on the port. They climbed to 6,000 feet to be able to see both the firing ship and the target and radioed, "Commence fire." Jopp directed the monitor's shells on to two steamers that lay side by side at the port. Samson recorded,

> The first shot fell about 800 yards short fortunately behind the hills so that no notice was taken by the Turks. The next shot fell on the beach and killed some Turks. The third shot fell into the sea. We now had got the range. A terrible panic occurred. The tugs that had got dhows in tow cut them off and steamed for the Asiatic shore. I was trying to get a hit on the two steamers which were still at anchor. The eighth shot hit one. Jopp said, "What correction must I signal?" I said, "Report O.K." (hit). The ninth shell hit the second steamer. When it is remembered that these two ships were lying alongside each other, the range was about 18,000 yards, that hills 800 to 1,000 feet were intervening, and that M.15 was just lying with her bows up against a little mark buoy and rolling in the swell, this shooting is really wonderful.[47]

Between the British submarines, floatplane torpedo attacks, 3 Wing bombing runs, and directed naval artillery, the Turks gave up Ak Bashi Liman as a resupply port, at least during the daytime. The joint operations enabled by the airmen forced the Turks to relocate to a port farther north and rely on overland transportation for logistics. This in turn created an opportunity for the Allies: if the route could be severed—by a successful land offensive or aerial bombing—the Turkish forces on the peninsula could be cut off from their supplies and isolated. Samson realized this and began planning strategic bombing attacks against the enemy. For Samson, aerial interdiction of the Turkish supply lines was a way his pilots and machines could help the troops on the ground. If he could cut off Turkish supply form the air, 3 Wing might be able to turn the tide of the battle raging below.

The Allies boasted about fifty aircraft by August, divided between the two wings and the two floatplane tenders. Of these, about thirty were operational. However, there was still a lack of coordination between the flyers and command. The floatplanes fell under the direct jurisdiction of the admiral, but there is no clear evidence that their missions were directed or coordinated. The land planes of 3 and 2 Wings were by this time under Sykes' direct command; he filtered orders through their respective commanders, Samson and Gerrard. But other than deciding that 2 Wing would fly observation—with their complement of obsolete aircraft—and Samson's men would be left to their own devices, there was little direction from above. The various personalities were interesting and strong, but none were willing or able to take charge and direct the campaign toward decisive victory. Further, it was obvious that the airplanes could manage long-range spotting for the naval guns, which was the original goal of the landings. The troops on the ground had intended to get to the high ground, in order to spot for the ships' fire, to clear the Dardanelles and race for Istanbul. By August, this idea had died. In hindsight, with the accomplishments of the airmen to that point, a renewed offensive with airpower and naval gunnery could have been mounted that may have accomplished the original goals. Hamilton and de Robeck were content to wage a protracted war on the peninsula, while the flyers plied the air above for tactical, not strategic, advantage. It seems as if only Samson and the 3 Wing pilots understood that they could have a strategic impact on the campaign by going after supply lines and Turk vulnerabilities.

By the end of August, 3 Wing had accumulated over 112,000 flying miles.[48] The core was the same group of men that had started the campaign, and only a few new machines had trickled in from England. It was a very impressive record: with an average of only seven active pilots, and a dozen or so planes, the Wing had been able to accomplish so much. They flew dated machines in a hostile environment in the face of overwhelming odds, and yet managed to accomplish and improve a number of aerial roles, successfully adding to the operational effectiveness of the campaign. In addition to photography and mapping, observation and spotting, submarine patrols and bombing, the wing had brought down a pair of enemy airplanes, destroyed enemy aircraft on the ground, and forced the Turks to give up an important supply port. The addition of the new 2 Wing gave Samson and his pilots the freedom of action to turn to strategic attack, within the limitations of the technology of the time. He had big ideas, and would continue to evolve the capabilities; 3 Wing prepared for a new chapter in the history of the air war over Gallipoli.

CHAPTER SEVEN

Autumn over Gallipoli

At the beginning of September, the Ottomans received much needed aviation supplies from Germany. An Albatros C.I arrived after flying across neutral Bulgaria. Another made the trip at the middle of the month. Although already eclipsed in the air war on the Western Front, they were a substantial upgrade for the Gallipoli campaign.[1] The Albatros C.I was a two-seat observation biplane, powered by a Mercedes D.III inline, liquid-cooled, six-cylinder engine. With the 160-horsepower engine, the Albatros could fly eighty-two miles per hour. The observer sat in the rear seat of the plane where he was armed with a 7.92 mm Parabellum MG14 machine gun attached to a ring mount, enabling him to swing it around to fire at targets behind and above. The Albatros, designated AK.1, and its sister ship AK.2, began to terrorize the Allied airmen and ground troops. The planes were sent to the new Turkish airfield erected near Tekirdag, closer to the front than Inci Tayyare Bölük, and to that point unidentified by the Allies.

At the same time, two new Gotha WD.1 floatplanes were delivered to the Naga facility, bolstering the number to four.[2] But the floatplanes were tempestuous; the German-Ottoman team was only able to keep two operational throughout the late summer and autumn. The floatplanes focused their attention on antisubmarine patrols in the Dardanelles and Sea of Marmara, hoping to challenge British submarines lurking in the area.

These aircraft brought the total force to six land-based aircraft and four sea-based planes for the Ottomans in the campaign. In September, Serno received more pilots and observers. The total contingent included nine pilots (four recently-graduated Turkish lieutenants: Cemal, Mehmet

Ali, Abdullah, and Ali Riza, as well as a new crop of eight observers) who arrived in September to replace five who returned to Germany. Of the new observers, three were trained Turksish lieutenants: Ahmet Fehmi, Orhan, and Sakir Hazim.[3] In addition to the pilots and observers for the land-based planes, there were five pilots for the seaplanes—all German—and two observers. Although the Ottoman air contingents were smaller in number than their Allied counterparts, they included some of the most recent aircraft available from the Western Front; they had better equipment.

On the Allied side, 2 Wing and 3 Wing continued their support for the ground troops. Both wings focused primarily on spotting and reconnaissance duties, while Samson concocted plans for further adventures. Through the first two weeks of September, 3 Wing continued attacks on the Turkish positions and any ships they spotted. On 5 or 6 September, Newton-Claire landed at Suvla with a misfiring engine, and although the plane was destroyed by Turkish shelling, the engine was recovered under cover of night, saving the valuable and scarce powerplant.[4] On 8 September, Samson was flying with St. Aubyn as his observer, when he spotted two Turkish capital ships on the straits and directed the HMS *Abercrombie* to fire on them. Although the directed fire scored no hits, the ships retreated beyond the *Abercrombie*'s guns to safer waters.[5]

The weather continued to be a factor in operational efficiency for the pilots on both sides. On 11 and 12 September, inclement weather—this time rain—halted operations, but allowed the mechanics to catch up on repairs and maintenance. By this time, Samson had fitted two of the Wing's Nieuports with machine guns, in fixed forward firing position. They were angled at 45 degrees upward, to avoid shooting through the propeller arc. The guns were useless against ground targets, but they could fire at targets above and in front of the Allied planes. The Nieuports were tasked with daily enemy aircraft patrols, searching for the Turkish Albatroses. Davies and Samson record numerous solo flights in the Nieuports and launched daily bombing and patrol flights.

On 18 September, Samson had a special guest at 3 Wing HQ. General Birdwood dropped in to get information on the ground situation. In response, Samson fired up a Maurice Farman (MF.25) and put the general in the observer seat. They took off and flew over ANZAC Cove for fifty minutes to give the commander a bird's eye view of the battlefield.[6] Samson recounted that "he was the only big noise that went up. I think it rather a pity that some more didn't."[7] The flight revealed two important factors in the campaign: the leadership did not understand the importance of airpower, and were late to recognize the important role it could play in the campaign, both over the water and over the land. Undeterred, Samson and his men soldiered on and tried to carry out effective operations in the campaign.

At the strategic level, the Gallipoli Campaign continued without progress. A renewed French attack on the Asian shore of the Dardanelles was scrapped when increased enemy activity in the Balkans erupted. French and British divisions were withdrawn from Gallipoli to deal with new threats around Salonika. The Germans sent additional submarines to the Mediterranean to combat the Royal Navy. Bulgaria was on the cusp of declaring war, unfortunately on the side of the Central Powers. And heavy fighting was taking its toll on the Western Front. Kitchener suggested to Hamilton that Suvla Bay should be abandoned, but Hamilton was reluctant to give up on the fight.[8] In light of the stalemate at Gallipoli, a lack of decisive action, and other threats, the French and British began to turn their attention away from the Gallipoli Campaign, not that there had been much attention paid to that point.

For the soldiers, sailors, and airmen already in theater, it meant that no new resources were forthcoming. They had to do with what they already had, and could not expect significant reinforcement. It meant that planners had to devise new ways to break the stalemate with existing resources and figure out ways to win.

The battle for Gallipoli and the future of modern Turkey nearly changed on 21 September. At 1650 that afternoon, Samson took off in his Nieuport with a machine gun mounted above the upper wing and three 20-pound bombs. The flying log records a "Recon and Bomb attack."[9] As he flew, Samson spotted an open touring car driving along the road with three occupants: a driver and two passengers. As cars were so scarce on the Turkish side, he knew it must be someone immensely important. Samson dived and let two bombs loose in an attack. Both bombs missed, but the car swerved to a stop and the occupants jumped into a ditch for cover. He flew on, knowing he could not hit the men laying in the ditch. Samson kept an eye on the car, viewing it through his binoculars to see when it resumed its route. After twenty minutes it did, and Samson returned with his last bomb for another attack. This attack was closer, and the bomb detonated immediately in front of the touring car. The explosion brought the car to a halt, with minor damage, but the occupants were only shaken. Samson returned to base after expending all his ordnance. The occupants of the car were Mustafa Kemal, his executive officer, and Kemal's driver.[10] Had Samson's bombs found their target, he would have personally altered the course of the campaign, the war, and the future of Turkey. However, Kemal survived the attack, was transferred a week later, and eventually went on to lead Turkey into the modern era.

Samson and his pilots focused their efforts on the Turkish supply lines running down the peninsula. They spotted for naval artillery firing on the port facilities and dropped bombs on the roadways. Frequent bombing raids forced the Turks to resupply by night from both sea and land routes, complicating their supply and logistics. It was one way the pilots tried to affect the Gallipoli campaign. In addition, both sides attacked the most vulnerable targets, the aerodromes. The German pilots stepped up attacks on the British aerodromes on Imbros as well as the French airfield on Tenedos. The Allies reciprocated with attacks on the Turkish airfields on a regular basis. Between 16 September and the end of the month, both sides attacked the others' airfields nearly every other day. The attacks were inconclusive and neither side reported significant losses, but the focus of the air campaign had shifted from attacks on ground and sea targets to attacks against enemy airfields.[11] Neither side recorded losses of men or planes, but the nuisance raids continued until early October; both sides mounted the attacks in order to reduce their opponent's airpower capabilities. The German-Ottoman forces averaged two flights a day, with a high of six flights on 16 September, flying mostly reconnaissance missions. They launched five bombing missions on the Allied aerodrome at Imbros, searching out the airfield and the newly constructed blimp hangar.[12] The British planes were more active, with an average of four flights a day and a high of eleven on 3 and 18 September. On 16 September, the British launched eight flights.[13] Even with three "no flying" days due to weather, the operational average was impressive. Most of the flights were for reconnaissance and spotting, with a number of entries mentioning bombing enemy emplacements. In September, the Flying Log records that the British pilots increased patrols for enemy aircraft, seeking out the enemy in the air. Both sides' logs record a significant event on

27 September, when the lone Turkish flight engaged in aerial combat over the peninsula. An Albatros C.I—flown by the German Lieutenant Pruessener, with Lieutenant Kettembeil as observer—was flying over the Gulf of Saros on an observation flight. Either Samson, flying Nieuport Number 24 or Davies in Nieuport Number 26 came into contact with the Albatros that morning.[14] The planes flew against each other and shots were fired, but the encounter was "indecisive, no damage sustained."[15] It was not the first time that the enemies faced off in the air, but it was the first time that two aircraft, both armed with machine guns, exchanged fire over Gallipoli. Both sides recorded increasing specific counter-air missions.

By the end of September, 3 Wing flying logs record that the pilots had flown 123,387 miles thus far in the war; they were adding over 10,000 miles every month. The record is impressive considering the limitations in manpower and machinery faced in the campaign.

At the start of October disaster struck the Turkish planes and their German pilots and observers. On the night of 6–7 October, a storm raged across the Gallipoli Peninsula, collapsing the main hangar at Galata. Five aircraft were damaged; only one remained operable, an Albatros AK.2. The broken machines were returned to Yeşilköy for repair, and were lost to operations for the rest of the month.[16] The remaining Albatros flew for a few days, but broke down on a flight to Izmir. It remained there under repair for the rest of the month, giving the Allies complete air superiority over Gallipoli. Fortunately for Samson's men, as well as the 2 Wing pilots, their planes were better protected and after the storm flights continued at a very hectic pace.

But even with absolute air superiority, the campaign suffered from decisions made in Paris and London. On 7 October, the French were recalled from Gallipoli; the land forces were evacuated from the campaign and sent to bolster troop strength at Salonika.[17] The HMS *Ark Royal* was ordered to prepare to sail from Gallipoli, and the floatplane squadron counted down its last few days in support of the campaign. By the end of the month, the *Ark Royal* sailed from Mudros to provide support for the Salonika campaign as well.[18] With increased activity in the Balkans, the Greeks demanded support from the Allies, shifting focus from the inconclusive Gallipoli campaign to a new front. Bulgaria declared war on the side of the Central Powers on 14 October. In London there was growing concern about the futility of the Gallipoli campaign, and Kitchener cabled Hamilton asking the latter's opinion on a full evacuation of the theater. Hamilton was incensed, and replied that it would be extremely costly in men and material, as well as prestige and purpose.[19] On 16 October Hamilton was recalled and replaced by General Sir Charles Monro, with Birdwood acting as temporary commander. Hamilton was given the opportunity to visit Egypt and Salonika to report on these areas and he replied that he would rather return to London forthwith to be able to give an accurate and immediate report on Gallipoli, to shore up doubts in London.[20] Monro arrived at Gallipoli on 28 October and gave a dire, yet frank, account of the situation. He was in favor of evacuation.

Concurrently, the weather took a turn for the worse. Flying was restricted because of both breakdowns and the winter weather closing in on the flyers. There was less activity every day as the October weather conspired against flights on the 17th and 19th as well as the 22nd through the 24th. Samson's 3 Wing could only launch two or three flights a day until the end of the month and were not able to take advantage of their air superiority.[21] They made the best of the situation, bombing enemy encampments and supply lines when they could, but diminishing operational effectiveness limited the wing's abilities to contribute. Marix was recalled to England in the middle of the month, leaving a noticeable absence in the pilot's mess. As autumn transitioned to winter, Samson came up with a daring plan.

November was a month of strategic aerial attacks; the intent was to cut off supply to the Gallipoli Peninsula with airpower. After Bulgaria joined the war, the Germans gained a direct rail route to Istanbul and had started sending more supplies. The Turks got stronger while the Allied forces became relatively weaker. The Germans began sending equipment to the Ottoman Empire across the newly opened land route including, most importantly, aircraft and supplies. Significantly, three new Albatroses were delivered in November, replacing lost machines. All of the material was sent by rail, as it was the fastest method for transport from central Europe to Istanbul. Consulting his maps, Samson realized that there were choke points where the rail lines crossed the Maritza River, running from north to south. One of these was twenty miles south of Adrianople (Edirne) at Kuleli Burgas. He planned and proposed an aerial attack on the rail bridge in order to halt the flow of supplies to Istanbul and hence Gallipoli.

On 8 November, the plan was ready. One of the Maurice Farmans was fitted with an extra fuel tank for the long flight, loaded with two 100-pound bombs, and readied for action. Samson flew with Captain Edwards as his observer. They took off on their momentous journey at 1000 hours. On the way Samson spotted encampments that Edwards noted, intending to revisit them on later missions. Samson was unsure of how high he should fly to avoid damage to his plane when the large bombs went off, so he only descended to 700 feet, to be safe. He recounted, "I knew about 200–300 feet was safe for a single one, so I doubled it and added 100 feet for luck."[22] They dropped their bombs as they flew along the bridge, straddling one of the piers. Although the bridge did not collapse, the attack did significant damage to the railway. Samson's attack was moderately successful—he put the bridge out of action for a week, forcing workers to reinforce the structure.[23] As they flew back, the engine gave them trouble, misfiring and shaking violently. Fortunately, Samson and Edwards returned safely and were able to report their successes and plan more trips against the railway bridge while the wing mechanics fixed the Maurice Farman. Samson was determined to drop the bridge to strangle the Turks at Gallipoli. The plan and execution were sound, and in the end the bridge was damaged with airpower. But in the final analysis, it is unclear how much it would have really influenced the ground campaign on the peninsula. But it was one way that Samson and 3 Wing could at least try to help the men on the ground, slugging it out with the Turks.

Two days later, Samson sent two planes on bombing missions north. Davies and Watson, in Maurice Farman Number 3 loaded with two 112-pound bombs and two 20-pound bombs, flew to attack the same railway bridge. Thompson and Jopp took to the air in MF.5 with two 100-pound bombs and four 20-pound bombs to target the large camp Samson had spotted on 8 November.[24] Due to low clouds and rain, Davies and Watson had to bomb from a higher altitude, but were still able to hit the rail line close to the station at Uzun Kepri. They reported "considerable damage."[25] But the Turks had reinforced the vital transport node with antiaircraft machine guns, and the flyers returned with a number of bullet holes in their machine. The bombing raid on the camp was also successful; Thomson and Jopp bombed the center of the congregation, and killed a "great many" of the Turkish troops.[26] Samson was impressed with the results. He was confident that his planes had the range and his men had the mettle, and he continued the bombing attacks on the strategic chokepoint. He commented that he had "always been a believer in the idea that once you start a job you should keep at it, until you succeed or circumstances arise which make it desirable to shift to something else."[27] Thus, he ordered a continuation of the bombing raids on the rail lines and the Maritza Bridge.

The next raid followed on 13 November after two inclement weather days with the entire wing participating. Samson and Davies flew the two single-seat Nieuports to the railway station at Ferejik. Each airplane carried three 20-pound bombs. Flight Commander Busk, with Samson's younger brother Bill riding along as the observer, set off in MF.3 to renew the attack on the railway bridge. Two other planes, each loaded with bombs, flew from the aerodrome searching for Turkish encampments. Heriot and St. Aubyn in MF.5 did not find the previous Turkish encampment, which had been evacuated, but spotted a different Turkish camp and bombed it. They killed a number of troops on the ground and set fire to several tents. Nicholson and Isaac in Henri Farman Number 5 found another Turkish camp at Keshan and bombed it. The main effort farther north against the railway bridge at Kuleli Burgas was the target for Busk and Bill Samson. The flyers placed their two 100-pound bombs close to the bridge, but were not able to destroy the bridge. They did, however, receive a "very hot reception." Between 8 and 13 November, the Turks increased defenses around the bridge with a number of antiaircraft and machine guns realizing that the British would return to attack. Excellent piloting skills by Busk kept the two safe from serious damage, but the plane returned riddled with holes.[28]

At Ferejik, Samson and Davies attacked the railway junction station. Although the bombs did not sever the vital lifeline, the attack caused havoc on the ground. One of Samson's 20-pound bombs landed in the midst of three cavalrymen, who "happened to be in the wrong place, unfortunately for them."[29] On return to the aerodrome, Samson was ecstatic. All of the pilots and planes returned, a few of the planes a bit worse for wear. The bombing raids were deemed a success, but Samson was determined to destroy the junction and the bring resupply to Gallipoli to a halt.

The wing attacked again on 16 November with four flights against the railroad line. Thomson and Annesley took off at 1045 to attack the bridge at Kuleli Burgas accompanied in the air by Samson, Nicholson and Walser, and Barnato and Boles, the latter three planes attacking Ferejik. Thomson and Annesley faced strong opposition from the ground and high winds in the air. They made three passes to find the right bombing line. They did not hit the bridge; the bombs drifted in the high winds. The three planes attacking Ferejik were more successful; they managed to disrupt the supply line and create general chaos with the attack. Hearing Thomson's report, Samson decided to forego attacks on the Maritza bridge at Kuleli Burgas for a while, as the defenses were proving too strong. He was happy that the wing had been able to tie up a number of resources there, instead of having the guns at the front facing the Allied troops. As well, the big bomber needed repairs, and Samson did not have the equipment to continue the attacks on the bridge.[30] Samson decided to focus on the easier and closer target at Ferejik.

On 18 November Samson sent Nicholson in HF.5 to reconnoiter the Ferejik junction to provide bomb damage assessment and report on the wing's previous activities. Nicholson returned and reported that the previous bombing had destroyed a few buildings, and that the arrival of his aircraft sent workers scurrying. The bombing attacks had been moderately successful in disrupting the transit point. Samson took the information and planned an operation to try to shut down the railway junction for good. He brought the wing together for a meeting where he detailed a plan to attack the station en masse. Each pilot was given a specific objective; the mission was set for the next day. If successful, Samson argued that they could destroy the supply line for the Turkish troops at Gallipoli.

On 19 November, five of the seven wing flights were tasked for the bombing raid on Ferejik railway junction. Each plane had a designated target, was loaded with bombs, and took to the air. Samson led in his Nieuport, loaded with two 100-pound and two 20-pound bombs; Davies followed in the second Nieuport with three 20-pounders. Barnato and Smylie followed in Henri Farmans (HF.3 and HF.5) flying solo, and Heriot flew the Maurice Farman MF.5 with Edwards in the observer's seat. Each of the latter three planes carried two 100-pound and two 20-pound bombs.[31] The five aircraft arrived on target with Samson in the lead. He let loose his bombs, then watched the rest of the wing in action. The wing laid waste to the targets. Samson turned for home, confident that the mission had been successful. He arrived back at the airfield first, and waited patiently for the others. Heriot and Edwards returned next, and gave a favorable report on the attack. Barnato landed with bad news; he reported that Smylie's plane had gone down close to the target. When Samson heard the distinctive engine noise of a Nieuport, he knew that Davies was coming back, which eased the tensions somewhat. Samson was afraid he had lost his best friend as well. Davies landed, got out of his airplane, and the men were surprised when Smylie unfolded himself from the single-seat Nieuport as well. He had returned, hidden in Davies' plane! Amidst the excitement, Smylie reported his adventure. His plane had been hit by ground fire and the engine died. He was forced to land, in extremely hostile territory. As he set fire to his machine, Davies alit aside the flaming craft, picked Smylie up, and took to the sky again before the enemy could capture them. Smylie was stuffed into the small compartment for a very cramped ride home, but it was better than being taken prisoner. Smylie's plane was lost, but the pilot was saved. In his memoirs, Davies recounted the incident with nonchalance, stating that he "decided to go down to pick him up."[32] Davies was awarded the Victoria Cross for his gallantry; Smylie received the Distinguished Service Cross for his actions under fire. The citation for the awards read:

> The KING has been graciously pleased to approve of the grant of the Victoria Cross to Squadron-Commander Richard Bell Davies, D.S.O., R.N., and of the Distinguished Service Cross to Flight Sub-Lieutenant Gilbert Formby Smylie, R.N., in recognition of their behaviour in the following circumstances:
>
> On the 19th November these two officers carried out an air attack on Ferrijik Junction. Flight Sub-Lieutenant Smylie's machine was received by very heavy fire and brought down. The pilot planed down over the station, releasing all his bombs except one, which failed to drop, simultaneously at the station from a very low altitude. Thence he continued his descent into the marsh. On alighting he saw the one unexploded bomb, and set fire to his machine, knowing that the bomb would ensure its destruction. He then proceeded towards Turkish territory. At this moment he perceived Squadron-Commander Davies descending, and fearing that he would come down near the burning machine and thus risk destruction from the bomb, Flight Sub-Lieutenant Smylie ran back and from a short distance exploded the bomb by means of a pistol bullet. Squadron-Commander Davies descended at a safe distance

> from the burning machine, took up Sub-Lieutenant Smylie, in spite of the near approach of a party of the enemy, and returned to the aerodrome, a feat of airmanship that can seldom have been equaled for skill and gallantry.[33]

The weather kept the wing grounded for most of the rest of the month, while the new commanders decided the fate of the campaign. In late November a shipment of new pilots with a few Henri Farmans had finally arrived and four sorties were launched on the 24th. But two flights were abandoned due to "dense clouds." There were only two other flying days, with one sortie each; the other seven days had no flights because of bad weather.[34] With stalemate on the ground, limited action at sea (because of the weather and hostile submarines), and the air component grounded with winter setting in, Monro was considering options for the British and ANZACs at Gallipoli. The situation was only getting worse; it was not going to get better any time soon.

Kitchener visited HQ and as he was departing on 23 November, forwarded his orders to his subordinates. Monro was put in charge "of all the British Forces in the Eastern Mediterranean, including Salonika, and General Birdwood in command of Gallipoli, to carry out the evacuation."[35] On 25 November de Robeck turned command of the naval component over to Admiral Rosslyn Wemyss and sailed for England on the HMS *Triad*, taking his entire staff with him. Keyes recounted, "Thus the Admiral and the General who were really entirely responsible for the lamentable policy of evacuation left the execution of this unpleasant task to an Admiral and General who were strongly opposed to it!"[36] High Command decided that the lack of clear successes on the ground, the wavering support at home, the presentation of new and dangerous liabilities in other fronts, and the winter weather closing in, it would be best to cut their losses at Gallipoli and get out. The plan was to evacuate Suvla and ANZAC beaches first, followed in turn by Helles.

When the orders were handed down, the wing's missions changed fundamentally. They were no longer concerned about stemming the supplies coming into the theater, but instead given the task of covering the beaches for the imminent evacuation. The troops on the ground prepared to evacuate the northern beaches at Suvla and ANZAC, which fell under the watchful eye of 3 Wing. 2 Wing was responsible for giving aerial support for Helles, which would be evacuated last. Samson prepared orders for his pilots at the start of December.

The wing continued to fly whenever weather permitted. On 1 December the wing launched eight flights. Four were practice flights for the new arrivals, but the seasoned veterans continued harassing the enemy. Vernon and Jopp took off in MF.3 to bomb the Ferejik station, "just to let them see we were still alive."[37] Samson was up once looking for enemy airplanes.[38] The operational effectiveness of the wing was impressive considering the weather that time of year. On 2 December, twelve flights were recorded, including three by Samson in his favorite Nieuport. Around noon on his first flight of the day, he spotted and chased a Turkish seaplane, but it escaped his grasp.[39] Five aircraft bombed Turkish transports off the port at Kilia Liman, and scored direct hits on ships and the port.[40] In their new Henri Farman (Number 7), Busk and Jopp were spotting for one of the monitors off Suvla when they noticed an enemy aircraft. They broke contact and gave chase. The two planes fought a running gun battle all the way back to the enemy's airfield at Galata, when the antiaircraft guns there put up stiff resistance to the British plane. They turned away and the enemy plane escaped. Upon return, Samson received word from the monitor's captain that he was angry about "the shoot being spoilt" when his aerial observer broke contact.[41]

Poor weather hampered flights on 3 and 4 December, but on the latter, three brand new pilots were able to make check flights on arrival at the wing. The 6th and 7th were also heavy flying days, but weather impeded anything more than check rides for the new pilots. Even though there were fourteen flights those two days, only one was a successful bomb attack. In that flight, on 7 December, Busk and Edwards were in HF.7. They spotted Turks moving toward the ANZAC trench lines, and even though it was a close call, they dropped a bomb on the enemy troops.[42] The trench lines were only twenty yards apart, and the flyers were flying a relatively high speed at only a few hundred feet. When they returned to the airfield, they were worried that they may have dropped their bomb on their own troops. At that same instant Samson received a message from the ground commander stating, "One of your aeroplanes bombed Turks' trench; bits of Turks seen in the air, remainder of occupants got on to the parapet, where we killed a lot with machine guns; please repeat bombing."[43] The reputation of the 3 Wing airmen soared among the troops on the ground, even if it was a very lucky shot. Thus, even in the closing days of the campaign, 3 Wing was able to add close air support to their list of proficiencies. The wing had done yeoman's work in the campaign, but the hardest part was about to begin.

As winter began to close in, pilots on both sides realized that the winter weather would hamper air operations. They fought with each other and with the environment. But they were able to accomplish significant effects, at least at the tactical level. While there was still little guidance from above, and while everyone waited for the flag ranks to make decisions, operations continued when weather permitted. 3 Wing harassed the Turks on the ground and continued bombing attacks against vital supply lines. 2 Wing mapped, observed, and spotted for the Helles beaches. The Ottoman forces flew to try to deny the Allies control of the air. But in the early days of aviation weather was the deciding factor in the third dimension.

On 7 December, the cabinet in London issued orders to evacuate Suvla and ANZAC between the 18th and 19th of that month.[44] It was the beginning of the end of the Gallipoli Campaign.

A Short Admiralty 135 being unloaded from the HMS *Ark Royal*. The seaplane tender would lower the aircraft to the sea and recover it after flying missions. *Imperial War Museum File SP 501*

Launching a kite balloon from the HMS *Manica* for an observation mission. *Imperial War Museum File SP 515*

Caudron G.IIIs were brought to Gallipoli by 2 Squadron at the end of summer 1915. It was an unarmed reconnaissance platform. *Library of Congress, LC-B2-34001-15*

The Sopwith Tabloid was brought to Gallipoli by the HMS *Ark Royal*, but had to wait for a land-based aerodrome for operations. When 3 Squadron built an airfield, the Tabloids were handed over for operations. *George C. Bain Collection, courtesy of the Library of Congress, LC-B2-3401-13*

MF.11 Shorthorns were used by 3 Squadron; upgraded HF.20s were used by the French. Flight Commander R. Marix is standing in the foreground, indicating the size of the plane. *Imperial War Museum File Q 44363*

RNAS 3 Squadron Nieuport 10 at Gallipoli. *Imperial War Museum File Q 44358*

RNAS 2 Squadron brought a few Morane Saulnier Type L parasol-wing monoplanes for observation. *Courtesy of San Diego Air & Space Museum*

The Ottoman air force began the campaign with the German-built Etrich Taube, a fragile, slow, unarmed observation platform. *Brown & Dawson to National Geographic*

German-built Albatros B.1 ready for flight. *Österreichische Nationalbibliotek File 15715729*

An Albatros C.1 in German scheme, most likely on the Western Front at the start of the war. Once this technology was eclipsed, it found service in the secondary theater over Gallipoli. *Public Domain*

The Germans received Fokker E.1 Eindeckers at the end of the Gallipoli campaign, the first true fighter aircraft to arrive on station. It had a synchronizer gear, which allowed the pilot to fire the machine gun through the propeller arc, creating a stable gun platform. *Public Domain*

Squadron (later Wing) Commander Charles Rumney Samson, who led 3 Squadron, at the Imbros aerodrome. *Imperial War Museum File CP 44351*

The Breguet Bre. 4 was 3 Squadron's "Big Bomber." Only Marix was willing to fly the temperamental machine. *Reprinted from J. M. Bruce,* War Planes of the First World War: Fighters, Volume IV *(Garden City, NY: Doubleday and Co., 1972)*

Used by both 3 Squadron and the French MF. 98(T), the Henri Farman HF.20 was a stable, reliable observation and bombing platform for the Allies at Gallipoli. *Photo taken by Etienne Labranche, 1912. Actia Nicopolis Foundation, Preveza, Greece*

Samson's favorite plane, RAF BE2a "Number 50" at the aerodrome on Imbros. The Gallipoli Peninsula and the Helles beaches are visible in the background. *Imperial War Museum File HN 67762*

The RAF BE2c, a substantial upgrade to the BE2a, was the workhorse for 3 Squadron over Gallipoli. *Imperial War Museum File MH 3235*

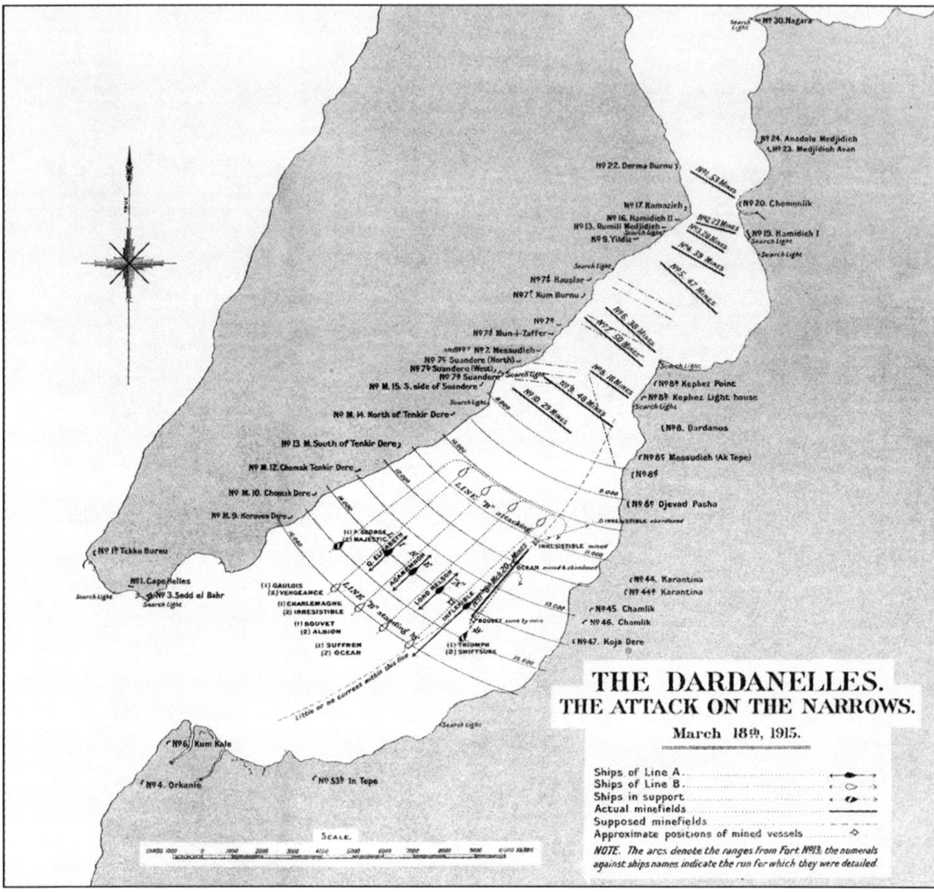

Map showing the Dardanelles defenses prior to the Allied naval attacks, including the forts and minefields. *Courtesy of historyofthegreatwar.com*

CHAPTER EIGHT

The Evacuation and the End of the Gallipoli Campaign

With the decision to evacuate, the role of aviation changed. The remaining British aircraft at Gallipoli had to provide valuable support for the evacuation of the peninsula. The French were gone, the Turkish-German force was getting stronger, and at the same time the weather became increasingly problematic. In addition to all of this, Samson had only ten days to plan for his wing's role in the evacuation; Gerrard at 2 Wing was given only a few weeks. Concurrently but separately, the wing commanders wrote orders for the best use of their aircraft in support of the troops and the evacuation from the Gallipoli Peninsula.

The Turks remained unaware of the Allied plans. There were rumors of an evacuation, but the Allies maintained strict secrecy—even Liman von Sanders did not receive definitive word that the evacuation was imminent.[1] Although he instructed his officers to watch for signs of an evacuation, the Turks did not have conclusive evidence of the movements off shore.[2] Instead, all the Turks saw was reinforcements coming in every day and continued activity in shoring up defensive positions. Thus, the Turks focused on bolstering their numbers along the entire line. That said, there were indications that airpower might have warned the German and Turkish commanders, who did not heed the warnings. In the Serno reports[3] and in subsequent research,[4] the record indicates that one German pilot-observer, Major Willhelm Siegert, took to the skies on an orientation flight after his arrival to the theater sometime around the end of December or early January. "The trained eye of an experienced old flier confirmed the

British preparations for a withdrawl."[5] This information was either not passed on to high command or was ignored. Historian Richard Layman suggests, "The [German and Turkish] ground command had held fast to the 'Gibralter [*sic*] Thesis' (i.e. that the British would hold Gallipoli like Gibralter [*sic*])."[6] Even at this late date, with seemingly incontrovertible evidence, the pilot reports were either undelivered or ignored. It seems as if the Turkish-German aviators might have been able to capitalize on the aerial intelligence that was available.

In the air, the Turks benefited from new reinforcements. Two new land planes—Albatros C.1s—were delivered in December, and a new batch of Fokker E.Is were on the way.[7] In addition, three new Gotha WD.12 float-planes arrived that month, bringing the sea-based plane total to six available for operations from the base at Çanakkale.[8] The resupplied German-Turkish air forces increased aerial operations against the Allies over Gallipoli. Of greatest concern to Samson and Gerrard was that the Turkish planes might observe and report on the evacuation operations from Gallipoli.

Samson issued orders to his men, focusing on covering the evacuation while at the same time providing aerial support for the beaches. He needed to keep the Turks away from the beaches and prevent them from complicating the Allied evacuation plans. At the start of the Suvla Bay and ANZAC Cove evacuation operations there were still more than 50,000 men on the beaches at Suvla with another 40,000 at ANZAC Cove. The plan was directed in stages. Before the final evacuation of the two beaches, set for the nights of 18 and 19 December, men, artillery, and animals were withdrawn under the cover of darkness every night. By the final night, only about 10,000 men remained on each beach.

Samson's 3 Wing pilots played a large role in the evacuation operations. Between 9 and 19 December, 3 Wing carried out fifty flights, an average of five a day. This included a no flying day on the 15th due to bad weather.[9] The wing bombed Turkish positions at Suvla and ANZAC to make the Turks believe that renewed offensive operations were at hand. The bombing and action also helped mask the noise of evacuation preparations. In addition to the overflight missions, the wing conducted a number of "enemy aircraft patrols" to prevent enemy observers from spotting the evacuation. Due to the combination of aerial bombing and harassment, naval artillery fire on shore positions, and continual land artillery bombardment, the Turks "could not tell if they were opposed by 10,000 or 40,000 troops."[10]

The wing kept up continuous air patrol over the beaches. Samson noted that he searched specifically for signs of the evacuation that might betray the actions to the enemy. But even in his advantageous position in the air, he did not see any signs of the impending evacuation.[11] Over the course of the week the airplanes covered daily movement toward the beaches, while men and materials were evacuated under the cover of night. During the day, British ships and planes kept up a steady bombardment to cover the operation, keeping the Turks unaware that the troops were being pulled back. On 16 December two 3 Wing planes took the fight directly to the enemy. Flight Sub-Lieutenant Heriot with Blackford in the observer's seat and Flight Lieutenant Wakeley with Lieutenant Boles went on a bombing mission against the Turkish airfield at Galata. On return from the mission the aircraft were shot at by Turkish gunners and one was hit, causing a forced landing at Helles.[12] The pilot and observer were fine, but the plane was damaged beyond repair.

Over the next few days the German records state that the weather was too poor to fly, keeping their airplanes grounded.[13] This was a bonus for 3 Wing, which continued air operations to cover the evacuation in spite of the inclement weather.[14] On 19 December, 3 Wing launched seven flights over the course of the day, to cover ongoing troop movements. Samson flew the first and last flights of the day, and all of the flights were labeled "patrol Anzac and Suvla."[15] That night, the last ten thousand troops on each location were evacuated from the beaches. The withdrawls from Suvla and ANZAC were complete; the ruse was successful. The planned evacuation went off without a hitch; neither the British (at Suvla) nor the ANZACs (at ANZAC Beach) suffered a single casualty in the overnight evacuation.

Samson took to the skies on 20 December—in addition to the other nine wing flights—for a "Reconnaissance of Anzac, Suvla & shipping"[16] to "see if the Turks had discovered our departure."[17] The Turks were still shelling the beaches, apparently unaware that the troops had been evacuated. As the British ships moved off-station, Turkish ground troops tentatively advanced on the empty beaches, surprised and frustrated that the Allied troops had departed. The evacuations were overwhelmingly successful. Not only did the Turks not respond to the evacuations, the Allied troops were taken off the beaches according to plan without losses. In the end, it was an impressive joint operation that combined air, sea, and land coordination. The role of the 3 Wing aircraft was significant in that they prevented the Turkish air and ground forces from deducing the plan. Airpower helped enable a successful withdrawl from the two northern beaches.

The next step was to evacuate the rest of the Allied troops from Helles. After the evacuation of Suvla and ANZAC, Liman von Sanders was concerned that the Allies would evacuate the entire peninsula, although he also thought that the British might stay—at least at the toe of the peninsula. He began to consider ways to spoil a potential Helles evacuation, or to use force to pressure the British to quit.[18] Sanders planned a ground offensive to try to force the British to leave, unaware that they were already planning to. Once again, airpower was called on to enable a successful evacuation.

With the evacuation of Suvla and ANZAC, 3 Wing's official role in the Gallipoli Campaign was done. Gerrard's 2 Wing was in charge of aerial operations over Helles, and 3 Wing prepared for new operations. They continued the fight for another nine days, to 29 December, but the bulk of the flying duties shifted to 2 Wing. During the last few days, 3 Wing flew another thirty flights over Gallipoli, mostly in support of 2 Wing operations and anti-shipping bombing raids and spotting against the port at Kilia Liman. 3 Wing pilots handed over most of their photography equipment to 2 Wing and helped instruct the latter on aerial photography. Thomson and Davies received orders to return to England, but spent their final days at Gallipoli dropping bombs on transport ships reinforcing the Turkish lines.[19] Samson flew every day, as usual, searching for enemy aircraft and targets of opportunity on the ground.

Between March and December 1915, 3 Wing flew over 2,600 hours and nearly 156,000 miles in support of the Gallipoli Campaign. At the end of December, Samson, Davies, and Thomson left for England, and the rest of the wing was folded into 2 Wing, who continued the fight against the Turks. In the final days of the campaign, 2 Wing took a page from Samson's book and pounded the forward Turkish positions into paralysis. The Turks—and Liman von Sanders—had an idea that the Allies might evacuate, but were prevented from launching spoiling attacks. With the combination of naval artillery, air-delivered munitions, and ground fire, the steady and well-planned evacuation proceeded. But the increased aerial activity opened up new dangers for the pilots.

Gerrard's 2 Wing received six new Bristol Scouts at the end of December; it was the first British plane with a machine gun that fired through the propeller arc. It finally gave the British pilots a fighter plane.[20] But they faced a worthy challenger in the new Fokker E.Is flown by the Germans under Turkish command. On 6 January, Flight Commander Busk of 3 Wing was shot down and killed while on a bombing mission, most likely by Lieutenant Buddecke in a Fokker E.I. Busk was the first British aviator lost to enemy action in the campaign.[21] That same day Buddecke allegedly shot down a second plane, but the British have no record of the loss.[22]

In spite of the loss of Busk and the increased enemy aerial activity, the Allies maintained the plan and the operational pace. Like the earlier evacuation operations, troops were pulled off Helles each night and every day the aircraft and naval artillery harassed the Turks. As the winter weather closed in, the Allies realized that time was not on their side. There were hundreds of pack animals—horses, donkeys, and mules—at Helles, and both Birdwood and Keyes wanted to keep them, but both were willing to leave them if it meant saving the troops.[23] In an effort to spoil British plans, Liman von Sanders ordered a full-on frontal assault on 7 January. But the 2 Wing pilots saw the build-up and preparation and informed high command of the enemy plan. The trap was set. When the Turks attacked on the 7th, British air power combined with naval artillery to spoil the enemy ground offensive. With the element of surprise gone, the Turkish attack stalled and was stopped. The attack "was repulsed with such ferocity that the German general [Sanders] became convinced the British were indeed planning a 'Gibraltar' defense."[24]

However, it did not fundamentally change the British plan; the failed attack simply put the Turks on the defensive in their trenches. On the night of 9 January the last of the Allied troops were evacuated from the Gallipoli Peninsula. And, it was not a moment too soon. As dawn broke, a terrible gale blew in bringing all movement on land, sea, or in the air to a screeching halt. But it was too late; the evacuation from Helles was an overwhelming tactical success. The fleet and 2 Wing prevented the Turks from any significant opposition to the evacuation and the plan went smoothly.

When the weather cleared two days later, the airmen resumed flying over the peninsula for a few days to reconnoiter the aftermath. As the fleet retreated, first to Mudros and later to Salonika, the Turks were left in complete control of the peninsula. The Gallipoli Campaign was over.

Ironically, the next few days brought the worst aerial losses for the RNAS. On 11 December, while flying observation to see the after-effects of the evacuation, 2 Wing pilot Flight Lieutenant C. H. Brinsmead and his observer Lieutenant N. H. Boles were shot down by two E.Is. The kill was shared by German pilots Schüz and Buddecke.[25] On the 12th, Flight Sub-Lieutenant J. S. Bolas and Midshipman D. M. Branson were shot down by Schüz; Buddecke also claimed another Allied plane.[26] Bolas was killed in the crash; Branson was taken prisoner on the ground that had been until very recently British-held Helles. Thus, it was only in the final days of the campaign—and the few days that followed—that there were any Allied losses in aerial combat. And as historian H. A. Jones points out, the final few days of aerial activity over Gallipoli "[gave] ominous distinction to the second letter of the alphabet,"[27] as the last three pilots and two observers lost at Gallipoli all had last names starting with "B."

After the evacuation, Commander Gerrard and 2 Wing remained on station for a few weeks. The wing was eventually transferred to the Salonika theater, to assist with offensive operations farther north on the Greek coast. Gerrard's 2 Wing set up an airfield at Thasos, and continued offensive operations in support of the Allied offensive. Gerrard, the last air commander at Gallipoli, was awarded the Distinguished Service Order for his leadership and efforts in the futile campaign.

Commander Samson returned to England on leave, and was ordered to see a doctor, despite his protests. After some rest and leave he was medically cleared to return to action. In April he was ordered to report to Egypt as the new captain of the HMS *Ben-my-Chree* seaplane tender. He arrived in May and assumed command from Acting Commander Cecil L'Estrange Malone, who became Samson's deputy.[28] The *Ben-my Chree* and two other ships—the *Anne* and the *Raven II*—became the East Indies and Egypt Seaplane Squadron, and were ordered to harass Central Powers ships and planes, ranging from the Mediterranean to the Red Sea to the Indian Ocean.[29] The *Ben-my-Chree* was shot out from under Samson and sunk on 9 January 1917, after succumbing to Turkish artillery based on the island of Castelorizo. It was the only aviation ship to be sunk by enemy action during the war.[30] Samson's career did not suffer from the loss; he was acquitted of culpability in the loss of the ship. After the war, Samson was integrated into the Royal Air Force when the RNAS was disbanded, and eventually promoted to chief of staff of the RAF's Middle East Command.

Erich Serno, the German pilot officer sent to Turkey to establish an air force in 1914, stayed on in Turkey, was promoted, and eventually helped build an entire air force. According to the records, he organized seventeen land-based and four seaplane squadrons for the Ottomans over the course of the war in his role as the general inspector of the Ottoman air force. At the end of the war, Serno returned to Germany.[31] Although it is unclear what Serno did in the immediate aftermath of the war, he later worked for the Arado aircraft company as an executive and designer.

Liman von Sanders was promoted to commander of the Ottoman army by the end of the war, but declining troop strength and morale led to a massive defeat at the Battle of Meggido in 1918. Sanders was arrested by the Allies in 1919 for war crimes, but released six months later. He retired from the German army that year and began writing his memoirs.[32]

Mustafa Kemal took over when Sanders left and attempted to organize the Turkish forces for the imminent postwar reconstruction of the Ottoman Empire. He led a military and political campaign to preserve the empire at the end of the war, as it was in political and social chaos after the defeat of the Central Powers. He eventually seized control of the Ottoman heartland, renamed it Turkey, and focused on political consolidation. He became the father of modern Turkey and is remembered as Mustafa Kemal Attatürk.[33]

***

Airpower played an important role in the Gallipoli Campaign. An interesting mix of fifty aircraft, as well as three balloons and a blimp, inaugurated the third dimension of warfare in the backwater theater. More importantly, it was the birth of joint warfare with the addition of the third dimension for the Allies, even though the combined air, land, and sea campaign ultimately failed. The Gallipoli Campaign was a test to see if the Allies were equal to the task of combining the three components in a coherent battle plan, which in the end they were not.

However, the aviation record is worthy of reflection. From the start of the campaign to the end, the aviators, mechanics, and support personnel served admirably, and introduced new ideas and methods into the exercise of warfare. The individual commanders were highly successful tacticians and operators, and very adaptive. In spite of all of the limitations from the environment, logistics, and technology, they were able to achieve incredible feats of military prowess on the periphery of World War I. Considering the limitations of technology and the painful logistics chain to the operational theater, the record of aviation at Gallipoli is very impressive.

The first use of airpower at Gallipoli included the floatplanes of the *Ark Royal.* The pilots, flying primitive and tempestuous machines, were able to observe, chart, map, and photograph the Turkish defenses. They spotted for naval artillery, searched for sea mines, and found Turkish hiding places that could not be seen from the sea. With no more than four machines they carried out the first phases of the campaign as the Royal Navy and Marine Nationale prepared for naval operations against the Dardanelles Straits. They were hampered by weather, maintenance, logistics, and inexperience. They failed to spot the minefield that stymied the 18 March attempt to force the waterway. When the plan was rewritten, they continued their pursuit of their traditional roles of spotting and observation and added new missions. In the following months they searched for enemy submarines, began bombing land and sea targets, and were responsible for the first torpedo attacks on enemy ships. When enemy submarines threatened the *Ark Royal* and she was forced to seek protection in Mudros Harbor, the British floatplanes continued to fly and harass the enemy. Their contribution was so important that the seaplane tender *Ben-My-Chree* was sent to support as well, bringing another handful of planes and pilots.

The balloon ships also contributed to the effort. The HMS *Manica* provided a necessary observation platform for naval bombardment, and provided a stable communications link for spotting artillery. Their contribution was so significant that the Royal Navy dispatched another two balloon ships, the *Hector* and the *Canning* for operations. In summer 1915 the Royal Navy also sent a blimp to Imbros, but it did not participate in combat operations.

The Royal Naval Air Service pilots were the true heroes of the campaign. From March until December, Squadron Commander Charles Samson and 3 Squadron—which was rechristened 3 Wing—led the fight in the air against the Turks. Samson's pilots were supplemented by 2 Wing in August, after Frederick Sykes' visit and reappraisal. Constantly harassed by the environmental conditions and a lack of spare parts, the small unit took the fight to the enemy on a daily basis. Samson's men and machines innovated a wide variety of aerial missions during the course of the campaign with great tactical success.

Over the course of the campaign, 3 Wing flew over 2,600 hours and 156,000 miles. In comparison to their counterparts on the Western Front, most of the wing's air miles were over water. H. A. Jones commented, "Never again in the war were seaplanes compelled to work so much over the land, nor aeroplanes so much over the sea."[34] Samson never had an overabundance of anything; he reminisced, "With a maximum of eleven pilots and an average of seven, sometimes with only four aeroplanes in action, I think it will be agreed that they one and all quitted themselves like men."[35] Over the course of the battle, 3 Wing mapped, observed, spotted for artillery, photographed the entire peninsula, and bombed the enemy on land and sea. They eventually included air-to-air combat, close air support, and long-range strategic bombing into their menu of competencies—all without losing a pilot to enemy action until the very closing days of the campaign.

The gallant efforts of the pilots at Gallipoli opened a new era of warfare and gave birth to the concept of joint operations in three dimensions. By the end of the campaign, it was clear that that neither Allied nor Turkish airpower changed the course of the fight, but the new technology initiated a new era of combat. Airpower forever changed the character of warfare during the Gallipoli campaign. The men who flew the missions realized they had fundamentally introduced a new era of warfare.

CHAPTER NINE

Campaign Evaluations and Lessons Learned

The dearth of information on the air war over Gallipoli is an understandable reason why the topic is so poorly addressed in the scholarship on the campaign. For historians who focus on official records and generals' and admirals' papers, it is very easy to see why this topic has been overlooked for over a century. Added to the fact that there were very few supporting documents, and that very little information was retained during or after the campaign, it is no mystery why the story of airpower over Gallipoli has not yet been addressed.

Looking closely at the documents, reports, and memoirs during and after the war, a narrative emerges. Militaries invariably try to assess performance during and after conflict to ascertain strengths and weaknesses, to assign kudos for victory and blame for defeat. In the final analysis, each of the four belligerents at Gallipoli—the Ottomans, the Germans, the French, and the British and Commonwealth nations—recorded the role of airpower in the campaign; some at the time, some after the guns were silenced. A main argument emerges that none of them fully understood airpower at the time, thus the importance was lost. In the official records it was more a matter of absence of assessment rather than a fulsome treatment.

This is due in part to the relatively minor role airpower played in the campaign. In the present narrative airpower has been the main focus, to illuminate the daring, bravado, and abilities of the airmen and the innovation of the machines they flew. But even the interesting anecdotes, the experimentation and abilities, and the influential evolution of tactics and employment did not rise to the level of mass carnage on the ground and sea. The fact that a handful of planes, with few losses and little real strategic influence on the outcome of the campaign, allowed wartime chroniclers as well as airmen at the time to overlook the historic role that airpower played in the Gallipoli Campaign. Compared to the 119,000 Allied casualties on land (40,000 killed), an untold number of Ottoman dead and wounded, and another 1,000 Allied sailors killed in the naval attacks, only a handful of airmen died in the entire air campaign on both sides—nearly all in accidents. The first losses in the air to enemy action only came at the very end of the campaign.

Still, this author believes that the oversight is significant. Aircraft and airmen did play a vital role in the campaign; airpower "earned its wings" over Gallipoli. But the lack of communication, commemoration, and acclamation during and after the campaign indicates that the sea and ground commanders on both sides overlooked the abilities and potential of the third dimension during the battle for Gallipoli. There was definitely a hierarchical aspect to this oversight: the generals and admirals overlooked the contributions of navy commanders and army majors and captains. An additional consideration was that the technology was simply too new; the higher-ups did not understand how to use the new machines to their advantage, let alone how to incorporate aircraft into tactical and strategic planning. Finally, the limitations of the machines themselves meant that in the early days of airpower, combined with the harsh environment of the Dardanelles and Gallipoli, created consternation for the pilots as well as the commanding officers. There was little consensus on what airpower could do, and even less consideration for how it could help.

The Ottomans

Unfortunately for the historical record, little remained from the government perspective at the end of the Gallipoli Campaign. Liman von Sanders left Turkey after the war, and took his entourage with him. During the Turkish War of Independence (1919–23) that followed immediately on the Ottoman Empire's battles in World War I, there was little time to write and reflect on the war that was lost, even considering the victory in Gallipoli. Mustafa Kemal was venerated, but little remained in the Turkish archives on the campaign, beyond the highlights of the German-Turkish successes in defeating and ejecting the Allies from Gallipoli. After Mustafa Kemal consolidated power, the new government went so far as to change the alphabet to Modern Turkish. Thus, by 1928, government documents transitioned from Arabic to Modern Turkish (Latin) script. In the same period, the archives were purged to create a doctored history of the Ottoman Empire for future historians. There was little in the Turkish archives on the Gallipoli Campaign (mostly in Arabic script) and no official government overview of the 1915 battles at all.[1] What was available was incorporated into this project as best as can be expected for the lack of resources, compounded by the language barrier. The archivists and graduate students in Ankara and Istanbul were immensely helpful and at the same time incredibly embarrassed that there were so few resources that survived the one-hundred-year gap from then to now.

The Turkish documents posed limitations. The Germans delivered the planes; German pilots flew the missions. Very few (three) Turk pilots participated in the aerial campaign and little remains of their records. Turkish maintainance personnel, construction crews, and workers were integral to the operation of the airfields, but there is almost no mention of them other than raw numbers. The official Turkish records of the Gallipoli Campaign focus on the exploits of Mustafa Kemal, the Sixth Army, and their efforts to counter the Allied naval and military (land) forces. The miniscule air efforts of the Turks were understandably understated.

Serno went on to continue the war with the Ottomans after the Gallipoli Campaign, but there is little indication that the few lessons from Gallipoli translated to ongoing tactical or operational acumen. The Ottomans naturally focused on counter-air over the course of the war, but Serno offers scant information on the air campaigns that followed Gallipoli. The Ottoman Turks provide no further insight into follow-on operations, other than the fact that their air force expanded to face threats in the other theaters of combat.

The Germans

At the very least, the Germans kept good records. While a lot were lost during the next war (to the consternation of my World War I historian colleagues), this author found a treasure trove of information for this project in both Berlin (Lichterfeld, Bundesarchiv Berlin), and Freiburg (Bundesarchiv

Militärarchiv, BA/MA).[2] The German documents in Berlin were mostly official government records on the military mission to Turkey produced by the Reichskanzlerei as well as some newspaper clippings on the actual conduct of the war. The diplomatic papers were informative, but limited to names and numbers. At Freiburg, the documents were more specific and useful. The *Kriegtagesbücher Dardanellen* (Daily War Reports—Dardanelles), in the RM 40/6 to /19 collection, recounted the daily reports from the front. It listed obscure references to "Air Attack" and "Air Activity," but from the opening day of the air campaign, when the first planes arrived for action at Gallipoli (27 March 1915), to the period immediately following the evacuation, the record shows extensive air action by all of the belligerents.[3] The German reports corroborate many of the same dates and events from the Allied records (see below), which was ultimately useful in building the narrative dominated by the Allies. But throughout, there is an underlying lack of understanding of the role of airpower from the German-Turkish side, little communication between German land (Von Sanders) and air leaders (Serno), and no cooperation between them. Major Serno—like his Allied counterparts—had complete control and command of his pilots and planes, without any significant guidance from above. It was however, a double-edged sword; airpower was not used for anything above tactical effect by the German-Turkish forces. Not that it could have been, but there was not even an attempt to do so. Interestingly, the Germans also recorded numerous attempts to secure more planes, parts, pilots, and supplies; they seemingly always wanted more, regardless of military effect of the weapons system. Indeed, usually once a week, one of the air commanders would add a line in the daily record that it would have been beneficial if Berlin could send more planes and parts.

Major Erich Serno, the officer in charge of the combined German-Turkish air effort, produced a pair of more official documents, one during and one after the war, also found at the BA/MA (MSG 2/10876 and MSG 2/10873).[4] The first—chronologically, not numerically (10876)—was his report on hitting the ground in Istanbul. Serno was given a Turkish uniform, promoted to major, and put in charge of organizing a Turkish air arm from the ground up. With nearly unlimited funds and official letters he set out to build a force, first writing on the state of Turkish aviation in 1915. This preliminary document is critical, but not harsh. He reported that there was nothing of note, all of the previous machines were already destroyed through overuse in the Balkan Wars, and the foreign contracted pilots returned to their home countries before the outbreak of World War I. Serno committed to paper the challenges and opportunities he faced in creating an air arm from scratch. In his initial 1915 report, Serno relayed the state of airpower before the start of the Gallipoli Campaign, upon his arrival in late January 1915. He started with nothing; all of the airpower at Gallipoli for the German-Turkish air arm came after he arrived, and on his authority.

A more interesting document is his postwar report *Sammlung Luftwesen vor 1918* (BA/MA MSG 2/10873).[5] The 168-page document recounts Serno's entire career and interaction with the Ottoman Turks, from his days immediately leading up to travel to Istanbul in January 1915 (to p. 33) and through the war, ending on the last page with his circuitous return to Berlin after the end of hostilities. Pages 33–91 deal specifically with the air war for Gallipoli and his role as the air commander. Serno had planes for the second naval attack in March and was able to warn the land commanders of an imminent attack after spotting seventy to eighty ships sailing around Tenedos (p. 44). Throughout the narrative, he relates the need for more aircraft, the limitations of the machines, men, and technology, and the frequent battles with the environment, especially the unpredictable weather. The narrative seems to follow the daily pilot's log, which may have been limited to the *Kriegstagesbuch* mentioned above, or some other pilots' logs lost to time. His narrative confirms most of the better-preserved British records, although there are some minor discrepancies on dates and events between the German and British records. Overall, this document provided the bulk of the evidence for the German-Turkish team and their air efforts over Gallipoli. What is painfully clear from Serno's postwar reports is the lack of coordination and cooperation between the land and the air.

Throughout the narrative it is clear that there was little guidance from Liman von Sanders and the land component even with regards to counter air against the Allies, or air–ground coordination. The German airmen fighting for the Ottoman Turks were on their own in the new domain of war. But even considering that it was written as a pseudo-memoir (secret and sealed for a number of years), it was able to recapture the successes and failures of the German-Turkish air arm over Gallipoli with impressive reliability. Interestingly, it was one of the few documents (this and his earlier report in MSG 2/10876) that could not be photographed by the researcher; the archivists at BA/MA were the only ones authorized to photocopy the document. German state secrets are still preserved even a hundred years after the events. Further, there is no indication, other than the expansion of the force, that any significant lessons were learned from the Gallipoli Campaign. Serno reported that more Turkish pilots were trained and pressed into service and more German planes arrived to expand the force. Throughout the rest of the war the command confusion continued, and the Ottoman air force remained a tactical organization. There is no indication that the theoretical or doctrinal use of airpower by the German-Ottoman forces improved. Hans Joachim Buddecke, Serno's best German pilot, remained with the Ottoman air force until late 1916, although he returned to fly for the Ottomans in 1917. He gained fame as an ace (thirteen kills), but was himself killed in early 1918. He is remembered as a great tactician, but there is no indication that any of his Gallipoli experiences were disseminated after that campaign.

The official German record of the Dardanelles-Gallipoli Campaign was printed in 1927 as volume 16 of the official history, *Schlachten des Weltkrieges* (Battles of the World War), titled *Der Kampf um die Dardanellen* (The Fight for the Dardanelles) by Dr. Carl Mühlmann, (Berlin: Oldenburg, 1927).[6] Mühlmann was Liman von Sanders's aide-de-camp during the campaign and had been a history professor before the war, which proved beneficial in the researching and writing of the official history. While he naturally focuses on the land campaign and his boss, he does reference the air war where it was important. In the 195-page volume (written in old German script, and with excellent maps) he mentions "enemy" Allied air twice, and introduces Serno on page 163. But even the intrepid historian recounts that there were too few German planes (three in spring 1915, p. 163) and too few throughout the campaign ("inferiority" in the air, p. 166). In the concluding pages of the official history Mühlmann argues that the German-Turkish aviators were overpowered in the air, with only "a few planes of limited ability" facing "60 English and 20 French machines" (p. 179). According to Mühlmann the Allies had complete control of the air and had the ability to fly over their territory at will, mostly because of better machines. Mühlmann does not offer any indication of the dissemination of information from the Gallipoli Campaign to the rest of the war. His narrative provides a straightforward account of the Gallipoli Campaign, but offers little in the way of analysis of how the Gallipoli Campaign influenced or guided the greater German war effort.

Significantly though, there were only a few references to airpower in the German official history. While airpower did get specific mention, it was only in a couple of paragraphs in the official record. For the Germans and Turks, airpower did not matter for the campaign. It was not much more than a footnote to the carnage on the ground. After Gallipoli, Mühlmann and Serno turned their attention to other fronts to battle the Allies on land and in the air in the Levant, Mesopotamia, and the rest of the shrinking Ottoman Empire.

The French

The French official record is equally frustrating. There was very little in the archives or the official records that shed light on the French contributions in the Gallipoli Campaign. Although there are a number of excellent books on the French in the Dardanelles, from both the sea and land perspectives, there was nearly nothing on the squadron of aircraft that participated on the French side. What was available was incorporated, but the resources were spartan.

Admiral Émile Paul Almable Guépratte commanded the French Marine Nationale in the Mediterranean, with complete authority and autonomy. Although the Allies agreed that the Dardanelles was part of his mission set, when the British sent the Royal Navy, Guépratte was instructed to "help out in any way he could, based on his best judgement." He worked in coordination with Royal Navy Admiral Sackville Carden and later de Robeck in the unsuccessful naval attacks on the Dardanelles, and commanded the Marine Nationale throughout the campaign. After the war, in 1935, he wrote his memoir of the campaign, *L'Expédition des Dardanelles, 1914–1915*, (Paris, France: Payot, 1935).[7] Unfortunately, he does not reference the air war at all, even though it fell under his command. This oversight conveys both the lack of interest and cooperation between the French air, sea, and land services.

The French official records at the Service Historique de la Défense, Château de Vincennes, Paris, include two collections in files 16N2135 (82 pp.) and 16N1205D2 (55 pp.) labeled "Dardanelles 1" and "Dardenelles 2."[8] These documents are collections of letters, memos, and reports to and from the front back to Paris during the war. In "Dardenelles 1," there are a mere four paragraphs reporting the arrival and location of the squadron. It included two references to missions: observation and reconnaissance of the enemy lines (June and December 1915). In the five references in the second collection, three documents discussed the enemy air forces and two referenced the work of the French, including the report on the combined British and French attack on the enemy airfield on 6 July 1915. The French documents corroborated the British record of the same events where fourteen French and three British aircraft flew to bomb the enemy airfield (no page number given).

These documents were supplemented by the official dossier of Captain Césari, the commander of the French squadron. It was helpful in that it established a timeline for his service, as well as some detail on the assignment to the Dardanelles front. The MF. 98(T) squadron set up camp on Tenedos and flew missions to support French land forces, first on the Asian coast and continuing after they were withdrawn from the Asian side and moved to the European coast of the Gallipoli Peninsula. The record, and relevance of the French squadron, ended when the squadron was withdrawn from Gallipoli to the Salonika Front in December 1915. Unfortunately for this project and for future historians, there are no log books, daily reports, or postwar narratives of this squadron to draw from. The best unofficial (and consequently questionable) record of MF. 98(T) at Gallipoli is an online article in French written by David Méchin.[9]

The lack of sources from the French perspective hampered an in-depth analysis of the French contribution to the air war over Gallipoli. However, these few sources, along with some creative research, allowed this author to construct a coherent narrative based on what was available. It was clear that the French high command did not think that the air contribution was very important and subsequently did not keep adequate records or lost them in the intervening years and wars. However, enough of the story was available to be able to relate that there was at least one French squadron at Gallipoli, and they were fairly active in prosecuting the war from the air against the German-Turkish enemy. To this day, there is virtually nothing on Césari and very little on the French air squadron during or after the campaign.

The British

Fortunately, the British have preserved a wealth of resources on the Gallipoli campaign. The British records proved invaluable for the information that the British maintained on not only their forces, but on the French as well as enemy action during the campaign. Whether it was because they lost, because they have a culture of preserving military records, or the fact that the British archives were not overrun during World War I or World War II, the British archive materials are extensive. From the initial six planes of the HMS *Ark Royal* to the records of 3 Squadron and later 2 Squadron, to in-depth analysis of the enemy activity, the British records were ultimately the primary basis for this project. It was also helpful that the records were in English, and mostly typewritten.

Thankfully, the British have a compulsive obsession with keeping—and maintaining—military records. This extends back hundreds of years, and was extremely helpful for this period as well. Not only did the British maintain records during the campaign, but they set up an official commission at the end of the war to analyze the defeat, consider the issues, and assess accountability.

The daily log of the HMS *Ark Royal*, drawn from the National Archives UK (formerly Kew Gardens), was beneficial for the project. Located in the AIR 1 files, the *Ark Royal* documents included "*Ark Royal* flying logs" (AIR 1/726/137/2) that chronicled Commander Robert Clark-Hall's squadron logs and daily flights.[10] The detailed record outlined the role of the six *Ark Royal* floatplanes at the very beginning of the Dardanelles operations, and the limitations and issues the pilots faced supporting the fleet in its first few attempts against the Turkish forts. Later, when the HMS *Ben-my-Chree* was sent to the Dardanelles, its flying logs complemented the earlier seaplane tender (AIR 1/665/17/122/714 and AIR 1/726/137/2).[11] These two ships provided a handful of airplanes for the fight—never more than ten—for naval artillery spotting and photography and mapping.

The heart of the story of airpower at Gallipoli was supported by flight logs of 2 Squadron led by Royal Naval Air Service (RNAS) Commander Charles Rumney Samson, located at the Imperial War Museum in Record Group 12080, File 33, titled "Samson, Private Papers, Flying Log."[12] The daily flying log of the squadron was extensive and detailed, and helped create the narrative of the actual events over Gallipoli. However, it was interesting to note what was not included in the documents, either Samson's personal papers or the flying logs: there was very little cooperation or coordination with either the naval or military (land component) command. In fact, throughout the squadron's documents, it is absolutely clear that the squadron was completely autonomous and self-contained. Even though they had the potential to provide a unique perspective and component for a new form of warfare, Commander Samson and the pilots of 3 Squadron fought a seemingly separate war from either the sea or land campaigns. Their efforts in the air in support of the other domains were frequently ignored or at least overlooked.

By summer 1915 it was clear that there were issues with the campaign. Colonel Frederick Sykes was dispatched to the Dardanelles to observe, study, and report his findings on improving the outcomes of the campaign. He was promoted before he went, in order to make him superior to Samson, so that Sykes could make actual changes. His report (AIR 1/669/17/122/788) suggested additional airpower, better coordination across the board, and more communication between the disparate commanders.[13] The sea and land commanders (primarily de Robeck, Hamilton, and Birdwood) seemed to take the suggestions to heart, and there was better communication between the admiral and generals. Sykes also requested (and received) additional air support; 3 Squadron was elevated to wing status, and received more planes and men, RNAS 2 Wing was dispatched to Gallipoli. But tensions grew between Samson and Sykes, neither worked well together. And even though the air commanders (Samson and Eugene Gerrard of 2 Wing) submitted weekly reports to General Headquarters at Imbros, neither received—nor took—much direction from their sea or land superiors. Thus they were able to continue the air war as they saw fit, for moderate tactical success, but without any strategic outcome.

After the war, Samson set out to recount the tales of his exploits before, during, and after the Gallipoli Campaign. In his book, *Fights and Flights* (first published London: Benn, 1930), Samson narrates his exceptional contribution to the war effort, highlighting his amazing leadership in the Gallipoli Campaign.[14] In his own estimation, his men and machines were the only highlight of the entire campaign, taking the war to the enemy in a new and profound way. His self-aggrandizement was not without merit, but also overlooked a number of institutional and organizational flaws that plagued the leadership during the fight. From the days leading up to the landings to the days immediately following the eventual evacuation, 3 Wing (RNAS) was able to accomplish amazing feats in the air at the very introduction of the third dimension of warfare. Fortunately for historians, Samson's recollections, along with the official documents from the archives, helped create an exciting narrative of airpower over Gallipoli.

In addition to the record of the pilots and squadrons, the British sat down at the end of the Gallipoli Campaign to figure out what had gone wrong. The government assembled the Dardanelles Commission for a critical analysis of the campaign and its failures. The board included nine politicians (some with previous military experience) who questioned a wide range of personalities to form an official government opinion of the Gallipoli Campaign. Their witnesses included commanders in the field, as well as luminaries such as Winston Churchill, former first lord of the admiralty, who made the decisions in London. By the first submission, "The First Report of the Dardanelles Commission" (12 February 1917, located at the UK National Archives CAB 19/1), Lord Kitchener, secretary of state for war at the time of the Gallipoli Campaign, was dead; he was killed when the ship he was traveling on struck a mine and sank.[15] Thus, Kitchener's personal secretary H. J. Creedy was called to testify, along with thirty-four other witnesses, all above the rank (or title) of navy Captain (O-6). Noticeably absent from the list were any of the British air leaders from Gallipoli, presumably because they were all still fighting the war. This initial report, at forty-three pages, only mentions aircraft three times, on pages 24 and 25. The three citations mention aircraft as spotters for naval artillery twice, but then comments, "The Fleet bombarding the Dardanelles had the important advantage over fleets previously engaged in the bombardment of forts that seaplanes were available for observation; but apparently they did not fulfill expectations, as the engine power was deficient, and there was much difficulty experienced in rising from the water when there was any sea" (p. 25). The only comments on airpower were negative, with no air commanders called to defend the new technology or to inform the commission of the extensive positive uses of airpower in the days leading up to the initial naval attacks.

In the "Final Report of the Dardanelles Commission" (same file), which was distributed on 4 December 1917, the findings were similar.[16] This report considered the entirety of the Gallipoli Campaign whereas the initial report focused mainly on the "naval only" option leading up to the landings. The "Final Report of the Dardanelles Commission" called more than 150 witnesses between 4 January and 5 September to answer questions about the campaign. In the 186 pages that followed, the minutiae of the military operations in Gallipoli was dissected, looking for problems and issues that led to failure. The commission considered everything from the mail to water to the problems with communications between ships and shore. Some generals—especially during the Suvla operations—were named as culpable for mixed orders and confusion, but there were only two references in the entire document on the contribution of airpower. On page eight, Sir Maurice Hankey argued that the old methods of warfare were no longer applicable to conditions in 1915 with the statement, "By the use of aircraft, the naval bombardment, especially by indirect laying, would be enormously increased." Unfortunately, subsequent testimony described a number of situations where aircraft could have helped, but were not even mentioned. Airpower was omitted (wittingly or not) from the discussions of the final naval attack (18 March), the landings (25 April), or the Suvla Offensive (6 August). Even though there are multiple pages on the role of RNAS armored cars and motorcycles, there is no further mention of either the *Ark Royal*'s or the *Ben-my-Chree*'s floatplanes or 3 Wing or 2 Wing aircraft. Even an extended review of the order of battle (p. 30) overlooks the very presence of aircraft during operations.

The final two mentions of airpower come from the rejoinder added by Sir Ian Hamilton. Hamilton knew he was being brought to task for the failure of the mission and was allowed to present his case in writing to the commission. He took much of the responsibility in his four appendices (totaling fifty-seven pages of the report), but also highlighted failures of his subordinates, who did not carry out his orders to his satisfaction.[17] His only references to airpower are two paragraphs that read:

> Much might be written on the exploits of the Royal Naval Air Service, but these bold fliers are laconic and their feats will mostly pass unrecorded. Yet let me thank them, with their commander, Colonel F. H. Sykes, of the Royal Marines, for the nonchalance with which they appear to affront danger and death, when and where they can.

> So doing they quicken the hearts of their friends on land and sea—and assist of greater military value even then their bombs or aerial reconnaissance, admirable in all respects as these were.

He continued:

> With them I also couple the *Service de l'Aviation* of the *Corps Expéditionaire d'Orient*, who daily wing their way in and out of the shrapnel under the distinguished leadership of M. le Captaine Césari.

And that was all of it. The entire Dardanelles Commission only referenced airpower four times (one mention of the insignificance of enemy aircraft) in the entire post-campaign analysis. No pilots or commanders were called to testify; no input came from the men who flew the missions from the first to the last day. The Dardanelles Commission did not include any substantial discussion of the role of airpower in the campaign or the effects of the third dimension on the outcomes, good or bad. The secret document was published for internal governmental use, but sealed to the public until 1968. The entire event was hidden away from public knowledge, even while commanders and politicians accepted blame and punishment. Hamilton retired from active service and Churchill was forced to step down from his post as first lord of the admiralty.

Furthermore, there is little indication that the lessons learned from the pilots were disseminated to the rest of the British RNAS, let alone the RFC. There was little cooperation between the navy and army pilots, and the Gallipoli air campaign was perceived as a sideshow, with obsolete weapons, in a far-flung battle. All of the Gallipoli pilots went on to future flying assignments, but the insular nature of the RNAS (and their competition with the RFC) indicate that few of the lessons, tactics, or doctrine were applied after the fateful evacuation. In fact, few of the RNAS airpower concepts transferred to the Western Front where the character of the fighting—and the RFC command hierarchy—was completely different.

After the war a few official records were published; some attempted to outline the story of airpower over Gallipoli. The first of these was Walter Raleigh's *The War in the Air* (London: Hamish Hamilton, 1922). It was followed by the second volume in the series by Henry Jones, *The War in the*

Air, Volume 2 (London: Hamish Hamilton, 1928).[18] The overview of the first air war included some information on the Gallipoli Campaign, but not a substantial analysis of the airpower tool in operations. Cecil Aspinall-Oglander expanded on the topic in volume 1 of *Military Operations Gallipoli*, (London: Imperial War Museum, 1929), but only offers a cursory analysis of the role of aviation.[19] Thus, even in the official British government documents and analyses after the war, airpower over Gallipoli was only mentioned in passing. It is unfortunate; the exciting and influential story of the role of airpower remained overlooked during and in the immediate aftermath of the campaign.

***

The final analysis of the entire air campaign had to wait more than a hundred years for full exposure. Airpower in World War I was studied extensively, but not over Gallipoli. The record was sealed and lost to time until now. Generals and admirals—to say nothing of politicians and government personalities—had other, more pressing issues. The German contribution to the Ottoman Turks was so insignificant that only a few documents were produced, and most of them appear to have been lost in the next war. Only the records of the major in command of the combined German-Turkish air service survived. Fortunately, it was enough to build a narrative from the perspective of the "enemy." The French records were also sparse, but they were supported by British records and obscure references in various documents.

The British kept the best records, but seemingly refused to deal with the loss with an in-depth analysis of the role of airpower. It was only through extensive searching that enough materials emerged to compose a story of the first attempts at warfare in three dimensions, regardless of the lack of "joint" cooperation and coordination. The exploits of the airmen over Gallipoli, while not enough to turn the tide of the campaign, were still important enough for the effort at researching, writing, and ultimately reconsidering the story of airpower over Gallipoli.

CONCLUSION

The Legacy of Gallipoli

Airpower over Gallipoli did not have a significant effect on the final outcome of the campaign for the Allies or the Central Powers. Airpower did not turn the tide of the battle, nor did it cause victory or defeat for either side. Although the Allies boasted air superiority for most of the campaign, they still lost. And even though the German-Turkish aviators lacked air superiority, they won. In the end, airpower was a fairly insignificant component in the battles around, on, and over the Gallipoli Peninsula from 1915 to 1916.

That does not mean that airpower was not important. In all the volumes written on Gallipoli airpower has received short shrift. It was present, it was interesting, and airpower "earned its wings" in the Gallipoli Campaign. The air war over Gallipoli involved the first use of combined and joint three-dimensional warfare at the beginning of a new era. The commanders and machines may not have been decisive, but they wrote the first chapter in the history of airpower.

Up to the Gallipoli Campaign land forces could be brought in by sea and supplied and supported from the water, but they did not enjoy the benefits of airpower. Earlier in the war, the British had experimented with airpower delivered from the sea, as was practiced in the Cuxhaven raid. On the Western Front, the first tentative experiments were conducted using airpower to support ground forces at the tactical, operational, and strategic levels of warfare. It was not until Gallipoli, and especially after the intitial landings, that airpower was combined with both land and sea forces in "modern" joint warfighting. Not surprisingly, it was younger officers who pioneered the use of the new technology for a holistic approach to joint warfare.

Winston Churchill grasped the strategic concept of joint warfare. He was a proponent of new technologies of air, land, and sea power, and enthusiastically supported the use of all the instruments of military power for decisive results. Although he did not directly influence tactics and operations, he did send the various components to the campaign for what he hoped would be a decisive victory against the Ottoman Empire. Churchill had his detractors, and he was forced to overcome opponents and critics. Field Marshal Kitchener was convinced that the war would only be won against the Germans on the Western Front, and refused to send vital men and aircraft to support "Churchill's Folly." Still, Churchill sent what he could. While the Royal Navy's contingent for Gallipoli included what could be spared from the North Sea and defense of the homeland, Churchill also dispatched the Royal Naval Air Service for the air component.

Fortunately for the campaign, Number 3 Squadron RNAS was one of the most innovative organizations available. With an inspirational leader and a cadre of battle-hardened pilots and observers, 3 Squadron was ideally suited for the campaign and environment. The air war for Gallipoli was hampered by serious difficulties, but overall performed magnificently when put to the test.

In addition to the British contribution, which was the largest, the French also dispatched sea-based and land-based aviation for the fight, in the form of a seaplane tender, the *Foudre*, as well as the MF. 98(T) squadron. A French army captain turned pilot commanded the French air efforts in the theater. Conveniently colocated with the British 3 Squadron, the British and French cooperated on missions and shared resources. Unfortunately for the Allies, there was more squadron-level coordination than direction from above, which led to breakdowns in the strategic effectiveness of the Allied air component.

As well, the German-Turkish team also suffered from a lack of strategic oversight, compounded by political hindrances and supply problems. Major Serno, the German commander of the air component for the Ottomans, had fewer resources, no strategic guidance, and little support.

At the beginning of the campaign, the Royal Navy had only a handful of planes for operations. The men and machines of the HMS *Ark Royal* began joint operations in an effort to defeat the Turkish forces at Gallipoli. The seaplane tender unloaded the planes to the water where they took off for operations. The pilots and observers flew reconnaissance and mapping missions in support of the fleet. Air supremacy fostered effective operations as the planes conveyed information to the fleet for operations. At the start of the campaign the *Ark Royal* planes mapped the locations of the Dardanelles forts and located nearly all of the underwater mines laid by the Turks. With the opening salvo, planes spotted for naval artillery, providing vital air-sea tactical cooperation. The floatplanes were able to guide naval gunners onto targets better than spotters on ships. The result was mass firepower towards the objectives.

Air-sea cooperation was not without problems. Aviation technology was brand new; the airmen had to be innovative in how to employ airpower. Air support for the naval bombardments on the Gallipoli forts was the first time the coordination had been attempted. The novel use of airpower took time to develop. As well, there were issues with communications between the aircraft and ships. In the years before the advent of reliable, compact, two-way radios, it was difficult for aerial observers to coordinate fire. In the early days of the Gallipoli Campaign, wireless radios were unavailable. When they did arrive, the large sets necessitated pilots leaving observers behind in lieu of the heavy radios. A more simple, reliable, expedient solution existed in the balloon ship HMS *Manica*, which sent a tethered balloon aloft for spotting. The benefit was a telephone line on the tether for communications, as well as an extended loiter time. The most significant drawback was that the balloon ship had to anchor away from the shore to protect the flammable hydrogen-filled balloon, and thus the observer was restricted to an oblique view of targets. The planes could fly over the entire peninsula, but had communications issues; the balloons were more stable, but did not have the visibility of the planes.

In addition to the problems of developing tactics, the early machines were temperamental. Underpowered and fragile, they only flew in ideal conditions. Pilots recounted inability to fly if the sea was either too calm or too rough. Early seaplanes and floatplanes had "short legs," pilot vernacular for very limited range. The fragile machines had a tendency to shake themselves apart when over-stressed. And because of their limited power—only a 100 horsepower engine in the Sopwith Type 807—could not carry more than about 500 pounds aloft. That meant that with a pilot and observer, and a full tank of fuel, there was little room for offensive weapons or a radio.

Finally, the elements conspired against the airplanes daily. High humidity compromised engine power and weakened adhesives; laminated wooden propellers fell apart. Early in the campaign the cold hampered operations, later the heat was equally unbearable. Sand and saltwater of the theater added to the mix and was a recipe for constant maintenance and overhaul of the fragile machines. At the end of a very long logistics tail, in a secondary theater of operations, planes were frequently grounded because of lack of fuel, lubricants, and spare parts.

But even with the limitations, the pilots performed yeoman service for the fleet. The first two naval bombardments of the peninsula—19 February and 18 March 1915—employed the floatplanes in support of the naval bombardment as the Royal Navy and French Marine Nationale first bombarded then tried to force the Dardanelles. Although moderately successful, the Ottoman defenses held and the Allies withdrew.

More men, aircraft, and ships arrived for the next phase of the campaign. RNAS 3 Squadron arrived in March, MF. 98(T) arrived shortly thereafter. It began operations in support of the impending landings. As all the pieces fell into place for joint operations, it is important to consider the personalities involved in the operations. A fifty-two-year-old rear admiral, John de Robeck, was the naval commander of the Eastern Mediterranean Squadron and all of the naval forces at Gallipoli, but he had no real appreciation for aircraft or their capabilities. In his defense, airpower was in its infancy, and he could not realistically expect much from it. That said, he did little in the way of orders or guidance to use airpower effectively as part of naval operations. The *Ark Royal* airmen, under Commander Clark-Hall, were left to their own devices to provide information for the fleet. De Robeck allowed the airmen to formulate their own tactics, techniques, and procedures. When 3 Squadron commander Charles Rumney Samson arrived, he was given the same free rein. Likewise, it is clear that French captain Césari had little guidance or oversight from his superiors.

On land, General Ian Hamilton commanded the Mediterranean Expeditionary Force, the men assigned to invade Gallipoli. He was put in charge of landing troops on a defended shore without sufficient planning, equipment, or preparation. Like de Robeck, Hamilton did not appreciate airpower's potential in fighting joint warfare in 1915. He too left Samson and Clark-Hall to their own devices, only asking for information from the air component, without realizing the potential advantages of a good joint plan.

That left the Royal Navy commanders in charge of developing separate operational plans for the use of airpower in the Gallipoli Campaign. Considering their lack of guidance, Clark-Hall and Samson's efforts were commendable. The latter was able to set up an airfield and operations; both began immediately to aid joint operations at Gallipoli. The airmen, with about twenty aircraft, flew whenever possible to assist the naval and land forces. Samson's trust in his pilots, observers, and mechanics was unbounded. He produced "Mission Command" orders, announcing priorities then allowing his pilots to operate according to opportunity. Samson coached de Robeck and Hamilton on the capabilities of his airmen, and offered closer coordination for both the sea and land components. But with three major commanders in the campaign, and a number of lower-level subordinate commanders, there was little clear structure, hierarchy, or control. As the campaign unfolded, it seemed more like a number of individual military adventures rather than a coordinated effort against the Turks.

Samson's 3 Squadron innovated the use of airpower at Gallipoli. He and his pilots developed tactics in a vacuum to enable success on the ground. His first missions mirrored the efforts of the *Ark Royal* seaplanes: 3 Squadron pilots observed, mapped, and photographed the peninsula from the air, providing accurate maps and photos for the fleet and land commanders. The pilots and observers were able to locate and map nearly all of the Turkish defenses, especially the forts and static guns, and even provided daily information on troop and mobile artillery movements. Unfortunately for the soldiers landing on the peninsula, the leadership did not consider the Turkish defenses in planning for the landings; instead they picked what they considered the best beaches for supply and ease of assault. This led to massive problems when the Allies landed in April. The troops at the Helles beaches faced substantial defenses on land, all previously mapped by the aviators. The Australians and New Zealanders at ANZAC Cove waded ashore at the base of insurmountable geographic obstacles, specifically the high cliffs overshadowed by the Sphinx. Had the land and naval commanders considered the intelligence provided by the airmen, they might have chosen better landing sites.

Once the landings were underway, Samson's men reported soft Turkish defensive positions, and locations where the Allies could have exploited gains. Whether through a blatant disregard for the information or through sheer confusion, the information went unheeded and the Turks were able to shore up defenses because of Allied inaction. The ensuing hesitation condemned the attacks and stalled offensives. Allied troops were held on the beaches and did not achieve first day objectives—Krithia from the southern tip and the Ari Brnu heights from ANZAC Cove—completely negating the strategic objectives of the offensive within the first few days of the attack. There is little evidence that by capturing the heights the Allies could have eventually forced the straits, but the outcomes may have been very different.

Samson and his men expanded their aerial repertoire. He decided that if the land and sea commanders would not make use of his intelligence contributions, he would simply take the squadron on the offensive directly against the Turks. He and his men took to the skies with whatever offensive weapons they could carry and tried to turn the tide of the battle on their own. They carried rifles, pistols, and 20-pound bombs aloft, in an effort to mount offensive attacks against Turkish targets of opportunity. As well, by the start of summer, there were a few reliable, small radios for direct communications between air and sea. With improved communications, the airmen were better able to direct naval fire on the Turkish ports at Çanakkale and Ak Bashi Liman, staging an important interdiction campaign. Nearly all of the supplies for the Turkish forces traveled by sea down the Dardanelles; the roads were too primitive to support Liman von Sanders' army. The British fliers directed naval fire on the port facilities manned by civilian stevedores who refused to work whenever they saw planes for fear of being bombed. British naval gunners, in coordination with Samson's pilots, sank a number of ships and effectively disrupted the vital supply network.

The French mounted a separate air campaign, although they sometimes worked with their British brethren. The French MF. 98(T) squadron concentrated their efforts on support for the French troops on the Asiatic side at the start of the campaign, and later coordinated with the RNAS for operations over the peninsula. But they were also hampered by a lack of coordination or guidance from the ranking French admiral. In his memoirs, he does not even mention the efforts of the air contingent in the theater.

Thus, with three air commanders—Clark-Hall on the *Ark Royal*, Samson and 3 Squadron RNAS, and Césari with the French—there was no single air commander to coordinate the air effort for the Allies. The Turks did slightly better. The land plane squadrons took orders from Army high command and the seaplanes took direction from the admiral, but they too lacked operational oversight. Both the land-based and the seaplane squadrons focused on denying air supremacy to the Allies and attempted raids on the combined Allied fleet. Like the Allied air component, the Turkish-German fliers lacked coherent guidance and coordination for a specific operational plan. Also, both the Allies and the Ottomans suffered from not enough aircraft and a lack of spares, and all were at the mercy of the prevailing environmental conditions.

At the same time, Samson's glorification needs to be tempered with an honest critique of his leadership style. He was not without blame for the lack of coordination with his army and naval superiors. In July 1915 Sir Frederick Sykes was dispatched to Gallipoli to ascertain the problems with command and coordination among the disparate commanders and components. Sykes was given the temporary rank of colonel in the Royal Marines and technically outranked Samson, then the highest-ranking air officer. Sykes immediately recommended reinforcements, and was optimistic that with additional men and machines airpower could turn the tide in the campaign. Sykes' requests were honored, to a point. Samson's squadron was renamed 3 Wing, and started to receive additional planes and pilots. RNAS 2 Wing, commanded by Commander Eugene Gerrard was dispatched to Gallipoli to bolster forces, but only arrived in August with obsolete machines and insufficient stores of parts. The requested reinforcements proved inadequate for the mission. Sykes moved the airfield closer to General Headquarters in an effort to foster better coordination, but again ran into difficulties with Samson. The latter did not respect the former's rank or efforts; Samson was openly hostile to Sykes. Coordination issues continued between the air, land, and sea components of the joint operation.

Sykes went so far as to fly sorties with the RNAS pilots. He quickly realized the limitations of the machines at Gallipoli, and was despondent that they could not achieve the lofty goals set for the air services. Throughout his tenure at Gallipoli he continued to request reinforcements that never materialized. Sykes even opined that the airmen could bomb Istanbul directly, but technological limitations prevented any attempts—not that it would have made a difference. There was no proof that attacking the capital would have changed the strategic outcome of the campaign.

At the height of the summer, in August, airpower once again presented an opportunity to turn the tide of the campaign. With the initial offensives stalled at both Helles and ANZAC, high command decided to launch a spoiling attack at Suvla Bay, hoping to outflank the Turkish defenses. Air intelligence confirmed that the Turkish defenses were light and the landings were successful, but the British needed to move quickly to exploit initial successes. However, even with this precious and timely knowledge, the ground offensive hesitated and the Suvla Bay offensive also stalled. It was a missed opportunity despite the favorable information provided by the British airmen.

Without oversight or guidance from high command, Samson continued to innovate. By his own efforts, he gathered all of the air commanders together for what could be considered a strategic air campaign in November. Through aerial intelligence and simple map reading, Samson divined that the Turks were moving massive amounts of supplies across the Maritza Bridge, and decided to launch an aerial bombing raid on the vulnerable point. Calling on his colleagues in floatplanes and the French airmen as well, they mounted a coalition air strike against the Turkish rail line. Even given the primitive weapons at hand, the Allied airmen were able to successfully attack the rail line, disrupting supplies for over a week. However, once again the land and naval forces were not able to capitalize on aerial successes. And even if the airmen had been able to sever the supply line, it may not have mattered at the front. A shortage of Turkish supplies probably would have not led to strategic victory. But it was an attempt to change the balance of the campaign using airpower.

Concurrently, the German-Turkish air arm gained strength of numbers. When previously neutral Bulgaria joined the Central Powers, Serno finally had a reliable cross-country supply route. By the late fall he started receiving more (and better) aircraft, more pilots, and regular supplies. He employed his airmen in reconnaissance roles, but also initiated a counter-air campaign to disrupt the Allied efforts in the air. It became clear that the German-Turkish force was gaining strength as summer turned to winter.

In late fall Sir Charles Monro quietly replaced Sir Ian Hamilton as the ground forces commander at Gallipoli. After a quick survey, Monro recommended the evacuation of Gallipoli. The Allied airmen had one final mission to perform. They flew constantly despite bad weather and lack of spares, to try to convince the Turks that a renewed offensive was at hand. But the aerial activity was a cover for the evacuation of the peninsula. The troops were pulled from Suvla Bay and ANZAC Cove with great success. The airmen of 2 Wing screened the final evacuation of Helles by the middle of January, ironically the most successful operations of the entire campaign. With the evacuation of the peninsula, the air components were relocated to facilitate operations elsewhere in the Mediterranean Theater. Samson was recalled to London and 3 Wing was disbanded. The entire Mediterranean hierarchy was reassigned to other operations in support of the Allied efforts in other theaters.

With the end of the Gallipoli Campaign, each side reflected on the outcome. The German-Turkish pilots celebrated, but quickly turned their attention to other theaters where fighting raged. There was little time to consider the importance of airpower, and there is little indication that they seriously reflected on the air component at Gallipoli. Serno wrote an after-action report, but it was stamped secret and hidden in the archives. Carl Mühlmann, von Sanders' aide de camp, later wrote the German official history, but made only a few references to the air effort. The Ottomans, who won Gallipoli but lost the war, endured a civil war immediately after World War I, and had little time and put virtually no effort into any in-depth analysis of airpower over Gallipoli.

The French likewise did not study airpower over Gallipoli in any depth. In 1916 they sailed away to face other threats, and paid little attention to the loss. Their resources were equally as sparse as those of the Ottoman Turks; hence, there is still very little information on MF. 98(T) or its commander, Césari. It is a research topic that is ripe for scholarly analysis.

The British were the most concerned with the outcomes of Gallipoli in that they wanted to figure out what had gone wrong, or at least discern where to place the blame. For a full eighteen months, the British government conducted interviews and took minutes from the leading politicians and military commanders for what would become the Dardanelles Commission Report. But in the two-volume findings they did not talk to any airmen or report on the air component beyond a handful of citations. Politicians and military commanders were blamed for the failed outcome of Gallipoli and the British resumed focus on the ongoing war. For their efforts, Samson, Gerrard, and Clark-Hall were promoted and continued to serve throughout the war and into significant postwar careers.

Even though it did not have a significant strategic contribution to the Gallipoli Campaign, airpower was still important. At the tactical level, airpower attempted a number of new and innovative missions that proved the viability of airpower in war. From mapping and reconnaissance (the original intent and obvious ability of airpower) to more exciting missions like antisubmarine warfare and torpedo bombing, the airmen at Gallipoli proved that airpower was an important tool in modern warfighting. Samson expanded his ideas of strategic bombing and put it into practice. Serno implemented defensive counter-air and his pilots harassed Allied flyers with increasingly proficient results. The French and British flew over water and land in the hostile theater. Both sides faced nearly insurmountable issues with supply and the environment. The story of Gallipoli included the first chapter in the development of viable airpower in war.

At the very least, this author thinks that it was an important and interesting history to write. Of all the tomes on Gallipoli—including the one from my former master's thesis advisor, Dr. Tim Travers—none mentions the air war over Gallipoli in more than a passing reference. It deserved more. My effort has been to uncover the history, the stories, and the narrative of the airmen and airpower over Gallipoli, and to explore the earliest days of airpower history, modern joint warfighting, and the fascinating legacy of the men and machines in the exciting secondary theater of World War I. Airpower over Gallipoli was not decisive—indeed, it was barely relevant—yet it was an exciting and interesting chapter in the birth and evolution of airpower at war.

Appendix I
Gallipoli Personalities

Albert d'Amade, 24 December 1856–11 November 1941. Very little is known about French General d'Amade. In 1908 he replaced General Drude in Morocco, and at the start of World War I he was put in command of the Corps Expéditionnaire d'Orient in the Eastern Mediterranean. He led this organization of French colonial troops in the land campaign in Gallipoli, until he was replaced by General Gourard in mid-May 1915. No known biographies or memoirs exist.

Mustafa Kemal Atatürk, 19 May 1861–10 November 1938. He was an Ottoman Turkish military officer, politician, and "Father of the Turks." Atatürk was born to humble parents: his father was a militia officer and his mother was a housewife. He enrolled in the Ottoman Military Academy and graduated in 1905 earning a commission in the Ottoman army as an infantry officer. He was arrested after graduation for anti-monarchist activities and was held for several months. He later played a role in the 1908 revolution that seized power from the sultan and restored the constitutional monarch. In the tumultuous Ottoman Empire he participated in a number of revolutions and counter-revolutions, always in the midst of the political upheaval that characterized the late Ottoman Empire period. He went to war against the Italians in the Italo-Turkish War (1911–12), and later served in the Balkan Wars (1912–13). He was a lieutenant colonel by the time that the Ottomans joined the Central Powers in World War I.

His exploits in the Gallipoli Campaign earned him recognition in the form of promotions and prestige. By the end of the war, Atatürk's military accomplishments earned him fame, and he returned to Istanbul. In the chaos after losing the war, Atatürk was instrumental in the rise of the Turkish Nationalist Movement, aimed at expelling the Allies from occupied Istanbul. As a highly decorated and experienced military officer, he led a reconstituted Turkish forces in the Turkish War for Independence (1919–22), leading to a series of victories that culminated in the Treaty of Lausanne (1923) and the declaration of the Republic of Turkey (29 October 1923).

Atatürk became the first president of Turkey and spent the rest of his life modernizing, secularizing, and democratizing Turkey. He instituted reforms that brought Turkey into the modern era. Atatürk died on 10 November 1938 from cirrhosis of the liver. He is remembered as the "Father of Modern Turkey." The two best biographies on Atatürk (in English) are: Patrick Balfour, Lord Kinross, *Ataturk: The Rebirth of a Nation* (London: Weidenfeld and Nicolson, 1964; now in reprint), and Andrew Mango, *Atatürk: The Biography of the Founder of Modern Turkey* (London: John Murray, 1999).

Maurice Bailloud, 13 October 1847–1 July 1921. Bailloud was the son of a French Navy officer and attended Saint Cyr, graduating in 1868. As a young army officer he fought in the Franco-Prussian War (1870–71). In the French Second Madagascar expedition he served as the chief of staff under General Jacques Duchesne. He later fought in the Boxer Rebellion, as the commander of the French 2nd Infantry Regiment. Bailloud was stationed in Algeria until his retirement in 1912. When war broke out in 1914, Bailloud was recalled and was eventually named the commander of the 156th Infantry Division. When General Gouraud was wounded, Bailloud took command of the French ground forces at Gallipoli. After the French evacuation, he continued campaigning in Greece until 1917, when he was named the inspector general of all French forces in the Eastern Mediterranean. He died in a plane crash in 1921. No known biographies exist in English.

Field Marshal William Ridell Birdwood (GCB, GCSI, GCMG, GCVO, CIE, DSO), 13 September 1865–17 May 1951. Birdwood was born in India to a minor British functionary in the Bombay Legislative Council. Birdwood returned to England where he attended Sandhurst, graduating and receiving a commission in 1885. He returned to India where he served in a variety of military roles. He fought in the Second Boer War, and eventually found his way to Lord Kitchener's staff in 1900. Kitchener described Birdwood as exceptionally able, and the latter continued to rise in rank. Birdwood once again returned to India, to serve under Kitchener there. He was a major general and the quartermaster-general of India by 1911. With the outbreak of World War I, Birdwood was given the task of forming an army group out of the colonial armies in Australia and New Zealand, later known as the ANZACs. Birdwood commanded the ANZACs during the Gallipoli Campaign. After the evacuation of the peninsula, Birdwood reorganized the ANZACs in Egypt into I ANZAC Corps and II ANZAC Corps, taking personal command of the latter. The unit sailed for France, where it was incorporated into the lines on the Western Front. Promoted to general in 1917, he became the commander of the British Fifth Army in 1918, and had a modicum of success in the closing days of the war. After the war Birdwood continued his service and was promoted to field marshal in 1925. That same year he was named commander-in-chief, India. He retired from active service in 1930, but remained active in titular roles, holding the title of colonel in the 12th Royal Lancers, 6th Gurkha Rifles, and 75th Heavy Anti-Aircraft Regiment, Royal Artillery. He wrote two autobiographies, *Khaki and Gown* (New York: Robert Speller and Sons, 1957; orig. published in 1941), and *In My Time: Recollections and Anecdotes* (London: Skeffington, 1948; orig. published in 1946). Birdwood died in 1951. The best biography of Birdwood is John Millar, *The Soul of Anzac: General Sir William Birdwood and the A.I.F., 1914–1918* (North Melbourne, Australia: Vic Australian Scholarly, 2015).

Hans Joachim Buddecke, 22 August 1890–10 March 1918. Buddecke was a German ace pilot in World War I with thirteen victories. He was awarded the Pour le Mérite (the "Blue Max"), the third pilot to receive the coveted medal. Born into an army family, he received his commission in 1910. He left the German army in 1913 and traveled to the United States to learn and master flying. With the outbreak of World War I, he returned to Germany to fight for the kaiser. He was recommissioned into the Imperial German Flying Corps. His initial posting was to the Western Front, as an observer, but he quickly transitioned to the pilot's seat in a single-seat fighter. He excelled in the Fokker Eindecker fighter and brought down three British planes before his reassignment to the Dardanelles. At Gallipoli he was credited with four more victories and a number of unconfirmed. He returned to the

Western Front in summer 1916 to continue his aerial exploits with Jagdstaffel 4. He was reassigned to Turkey in late 1916, but in 1918 traveled back to France to fly with Jasta 30. He was shot down and killed on 10 March 1918, by Sopwith Camels of 3 Squadron RNAS, his old adversaries from Gallipoli. There is no biography of Buddecke, but he is mentioned in most books that list pilot aces of the Great War.

Admiral Sir Sackville Hamilton Carden (KCMG), 3 May 1857–6 May 1930. Carden was born into a military family, but instead of choosing the army like his father and grandfather, he chose the Royal Navy. He joined the navy in 1870, and rose through the ranks; captain in 1899, rear admiral in 1908. When the war began in 1914, he was named the commander of the British Mediterranean Fleet. Carden helped plan the first ill-fated attacks against the Ottoman Empire at the mouth of the Dardanelles, including the disastrous March attacks. He fell ill right before the March attempt, was relieved of command, and replaced by Admiral John de Robeck. Carden served for two more years, in shore assignments in England before retiring as an admiral. He died in 1930. There are no known biographies of Admiral Carden.

Antoine Marie Césari, 18 May 1885–(?). The record of the French pilot and commander of the Escadrille at Tenedos is woefully incomplete. His service records piece together a chronology of the airman for a better picture of his life. He was born in 1885 in Bastia, a commune on Corsica. He enlisted in the army in 1903, and rose through the ranks very quickly. He was commissioned in 1908, and transferred from the infantry to the aeronautical service in October 1911. Presumably Césari received pilot training immediately before or after his transfer. When war broke out, he was flying with Escadrille 16 on the Western Front, where he made a name for himself as a bomber pilot. Ian Sumner records in his book *The Kings of the Air: French Airmen and Aces of the Great War* (South Yorkshire, UK: Pen and Sword Aviation, 2015) that Lieutenant Césari bombed the Metz zeppelin sheds on 14 August 1914 with great success, destroying the zeppelin in its hangar. Césari was promoted to captain in April 1915 and put in command of MF. 98(T) sent to Tenedos to support the French efforts at Gallipoli. After the Gallipoli Campaign, he continued to command French escadrilles in the war. Césari stayed in the service after the war, including a command in

Algeria, working in the Defense Ministry, and as the commander of a training wing. His final rank, according to his service records was colonel, in 1942. It is unclear what position he filled in World War II or when he died. There are no known biographies of Césari.

Sir Winston Churchill (KG, OM, CH, TD, PC, PCc, DL, FRS, RA), 30 November 1874–24 January 1965. Churchill was an immensely important figure in British military and political history. He began his career with the military when he entered Sandhurst, graduating in 1894. He was commissioned as a cavalry officer in 1895. He observed the war in Cuba in 1895, and was assigned to India in 1896. It was at that point he began his prolific writing career. He traveled to Egypt in 1898 to serve there, but had other plans. He wanted to follow his father's footsteps in politics and resigned his commission in 1899 to pursue civil service. He failed to be elected and decided to try his hand as a war correspondent for *The Morning Post*.

Churchill traveled to South Africa to report on the ongoing Boer War, where he was captured. He escaped and returned to the front to continue as a correspondent. He was given a commission in the South African Light Horse regiment while still sending reports on the war back to London. After the Boer War, he resigned again, but gained a commission in the Imperial Yeomanry, serving as an officer in the Queen's Own Oxfordshire Hussars. He ran for election once again, winning the seat for Oldham in 1900. Beginning as a conservative, he crossed party lines in 1904 to the liberals. He rose through the ranks in the British government, and was named first lord of the admiralty in 1911.

Blamed for the ill-fated Gallipoli Campaign, Churchill was marginalized in the government and eventually resigned from public life in November 1915. He took a commission as a lieutenant colonel in the army and went to the Western Front in France. Bored, he returned to England, to reignite his political career. Churchill was named minister of munitions in 1917, then secretary of state for war and secretary of state for air in 1919. Continuing his political life, he rejoined the conservatives in 1924, increasing his political power. But at the end of the decade he was once again marginalized within his own government for his outspoken and controversial positions. But he stayed on in the British government and was once again named first lord of the admiralty when war broke out on the continent in 1939.

When Germany invaded France in May 1940, Prime Minister Neville Chamberlain resigned, and Churchill became the new prime minister for wartime Britain. At the end of World War II in Europe, Churchill stepped down as PM, and elections were called for the first time in almost a decade. He was replaced by Clement Atlee, but Churchill served as the leader of the opposition. Churchill once again won the post of prime minister in 1951, and remained until 1955. After that, even though still a member of Parliament, Churchill attended fewer official events until his death due to a stroke on 24 January 1965. Churchill was a prolific writer and historian, and contributed a number of volumes on the Boer War, World War I, and World War II including his *World at War* series. The best biography on Churchill is Geoffrey Best, *Churchill: A Study in Greatness* (Oxford, UK: Oxford University Press, 2003).

Air Marshal Sir Robert Clark-Hall (KBE, CMG, DSO), 21 June 1883–8 March 1964. Clark-Hall was a career Royal Navy officer who fought in the Boxer Rebellion (1899–1901). He rose through the ranks and was named the commander of the HMS *Ark Royal* when war broke out in 1914. In 1916 he became the commander of 3 Squadron RNAS, after the ill-fated Gallipoli Campaign. He continued his service through the Great War, eventually commanding No. 1 Wing RNAS, assigned to the Dunkirk front. Under his command, the wing harassed German shipping and ground targets from 1917 until the armistice. He held a number of commands in the interwar period, most in the Mediterranean Theater, as the British fought to control their empire. He retired to New Zealand at some point in the 1930s, and when war broke out again he volunteered to serve in the Royal New Zealand Air Force. He was named a wing commander and took charge of RNZAF Harewood. He was promoted to commodore in 1943 and took command of Southern Training Group. In 1944, Clark-Hall was named the commander of Number 1 Islands Group with the rank of air marshall. At the end of the war, he retired a final time on 12 September 1945 and lived out his life in New Zealand. There are no significant, reliable biographies of Clark-Hall.

Vice Admiral Richard Bell Davies (VC, CB, DSO, AFC), 19 May 1886–26 February 1966. Davies enlisted in the Royal Navy in 1901, learned to fly in 1910, and was one of the first RNAS pilots, attached to the Eastchurch

Squadron in 1913. He flew for Samson from the start of the war through the Gallipoli Campaign. Davies was Samson's second in command, and took temporary command of 3 Wing when Samson went on R&R. Davies was in charge of the wing when it was moved from Tenedos to Imbros. He was awarded the Victoria Cross at Gallipoli, when he saved the life of another airman, Smylie, when the latter was shot down. After Gallipoli, Davies flew for the RNAS. After the war, Davies was instrumental in the development of British aircraft carrier aviation, and also served in a number of administrative roles in the admiralty. He was posted to the Mediterranean, then the Air Ministry, then China, retiring in 1941. Upon retirement he was promoted to vice admiral, but accepted a commission as a convoy commodore in the reserves and helped coordinate convoys during World War II. He retired fully in 1944 and died in 1966. His own memoirs are excellent: *Sailor in the Air: The Memoirs of the World's First Carrier Pilot* (Barnsley, UK: Seaforth Publishing, 1967) and he is mentioned in a number of books on British World War I pilots.

Air Commodore Eugene Louis Gerrard (CMG, DSO), 14 July 1881–7 February 1963. Gerrard earned his commission in 1900 as a Royal Marine, serving for a number of years on ships. He was offered the opportunity to go to flight school, and earned his wings in 1911. He was named a squadron commander of a training school and set records for high flights, including one flight to 10,000 feet, with then-major Hugh Trenchard as a passenger. When World War I broke out, he was named commander of No. 1 Squadron RNAS. Later he transferred to 2 Squadron and sent to the Gallipoli Campaign. He continued in command roles throughout the war and was the commander of the Mediterranean Group from 1920–21. He stayed on in the Mediterranean Theater in the interwar years, ending his career with retirement from the No. 1 Defense Group as Air Commodore in 1929. There is no known biography of Gerrard.

General Henri Joseph Eugéne Gouraud, 17 November 1867–16 September 1946. Gouraud was born in 1867, and attended Saint Cyr Military Academy. He earned his commission in 1890 and fought in the French colonies in Africa, earning distinction and promotion. Gouraud was a friend of the British general Hamilton, and worked closely with the latter after assuming command from d'Amade. He was wounded in battle at Gallipoli, and replaced by General Bailloud. Despite losing his right arm, Gouraud went on to command the French Fourth Army on the Western Front in 1917. He ended the war on the Western Front with distinction. After the war, he was named the high commissioner for Syria and Lebanon, where he served from 1920–23. He was named the military governor of Paris in 1923 and held that post until his retirement in 1937. He lived through the occupation of Paris during World War II and died there in 1946. His memoirs include a number of books on his time in Africa (in French), but nothing on his time at Gallipoli. Likewise, there are very few mentions of his service at Gallipoli and no known biography in English.

Admiral Émile Paul Aimable Guépratte, 30 August 1856–21 November 1939. Guépratte was a career French naval officer, from a family of French naval officers. He studied at the French Naval Academy (École Navale) and after graduation in 1874 received his commission in the French navy. He served on a number of ships, mostly in the Mediterranean, and was an authority on the use of torpedoes in war. At the outbreak of World War I, Guépratte was a rear admiral in charge of the Mediterranean Fleet. He was ordered to coordinate with the British as he saw fit, for the Dardanelles (and later Gallipoli) Campaign. He was promoted to vice admiral in 1915 and retired at the end of the war. In 1919 he was elected to the National Assembly as a left-leaning socialist. He excelled in keeping government attention on French naval budget and procurement. Guépratte retired from public service in 1924 and died in Brest in 1939, just after the outbreak of World War II in Europe. While there is no single biography on him, his memoirs on the Dardanelles and Gallipoli Campaigns, *L'expédition des Dardanelles: 1914–1915* (Paris: Payot, 1935), is a useful reference on his role in the theater.

General Ian Standish Montieth Hamilton (GCB, GCMG, DSO, TD), 16 January 1853–12 October 1947. Hamilton was born into a military family; his father had been a colonel and commander of the 92nd Highlanders. Hamilton attended Sandhurst, graduating in 1871. He fought in the First Boer War, where he was wounded in action. He returned to England for recovery and was even introduced to the Queen. After recovering he was assigned to India, where he learned to speak Hindi (having already mastered English, German, and French). In 1899 he fought in the Second Boer War, by then a major general. He was assigned to the War Office in 1901, but was quickly transferred back to South Africa to serve as Lord Kitchener's chief of staff. In 1904, he was the military attaché of the British Indian Army sent to observe the Russo-Japanese War, and wrote a short memoir on his time there, *A Staff Officer's Scrap-Book During the Russo-Japanese War* (London, UK: Edward Arnold, 1907). He continued to serve in staff positions until the outbreak of World War I. In March 1915, Kitchener called on Hamilton to command the Allied Mediterranean Expeditionary Force, gathering the land forces that would eventually be used in the Gallipoli Campaign. But when the offensive faltered and did not prove decisive, Hamilton was replaced by General Charles Monro. The Gallipoli disaster effectively ended Hamilton's military career. In his postwar retirement he became an advocate for the rise of Germany, expressing his admiration of Adolf Hitler. He was effectively marginalized and died at his home in 1947. Hamilton's own writing on Gallipoli includes *Gallipoli Diary* (London, UK: E. Arnold, 1920, 2 Vols.), as well as *Sir Ian Hamilton's Despatches from the Dardanelles, etc.* (London, UK: G. Newnes, 1916). He was a prolific writer; in retirement he was known for his poetry. The best biography on General Hamilton is John Lee, *A Soldier's Life: General Sir Ian Hamilton, 1853–1947* (London, UK: Pan, 2001).

Carl Mühlmann. Little is known about Dr. Carl Mühlmann other than he was Liman von Sander's aide de camp during the Gallipoli Campaign. He was an army officer (major), and was a history professor before the war. He recorded his thoughts and memoirs in a pair of books on the German military mission to Turkey, and the campaigns focused on the Dardanelles and Gallipoli. Although the rest of his life is lost to obscurity, Mühlmann's contributions to the research and resources was invaluable, although still in German. In Old German script, *Der Kampf um die Dardanellen 1915* (Oldenburg, Germany: Stalling, 1927, vol. 16 of the German Official History of the Great War) is excellent; and in modern German script, *Oberste Heeresleitung und Balkan im Weltkrieg* (Berlin: Wilhelm Limpert, 1942) provides a good context.

General Sir Charles Carmichael Munro (GCB, GCSI, GCMG), 15 June 1860–7 December 1929. Munro attended Sandhurst and was commissioned in 1879. He rose through the ranks in the infantry, and served in the Second Boer War. By the outbreak of World War I, Munro was major general in command of the 2nd Division, and dispatched to France. He commanded I Corps after December 1914, and was promoted to lieutenant general in command of Third Army in July 1915. When Hamilton was dismissed, Munro replaced him at Gallipoli to oversee the evacuation. After Gallipoli, he returned to France to command the First Army on the Western Front. He was named commander-in-chief, India in 1916, and led troops in the Mesopotamia Campaign. He was promoted to general in 1916 and continued his campaigns in Mesopotamia, including the capture of Baghdad in September 1916. After the war Munro was named governor of Gibraltar. He died in 1929. The best single biography is Patrick Crowley, *Loyal to Empire: The Life of General Sir Charles Munro, 1860–1929* (Stroud, UK: History Press, 2016).

Admiral of the Fleet Sir John de Robeck (GCB, GCMG, GCVO), 10 June 1862–20 January 1928. Born into royalty (his father was a Swedish noble), de Robeck entered the Royal Navy as a cadet in 1875. He served on a number of ships and was promoted through the ranks to rear admiral in 1911. At the start of the war de Robeck was the commander of the 9th Cruiser Squadron. He was reassigned to the Eastern Mediterranean Squadron in February 1915, second in command to Admiral Sackville Carden. When Carden fell ill in March, de Robeck was promoted to the former's position in command of the fleet. He was the naval commander of the Gallipoli Campaign and ultimately planned the naval component of the evacuation from Gallipoli. Even in failure he continued to succeed: he was named the commander of the 3rd Battle Squadron of the Grand Fleet, and later the commander of the 2nd Battle Squadron. He was promoted to vice admiral in 1917. After the war de Robeck was named the commander-in-chief of the Mediterranean Fleet and British high commissioner to Turkey. He was made a full admiral in 1920 and commander of the Atlantic Fleet in 1922. De Robeck retired from the Royal Navy in 1924 and in retirement was given the honorary title of admiral of the fleet. He died in 1928. Although there is no specific biography of de Robeck, he is mentioned in most books on the British Royal Navy and its commanders.

Air Commodore Charles Rumney Samson (CMG, DSO and Bar, AFC), 8 July 1883–5 February 1931. Samson was born into a relatively wealthy family; his father was a lawyer (solicitor). He joined the Royal Navy at a young age; he was a 13-year-old cadet on the HMS *Britannia* in 1896. He rose through the ranks serving on a number of Royal Navy ships before being selected to be a Royal Navy pilot in 1911. He earned his wings at the Eastchurch training center and was immediately promoted to commander of Naval Air Station Eastchurch.

An innovator in the air, Samson was the first to take off from an anchored ship when he flew off an improvised flight deck on the HMS *Africa* on 10 January 1912. He was the first to take off from a moving ship in May 1912. He was instrumental in developing tactics for the Royal Navy's air arm, and was the commander of the Eastchurch Squadron (later renamed the No. 3 Squadron) when the Royal Naval Air Service divorced from the Royal Flying Corps. At the start of World War I, the Eastchurch Squadron was sent to the continent to fight the Germans. Samson continued innovating air tactics, and was instrumental in developing armed cars, trucks, and motorcycles on the ground. His squadron gained notoriety when it successfully bombed zeppelin sheds in the first months of the war.

The squadron was sent to Gallipoli in early 1915 and formed the nucleus of airpower in that campaign. After the evacuation, Samson was promoted to commander of the HMS *Ben-my-Chree* seaplane tender and assigned to the Mediterranean and Red Sea. The *Ben-my-Chree* was sunk in 1917 by Turkish land artillery, but he was absolved of culpability and continued his service in the war. When the RNAS was folded into the Royal Air Force in 1918, Samson was promoted to Group Captain of 4 Group RAF. He continued his service with the RAF as Air Officer Commanding–Mediterranean in 1921–22, and chief staff officer of Middle East Command, 1926–27. He retired from the RAF in 1929 with the rank of air commodore, and died in England on 5 February 1931. There is no single biography of Samson, but he did write two memoirs of his exploits, including *Fights and Flights* (Nashville, TN: The Battery Press, 1990), which deals specifically with the early years of World War I, including his service in the Gallipoli Campaign.

Otto Viktor Carl Liman von Sanders, 17 February 1855–22 August 1929. Sanders was born to a businessman and his wife and gained his commission after attending the German Kriegsakademie in 1877. Originally a cavalry officer, he rose through the ranks and was elevated to the nobility (the "von" in his name) in 1913. As a general, he was assigned to the German military mission to Turkey. He commanded the Turkish forces in the defense of Gallipoli and later served in other roles for the Turks during the war. He replaced German General Erich von Falkenhayn for the Palestine and Sinai Campaign, but was defeated by the British (Allenby and T. E. Lawrence) at the Battle of Megiddo in 1918. He fled Turkey and was arrested on Malta in February 1919 for war crimes. He was released and returned to Germany, retired from the army, and wrote his memoirs. He died on 22 August 1929 in Munich. Although there is no good biography of this German general, his own memoirs, *Five Years in Turkey* (Nashville, TN: Battery Press, 2000, translated from the original German), are an excellent source on Gallipoli and his exploits in the war.

Erich Serno, 1886–1963. Not much is known about Serno. He was in the German army aviation branch, and an accomplished pilot leading up to and in the first months of World War I. He was assigned to the German military mission as an aviation expert, with the rank of captain. When he got to Turkey, he was given a commission in the Turkish army as a major. He organized all of the Turkish aviation assets for the Gallipoli Campaign as well as the central training facilities at Yeşilköy and the rest of the Turkish air force. After Gallipoli, Serno organized another seventeen land-based squadrons in addition to four more seaplane squadrons. He served out the war in Turkey, then returned to Germany. The only other information on Serno is that he later worked for the German aircraft company, Arado Flugzeugwerke, in the lead-up (and presumably during) World War II. He died in 1963 in Germany. There are no existing biographies of Serno, although it would make an interesting study, provided there are adequate resources in the German archives.

Air Vice Marshal Sir Frederick Hugh Sykes (GCSI, GCIE, GBE, KCB, CMG), 23 July 1877–30 September 1954. Sykes did not come from a military family, instead he took a circuitous route into the services. He enlisted in the Imperial Yeomanry and fought in the Boer War, where he was captured. He escaped and returned to the British lines after a forced march. He was commissioned in 1900. In 1904, he earned a ballooning certificate, the first step in satisfying his interests in aviation. He worked in intelligence before he earned his heavier-than-air pilot's wings in 1911. Thanks to his experience in the air and with intelligence, he worked in the Directorate of Military Operations, where he was a strong proponent of aerial observation and reconnaissance. When war broke out, he was too senior to be a line pilot, but too junior to command. He was appointed as the chief of staff to General David Henderson, commander of the Royal Flying Corps in the field in France. Noted for his influence in organizing the RFC on the Western Front, he was sent to the Dardanelles to reorganize airpower during the Gallipoli Campaign. He continued to serve in staff positions throughout the conflict, ending the war as the chief of the air staff. But with a change in government after the war, he retired in 1919 at the rank of major general, converted to air vice marshal in the Royal Air Force after the latter's independence.

As a civilian, he was the controller of civil aviation in Britain from 1919–22, and began writing his version of the history of aviation, which was published in 1922 as *Aviation in War and Peace* (London, UK: Read Books, 2016). In 1922 he entered the public sector, winning local elections in 1922, 1923, and 1924. He resigned in 1928 when he was named the governor of Bombay and subsequently the knight grand commander of the Order of the Indian Empire on 3 November 1928. He returned to England and political life in 1933, and was a member of Parliament when war broke out again in 1939. He offered to return to military service, but his services were not needed in that capacity. He continued to serve in the British government until his death in 1954. Sykes wrote an autobiography, *From Many Angles* (London, UK: G. G. Harrap, 1943) and is mentioned in a number of excellent works on British military and political history. The most relevant to this project was Eric Ash, *Sir Frederick Sykes and the Air Revolution, 1912–1918* (London: Frank Cass, 1999).

Appendix II
The Aircraft of Gallipoli

Significant Prewar Aircraft

Zeppelin. The German zeppelins were massive rigid airships, built by the Zeppelin Company, named for its owner and founder, Count Ferdinand von Zeppelin. The count had become enamored of flight and air travel after seeing balloons in the U.S. Civil War as an observer in 1863. In early retirement, he began sketching out ideas for large, steerable airships. He took out a patent in Germany in 1895 and began construction in 1899. The biggest hurdle was financing. Even his vast sums of personal wealth were not enough for a project that massive, so he started The Society for the Promotion of Airship Flight (*Gesellschaft zur Förderung der Luftschiffahrt*).

With additional interest and money, he set out to build his first prototypes. The lighter-than-air vehicles were aluminum alloy superstructures covered with canvas. The superstructure held up to sixteen individual gas bags made from cow's intestine to contain the flammable hydrogen. Although other designs had been flown, the first zeppelin made its debut in 1900. By 1914 the Zeppelin Company had proven the viability of the airship for commercial use; between 1910 and 1914, zeppelins had already carried 10,000 passengers. When the war broke out, Zeppelin was building M-class ships with the following flight characteristics: the M-class zeppelin, starting with Z.1, was 518 feet (158 m) long, with hydrogen capacity of 794,500 cubic feet (22,500 cubic meters). It could lift (useful load) up to 20,000 lbs. (9,100 kg). The Z.1 was powered by three Maybach C-X engines, rated at 630 hp each, and could reach speeds of 52 mph (84 kmh). With a crew of twenty-four (fewer in wartime), the zeppelin could stay aloft indefinitely—limited only by fuel for the gasoline engines and food for the crew.

Just before the war, a zeppelin launched a successful twenty-four-hour endurance flight. The zeppelins were especially susceptible to the weather and could not fly in high winds. Furthermore, they were full of flammable hydrogen, so fire was a constant concern. But their lifting capacity showed promise. The first "strategic" bombing raids by the Germans against the British were launched with zeppelins. Initially they were invulnerable to all forms of air defense; they could fly higher and farther than contemporary airplanes. Thus, the British and French tried—at times successfully—to destroy the zeppelins in their massive hangars, attractive targets for the early airmen. The Germans constructed eighty-four zeppelins during the war; three-quarters were lost in combat, to bombing, or to accidents (usually attributed to bad weather). The Germans launched more than fifty zeppelin bombing raids against England during the war.

Wright Flyer. The first powered, heavier-than-air prototype built by the Wright brothers to prove the feasibility of airplanes was a marvel of technology. The Wrights began as bicycle builders in Dayton, Ohio, before they turned their attention to heavier-than-air manufacturing. Improving on concurrent designs, they first built and flew unpowered gliders to confirm their novel aerodynamic theory. Their first powered prototype was a single-passenger biplane with a wingspan of 40 feet 4 inches (12.31 m). The wings could be "warped" by the pilot controls for directional control of the airplane. It was 21 feet 1 inch (6.43 m) long, with a canard elevator in front and a stabilizer in the rear. It was 9 feet (2.74 m) tall. It was powered by a 4-cylinder in-line engine, designed and built by the Wright brothers. They had considered other engine designs, but none were light enough for the aircraft. So the brothers designed and built their own engine with an aluminum block. It gave 12 horsepower, and weighed only 180 pounds (81.8 kg). Two bicycle chains were attached to the engine crankshaft, each powered a propeller attached to the rear of the wings. They rotated counter to each other to cancel out the yaw effect of two propellers. Empty, the plane weighed 605 lbs. (338 kg) and had a maximum takeoff weight of only 745 lbs. (338 kg)—not a lot of room for the pilot and fuel. The maximum speed was only 30 mph (48 kmh), so the brothers rigged a pulley system on a launch rail to get the plane up to flying speed. On 17 December 1903, they launched the first official powered flight, for a total distance of 120 feet (36.5 m), lasting 12 seconds, and reaching an altitude of 10 feet (3 m). In four flights that historic day, the Wrights flew for another 175, 200, and 852 feet (260 m). On the last flight, the hard landing broke the front elevator supports and the testing was suspended. With the successful tests, the Wrights returned to their workshop in Dayton, Ohio, to improve their designs.

Blériot XI. Louis Blériot began building aircraft in 1905 with Gabriel Voisin, another French aircraft designer. Together they built a number of unsuccessful designs before dissolving their business relationship. Blériot then reimagined his designs, finally coming up with successful aircraft, beginning with his Blériot V in 1907. The V was a powered canard monoplane. His follow-on models VI, VII, and VIII further proved the concept of powered flight, and by 1909 at the Paris Aero Salon—the first air show and manufacturer's exhibition—he had three new designs on display, a monoplane IX, a three-seat pusher biplane X, and his most successful design, the XI. The Blériot XI was an improvement on the previous Blériot VII, with a better engine and longer wingspan. The XI was a single-seat, tractor (engine in front) monoplane, constructed from wood, metal tubing, wire, and fabric. The 25 feet 7 inch (7.79 m) wings used "warping" for directional control; the rudder and elevator were at the rear of the plane. The new engine, designed by the Italian motorcycle engine master Alessandro Anzani, was a 3-cylinder fan radial that produced 25 hp. The plane was 25 feet (7.62 m) long, and 8 feet 10 inches (2.69 m) tall. Although it only flew at 47 mph (75.6 kmh), and only to a maximum height of 2,200 feet (1,000 m), it was powerful and reliable enough to fly for more than an hour—which was enough. On 25 July 1909, Blériot crossed the English Channel in just over 36 minutes, flying from Calais to Dover, and won the *Daily Mail* prize of £1,000 for the feat. The paper recorded that "Britain was no longer an island." Blériot built a number of copies of the Type XI and licensed it out to a number of other manufacturers as well, making it one of the most prolific aircraft designs before the war. The Type XII was basically the same aircraft, but had room for a two-man crew, a pilot and an observer.

Wright Military Model B. The Wrights' Model B was intended to secure coveted government contracts and the funding necessary to support their expensive endeavors. The Model B was an improvement on their earlier prototype experimental Flyer, and intended to prove their design. It was a biplane in a similar configuration to earlier designs, but the Model B had seats for two, a pilot and a passenger. Retaining the canard elevator and rear stabilizer, the Model B was more powerful. They decreased the wingspan to 39 feet (11.89 m) and increased the length to 26 feet (7.93 m), and added a more powerful engine producing 35 hp (Wright Vertical 4). Even with a shorter wing, the new engine design had the power to lift the fully loaded (1,250 lbs., 567 kg) plane off the ground. The first flight was in 1910, and the U.S. Army was interested enough that they bought one. The Navy bought a pair and attached floats to them. The Wrights sold a couple to Germany, and sold licenses to the Burgess Company and Curtiss, both of whom built a number of Model Bs. The new design had a top speed of 45 mph (72 kmh) and a range of 110 miles (177 km).

Etrich Taube. Igo Etrich was a fan of Otto Lilienthal and the latter's work on gliders. Igo's father was a wealthy businessman, and set Igo up with a workshop to experiment on aviation. When Lilienthal was killed in a glider accident in 1896, the elder Etrich acquired a significant amount of Lilienthal's data and remaining projects. Igo began his early experiments with aircraft manufacture by building gliders. In 1910, he made his first flight with a prototype *Taube*, but crashed, nearly killing himself. Undeterred, he moved to Liebow, Germany (today Lubawka, Poland) and opened *Etrich Fliegerwerke*, and began building his airplanes. Several companies began building copies of the Taube; Rumpler built them without license. Etrich sued, but dropped the suit in 1914 at the outbreak of war.

By the start of the war, at least three companies were building Taubes for the German military, including Etrich, Rumpler, and Lohner. The Taube (German: "dove") was a two-seat monoplane tractor aircraft, built specifically for military use. It was mass-produced and the mainstay of the German and Austrian forces at the outbreak of war. With a pilot and observer, the Taube had a gross weight of 1,874 lbs. (850 kg). It had a wingspan of 46 feet 11 inches (14.3 m); the wings' shape resembled a birds'. It was 32 feet 6 inches (9.9 m) long and had a height of 10 feet 6 inches (3.2 m). Powered by a Mercedes Type E4F 4-cylinder, in-line, water-cooled engine (86 hp), the Taube flew at 62 mph (100 kmh). Service ceiling was an impressive 6,600 feet (2,000 m). The Taube was the first to drop bombs in combat when an Italian pilot bombed Turkish troops with hand grenades in the Italo-Turkish War 1911. At the outbreak of World War I in 1914, the Germans and Austrians still had Taube squadrons, but they were replaced quickly as the type became obsolete.

Aircraft of the Dardanelles/Gallipoli Campaign

The Aircraft of the HMS *Ark Royal*

Wight Type A.1 Navyplane. Also known as the Wight Pusher Seaplane, the Type A.1 was a British pusher (engine behind the pilot's nacelle) floatplane with twin floats for sea duty. Wight aircraft were built by the famous J. Samuel White shipbuilding company, on the Isle of Wight, hence the name of the aircraft division. They began building aircraft in 1912, and specialized in seaplanes and floatplanes. The Navyplane's biplane wings were unequal; the lower wing was slightly shorter than the upper, the longer wing was 63 feet (19.2 m) long. The relatively massive plane was more than 44 feet (13 m) long with a height of 16 feet (4.88 m). Powered by one of the finest engines of the time, the Salmson 2M7, 2-row, 14-cylinder water-cooled radial (200 hp), the plane could fly at 72 mph (116 kmh) for more than 6 hours. It had a crew of two: a pilot and an observer, with a gross weight of 5,732 lbs (2,600 kg). The Type A.1 was a later improvement on the original design, with slightly longer wings, that could be folded back for transport at sea on board the seaplane tender.

Sopwith Admiralty Type 807. The Sopwith Aviation Company opened in June 1912, by the 24-year-old Tommy Sopwith. He was an eccentric and wealthy sportsman who was interested in speed: planes, boats, and cars. With his designers, he engineered and built a number of flying boats and seaplanes before delving into land-based aircraft. When war broke out in 1914, the Sopwith Company began building aircraft for the Crown, producing more than 16,000 during World War I. The Type 807 was a British two-seat tractor biplane floatplane powered by a Gnome Monosoupape 9-cylinder air-cooled rotary engine (100 hp). With a length of 30 feet 9 inches (9.37 m), a height of 11 feet 2 inches (3.35 m), and a wingspan of 43 feet 6 inches (13.1 m), the plane flew at 80 mph (128.7 kmh). The floats were especially delicate, and required constant attention. Furthermore, the aircraft was severely under-powered, and could not fly in other than ideal conditions.

Short Admiralty No. 135. Also known as the Type 166, the Short was a two-seat tractor biplane floatplane, manufactured by the British Short Brothers Company. The Short Company began in 1897 when the brothers bought a coal-fired balloon. Their earliest manufacture and sales were balloons. With balloon contracts from the British government, they transitioned to aircraft manufacture in 1905. They were the first company to build series production aircraft when they received an order for six Short No. 1 biplanes, British copies of the Wright 1908 Military Flier. The No. 135 first flew in 1914, and was bought by the government for the RNAS. It had wings that folded back for storage on the seaplane tender, and served as an observation platform. With a wingspan of 57 feet 3 inches (17.45 m) and a length of 40 feet 7 inches (12.38 m) it was the largest plane carried by the *Ark Royal.* It was 14 feet 1 inch (4.29 m) tall, and was powered by a Salmson 2M7 14-cylinder (2 rows of 7 cylinders) water-cooled radial engine (200 hp). It could fly at 65 mph (105 kmh) for four hours. The Short could be equipped with a radio, and could also if weight allowed, be fitted with a Lewis machine gun, in the rear cockpit for use by the observer. The Shorts were the favorite aircraft of the *Ark Royal* pilots. Short aircraft were also involved in a number of other "firsts"; before the war RNAS Flight Commander Charles Samson flew a Short floatplane off a ship underway, proving the concept of aircraft carriers. During the Gallipoli Campaign, a Short S.184 was the first to air launch a torpedo at an enemy ship.

Sopwith Tabloid. The two Sopwith Tabloids that the *Ark Royal* carried were not equipped with floats, and sat in the hangar deck until they were transferred to 3 Squadron RNAS, for use from the land base. The Tabloid was a single-seat tractor biplane, powered by a Gnome Monosoupape 9-cylinder rotary engine (100 hp). It could fly at 87 mph (140 kmh). The wingspan was 25 feet 8 inches (7.83 m), with a length of 22 feet 10 inches (6.96 m) and a height of 10 feet (3.05 m). The gross weight was 1,700 lbs. (773 kg), and the range was 315 miles (510 km) under ideal conditions.

The Aircraft of No. 3 Squadron RNAS

Royal Aircraft Factory BE2a. The Royal Aircraft Factory began as the Army Balloon Factory in 1904. In 1909, the government ceded direct control of the factory and turned it over to civilians, directed by Mervyn O'Gorman. His chief designer was Geoffrey de Havilland, who would later open his own aircraft company. In 1912, the company was renamed the Royal Aircraft Factory, and began design and production of military aircraft. Commander Samson's favorite plane was his BE2a No. 50. It was a single-seat tractor biplane that was ubiquitous in the RFC and RNAS throughout the war. Although it was obsolete very early, the reliable aircraft found its niche as a trainer after its usefulness as a combat platform had been eclipsed. The BE2a had unequal span wings; the wingspan of the upper and longer wing was 36 feet 11 1/8 inches (10.97 m), its length was 28 feet 4 inches (8.53 m) with a height of 10 feet 2 inches (3 m). It was powered by a Renault WB V-8 air-cooled engine providing 70 hp. The BE2a could fly at 78 mph (125 kmh) and had a range of 210 miles (337 km). Samson first flew No. 50 as commander of the Eastchurch Squadron before the war, and subsequently brought it to Gallipoli for operations during that campaign. As far as the existing records show, he was the only pilot to fly that particular plane.

Maurice Farman MF.11 Shorthorn. The Farman Aviation Works was a French aircraft manufacturer built by the three Farman brothers: Richard, Henri, and Maurice. They opened in 1908 and began building airframes and engines. At the outbreak of war, in order to bolster numbers, the British bought dozens of aircraft from the French, who at the time had quantitative as well as quantitative advantage. The planes that were designed and built by Maurice carried the prefix "MF." The Shorthorn was a two-seat pusher biplane used for reconnaissance and light bombing. The observer sat in the front, and because the engine was behind the pilot (between the wings and the tail in the rear of the aircraft), he had an unobstructed view to the front. Powered by a Renault WB V-8 air-cooled engine (70 hp WB or 100 hp 8G), the Shorthorn could achieve 66 mph (106 kmh) in the air. Its wingspan was 53 feet (16.15m), length 31 feet (9.45 m), and height 10 feet 5 inches (3.18 m). The Shorthorn could lift a gross weight of 2,045 lbs. (928 kg) to a service ceiling of 12,467 feet (3,800 m). Its range was nearly 150 miles (240 km).

Henri Farman HF.20. Another plane built by the Farman Aviation Works, but also used by the British was the HF.20, designed and built primarily by Henri Farman, hence the "HF" prefix. The HF.20 was an updated version of the Shorthorn, with a Gnome Lambda 7-cylinder air-cooled rotary engine (80 hp). The rotary engine had the propeller fixed to the engine, the whole engine rotated on a central shaft, attached to the aircraft. The rotation of the engine helped with cooling as it spun. The two-seat pusher configuration had the observer in the front and the pilot behind, with the engine behind the pilot. The wingspan was 45 feet 11 inches (14 m), length 27 feet 3 inches (8.3 m), and height of 10 feet 6 inches (3.2 m). The plane could fly to 1,050 feet (315 m) comfortably, with a max speed of 70 mph (110 kmh). Its range was 160 miles (250 km).

Royal Aircraft Factory BE2c. Another Royal Aircraft Factory product, the BE2c was a substantial upgrade to the BE2a, the 2c was a bit bigger and more powerful. Its wingspan was increased to 37 feet (11.28 m), length shortened to 27 feet 3 inches (8.31 m), and a bit taller at a height 11 feet 1½ inches (3.39 m). A new engine replaced the Renault of earlier designs. The RAF 1a V-8 air-cooled engine gave 90 hp for a top speed of 72 mph (116 kmh). It could fly for 3 hours and 15 minutes, and its service ceiling was 10,000 feet (3,050 m). The upgraded versions were used for reconnaissance as well as harassment bombing.

Sopwith Tabloid. The Sopwith Tabloids from the HMS *Ark Royal* were uncrated and handed over to the squadron. They are listed above.

Breguet Bre. 4. Louis Charles Breguet opened his namesake aircraft manufacturing company in 1911, after experimenting with aviation design and construction. His RU.1 in 1911 catapulted his company to success with massive government contracts and money. The tempestuous Bre. 4 was RNAS 3 Squadron's big bomber, and was known as "Marix's Breguet" because he was the only one brave enough to fly it. The massive plane was the main bombing platform for the squadron. The two-seat pusher biplane was powered by a Salmson 2M7 14-cylinder (2 rows of 7 cylinders) water-cooled radial engine producing 200 hp, impressive at the time. The wingspan was 53 feet 10 inches (16.4 m), length 31 feet 2 inches (9.5 m), and height 12 feet 2 inches (3.7 m). It flew at a maximum speed of 86 mph (138 kmh), and had a range of 248 miles (399 km). The most impressive feature of the plane was that it could carry a massive bomb load—up to 660 lbs. (300 kg). This was the plane that Samson and Marix tried to use to bomb Istanbul, but could not complete the mission because of engine problems. It was used on other bombing raids against the enemy.

Canton-Unne Maurice Farman Shorthorn. The Canton-Unne *Shorthorn* was the same airframe as the Maurice Farman MF.11 Shorthorn (above) but with a Salmson M9 9-cylinder water-cooled radial that produced 120 hp. The engine upgrade improved the plane's performance from 66 mph (106 kmh) to 70 mph (110 kmh). Range was also extended to 250 miles (400 km) more than the earlier version. It could carry a 7.62 mm machine gun in the front observer's cupola for offensive and defensive fire.

Voisin III. The Voisin Company opened in 1906 by brothers Gabriel and Charles. Nearly all of their early aircraft were experimental prototypes, but Gabriel continued improving on designs, even after his brother died in an auto accident in 1912. By 1914, he came up with the design for a military aircraft, hoping to cash in on lucrative government contracts. The Voisin III was a two-seat pusher biplane bomber-reconnaissance aircraft that arrived at 3 Squadron late in the campaign. The plane had a 48 foot 4 inch (14.74 m) wingspan, was 31 feet 2 inches (9.5 m) long and 9 feet 8 inches (2.95 m) tall. The Salmson M9 9-cylinder water-cooled radial engine produced 120 hp, pushing the plane to 65 mph (105 kmh), and a max ceiling of 11,485 feet (3,500 m). When the Voisins arrived at the squadron, they came with Lewis guns (British .303 caliber) that could be fitted to the forward observers' seat on a ring mount. It could also carry up to 200 lbs. (91 kg) of bombs.

Nieuport 10. The Nieuport Company was originally set up as an engine components manufacturer in 1902. They specialized in ignition components and magnetos. In 1909 they began building airframes, and in 1911 aero engines. Unfortunately, Edouard Nieuport was killed when he was thrown from his plane in 1911, and the company almost collapsed. The aviation enthusiast magnate Henri Deutsch de la Meurthe stepped in with substantial financial backing to revive the failing company. Another Nieuport brother died in 1912; Charles was killed in an airplane accident. But the Nieuport Company continued, with renewed interest from the French government. Gustave Delage was named chief designer in 1914 and came up with the design for a fast, agile racing plane, which at the outbreak of war became the basis for a successful military fighter.

The Nieuport 10s were the last reinforcements to arrive for (by then) 3 Wing at Gallipoli. The single-seat fighter biplane was reaching obsolescence on the Western Front, but was greeted with favor in the backwaters of the Mediterranean. With the arrival of the Nieuports, the Wing finally had fighter planes for air-to-air combat. Powered by a 92 hp le Rhone 9C 9-cylinder single-row rotary engine, the plane had a top speed of 86 mph (138 kmh). The wingspan was 26 feet 11 inches (8.2 m), length 23 feet 3 inches (7.09 m), and height 8 feet 11 inches (2.7 m), making it a small, fast mount. Although the range was limited to 155 miles (250 km), it could climb to 15,000 feet (4,572 m) if it needed to. It carried one Lewis gun (British .303 caliber) above the upper wing that could be swung down so that the pilot could change the magazine. The Nieuports offered an air superiority platform in the closing days of the campaign.

The Aircraft of No. 2 Squadron RNAS

Royal Aircraft Factory BE2c. Mentioned above, it was the same platform that 3 Squadron was already flying in theater.

Morane-Saulnier Type L. Brothers Leon and Robert Morane joined with Raymond Saulnier to form an aircraft manufacturing company in 1911. They specialized in monoplane designs while seemingly every other manufacturer was building biplanes. The Type L flown by No. 2 Squadron was a French-built two-seat parasol monoplane reconnaissance platform. The Parasol wing was attached above the fuselage with struts, giving the observer a clear view of everything below the aircraft. The wingspan was 36 feet 8 7/8 inches (11.2 m), length 22 feet 6 3/4 inches (6.88 m), and height 12 feet 10 5/8 inches (3.93 m). The plane was powered by a le Rhone 9c 9-cylinder single-row air-cooled rotary engine that produced 92 hp. It could reach 78 mph (125 kmh) and had a range of 312 miles (500 km). The Squadron brought Lewis guns (British .303 caliber) with the shipment of Type Ls.

Caudron G.III. Founded by another team of brothers, Gaston and Rene Caudron began manufacturing aircraft in 1909 in Romiotte, France, on their family farm. In addition to building airplanes, they also set up a flying school, based in Le Crotoy, close to their new factory. By 1913, the French military began sending students to learn to fly at the Caudron facility in their training aircraft. In addition to trainers, they also manufactured military planes, specializing in observation platforms. The G.III was a single-seat biplane, most likely built under license in Britain. Interestingly, the Caudron brothers did not charge a fee for building their aircraft, citing wartime necessity and patriotism. 233 copies were built in Britain during the war. The G.III was powered by the le Rhone 9c engine (92 hp). It had a wingspan of 44 feet (13.4 m), with a length of 21 feet (6.4 m), and a height of 8 feet 3 inches (2.5 m). It flew at 68 mph (106 kmh). It was unarmed, and served primarily as a reconnaissance platform.

Bristol Scout. After meeting Wilbur Wright in 1909, George White decided to expand his railroad empire into aviation. He founded the British and Colonial Aeroplane Company in 1910. At the start of the war, Bristol (as it was then called, sharing facilities with Bristol Tramways Company) was producing Royal Aircraft Factory BE2s, under license. The government insisted on only buying aircraft designed by the Royal Aircraft Establishment. But uproar from pilots, and a need for more airplanes allowed Bristol to begin manufacture of their own designs, specifically the Scout. The Scout was a single seat biplane flown by No. 2 Squadron for reconnaissance and mapping. It was also powered by the le Rhone 9c, making supply and maintenance somewhat easier for that squadron; three out of four of their plane types had the same engines. The plane had a 24 foot 7 inch (7.49 m) wingspan, was 20 feet 8 inches (6.3 m) long, with a height of 8 feet 6 inches (2.59 m). It could reach 94 mph (151 kmh), and had a range of 235 miles (376 km). The Scout was equipped with either a Vickers or Lewis gun (British .303 caliber) attached to the upper wing.

French Aircraft at Gallipoli

Voisin le Canard. The *Foudre* aircraft tender began operations with *le Canard* biplane floatplanes. Eventually there were two Canards on the *Foudre*. The Voisin le Canard (French: Duck) seemed to be built backwards;

the elevator was in front, with a fuselage that ended in biplane wings, with the engine in the rear of the plane. It was a fragile machine, especially when floats were attached for water landings. The single-seat plane had a wingspan of 40 feet (12 m) and a length of 26 feet (7.9 m). The second prototype sold to the French Navy could seat a pilot and observer; a crew of 2. It was severely underpowered with a Gnome 7-cylinder air-cooled radial that only produced 70 hp, thus limiting it to only 56 mph (90 kmh). Although it was the first French seaplane, on the first seaplane tender (according to the French records), the le Canard was obsolete by the start of the war and replaced with Caudron Type J floatplanes.

Caudron Type J. The *Foudre*'s replacement aircraft for the le Canard included the Caudron Type J. The Type J was a two-seat biplane that had floats, but also wheels on the floats. It was listed as an "amphibious aircraft." Powered by the same le Rhone 9c as the British aircraft, the underpowered (92 hp) engine had a tough time getting the floatplane into the air in all but ideal conditions. Its size and weight affected flight characteristics as well; it was a big airplane. With a wingspan of 48 feet 3 inches (14.7 m), a length of 26 feet 5 inches (8.05 m), but exceptionally light at only 990 lbs (450 kg) dry weight, the le Rhone had just enough power to pull it into the air. It could not lift much, with a max weight of 1540 lbs. (700 kg), but in the air it could fly at 71 mph (115 kmh). The Type J made up the entire compliment of the *Foudre*'s air component of four machines.

Henri Farman HF.20. An improvement on the *Shorthorn* that the British were flying at the same time, the HF.20 was a two-seat pusher biplane, with an observer in the nose and the pilot behind him. With a 45 foot 11 inch (14 m) wingspan, 27 foot 3 inch (8.3 m) length, and 10 foot 6 inch (3.2 m) height, it was a fairly large airplane. It was powered by a Gnome Lambda 7-cylinder air-cooled rotary engine that produced 80 hp. The HF.20 had a maximum speed of 70 mph (110 kmh) and a service ceiling of only 1,050 feet (315 m). But it had good range, and could fly 160 miles (250 km) on one tank of fuel. The entire escadrille MF. 98(T) was made up of HF.20s, simplifying supply and maintenance. In addition, the HF.20 could carry a light machine gun in the observer's seat on a ring mount. But the pilot, observer, machine gun, and maybe a few small bombs were all it could hope to carry.

German Aircraft in the Dardanelles/Gallipoli Campaign

Rumpler/Etrich Taube. The Taube, detailed above, was the same type that the Germans employed first in the Gallipoli Campaign. Serno's first available aircraft included four Taubes, all of which were destroyed over the course of the campaign, either by Allied bombing raids, or by the frequent, violent storms.

Albatros B.1. The Albatros Aircraft Manufacturing Company opened in 1909 in Berlin, founded by Walter Huth and Otto Wiener. Their first airplane was a license-built French Antoinette monoplane. At the outbreak of the war, they were building their own designs, including a number of important observation platforms. The B.1 was a two-seat tractor biplane, built for reconnaissance and observation. It was powered by a Mercedes D.1 6-cylinder in-line water-cooled engine (100 hp). The wingspan was 47 feet 6 1/8 inches (14.48 m), length of 28 feet 1 1/2 inches (8.57 m), and height of 10 feet 4 inches (3.15 m). Top speed was 65 mph (105 kmh), but the craft had a 400 mile (650 km) range. Although unarmed, the B.1 was a useful mount for observation over the peninsula.

Gotha WD.1. The German Gotha company transitioned from train rolling stock (*Gothaer Waggonfabrik*) to aircraft manufacturing just before the start of the war. Gotha was building the British Avro 503 floatplane under license, and renamed it the WD.1, for *Wasser Doppeldecker* ("water biplane"). The WD.1s were the first floatplanes to arrive for the Turkish-German contingent at Gallipoli. The WD.1 was a two-seat floatplane biplane powered by a Gnome Omega-Omega 14-cylinder (two rows of 7) air-cooled rotary (100 hp), in a tractor configuration with the engine in front. It had a wingspan of 47 feet 6 inches (14.48 m), a length of 33 feet (10.06 m), and a height of 12 feet 6 inches (3.81 m). The large plane, combined with the Gnome engine, had a top speed of 55 mph (89 kmh) and could climb to 8,200 feet (2,500 m). The plane had impressive range at 5 hours endurance, equaling 275 miles (440 km). Even though it was unarmed, it was an adequate observation platform.

Gotha WD.2. The WD.2 was an improvement on the WD.1, but carried many of the same characteristics. The two-seat German reconnaissance biplane floatplane was larger and more powerful than its predecessor. With a wingspan of 53 feet 11 inches (16.43 m) and a length of 34 feet 5 inches (10.5 m), it was bigger and heavier than the WD.1. It also got an engine upgrade; the WD.2 was powered by a Benz Bz.III 6-cylinder inline water-cooled engine that gave 150 hp. Speed was better too, at 69 mph (112 kmh). Range was extended to 416 miles (670 km) offering more time for observation. It too was unarmed.

Gotha WD.12. The WD.12 was another improvement on the earlier WD. 1 and WD. 2 models. Built in Germany, the WD. 12 got a new engine; a Mercedes D.III 6-cylinder in-line water-cooled 160 hp motor. The wingspan was 49 feet 2 5/8 inches (15 m), length was 32 feet 9 3/4 inches (10 m), and height was 12 feet 6 1/2 inches (3.825 m). It could fly at 88 mph (141 kmh), with a range of 484 miles (774.4 km). It was not armed, but loiter time was impressive for this reconnaissance floatplane.

Rumpler B.1. Edmund Rumpler opened his aircraft manufacturing company in Berlin in 1909. He began license-building Etrich Taubes, the latter based in Vienna. By 1914 he was building airplanes of his own design. The B.1 was a two-seat reconnaissance biplane powered by a Mercedes D.1 (100 hp) engine just like the Albatros B.1. Its wingspan was 42 feet 8 inches (13 m), length 27 feet 7 inches (8.4 m), and height 10 feet 2 inches (3.1 m). It had a top speed of 90 mph (145 kmh), a substantial improvement on the Albatros. Unarmed, it was relegated to observation roles.

LVG B.1. The *Luft-Verkehrs-Gesellshaft* (LVG) aircraft manufacturing company was based in Berlin, and originally opened in 1912 to license-build French Farman aircraft. By the start of the war they had transitioned to domestic design manufacture. The LVG B.1 was a two-seat reconnaissance aircraft that once obsolete on the Western Front was assigned to other theaters. The Gallipoli LVGs were powered by Mercedes D.1 engines (100 hp), mentioned above. The wingspan was 39 feet 9 ¼ inches (12.12 m), length 27 feet 2 ¾ inches (8.3 m), and height 8 feet 8 ¼ inches (2.95 m). It flew at 65 mph (105 kmh), with a range of 260 miles (416 km). It too was unarmed, but like most of the other German models the pilot would usually carry a pistol or carbine, and maybe even a few small bombs.

Albatros C.1. The Albatros C.1 was an evolutionary improvement on earlier designs. Built in Germany, the two-seat biplane switched the pilot and observer cockpits, putting the pilot in front and the observer in tandem to the rear, supplied with a 7.92 mm Parabellum MG 14 machine gun on a ring mount. Equipped with a new engine—a Mercedes D.III 6-cylinder in-line water-cooled 160 hp—the plane flew at a maximum speed of 82.5 mph (132 kmh). The wingspan was 42 feet 4 inches (12.9 m), length 25 feet 9 inches (7.85 m), and height 10 feet 3 5/8 inches (3.14 m). But even though it was more powerful, its range was limited to 206 miles (330 km). With the C.1, the German and Turkish flight teams could finally shoot back at the Allied machines.

Fokker Eindecker. At only twenty years old, Dutchman Anthony Fokker built his first airplane. He was studying to be a mechanic in Germany, but was bored, so he built an airplane he called "The Spider" (Dutch: *de Spin*). His friend crashed it. So Fokker built a new one. His friend crashed that one, too, and the friendship crumbled. So Fokker built another one. He became famous in his hometown of Haarlem (in the Netherlands) when he flew it there; the first Dutch airplane, built by a Dutchman, flying in the Netherlands. But he realized that he could make more money in Germany, so he returned to Berlin and founded *Fokker Aeroplanbau*.

Even though his company was taken over by the government at the start of the war, Fokker stayed as its director and designer. He built (or designed for other companies) several important aircraft for the Germans during the war. His most significant contribution to the war effort was the synchronizer gear (or interrupter gear). The Fokker Eindecker was the first true fighter plane dispatched to the Gallipoli Campaign. The single-seat monoplane was a tiny, fast, maneuverable aircraft that incorporated the synchronizer gear that allowed the 7.92 mm Spandau MG 08 machine gun to fire through the propeller arc along the axis of the aircraft, for stability and accuracy. The synchronizer gear interrupted the stream of bullets so that they would not shoot off the propeller. The plane was powered by an Oberusel U.0 7-cylinder air-cooled rotary engine that produced 80 hp. But even though the engine seemed small, the light frame (1,345 lbs [610 kg]) meant that the engine was enough to power it to 81 mph (130 kmh). The wingspan of the tiny craft was 29 feet (8.85 m), length 23 feet 7 inches (7.22 m), and height only 9 feet 5 ½ inches (2.9 m). It had a short range of only 123 miles (198 km), but it was enough to contest the skies over Gallipoli. At the very end of the campaign, Buddecke flew his Eindecker to fame when he shot down four Allied aircraft, confirmed (seven claimed).

Appendix III
The Literature of the Gallipoli Campaign

The corpus of volumes produced about the Gallipoli Campaign (aka, the Dardanelles Campaign) is extensive. Fortunately for the English-speaking world, nearly all the primary and secondary resources are in English, from British historians and authors. There are important works in other languages, but the bulk of the literature is in English. It largely casts a critical eye on the British and ANZAC failures during the campaign. Although there are some accounts that glorify the tactical, most concede that the campaign as a whole was a failure for the British, with few giving corresponding praise to the victors.

In the research for this project, I was fortunate to receive funding and time (to say nothing of an understanding editorial staff) to travel the world and research in nearly every relevant archive. An excellent interlibrary loan staff helped me gather an seemingly endless supply of secondary sources. I did not confine myself to English language documents and resources, but instead sought out the most obscure materials for what I hope is a comprehensive consideration of the topic. It is true that this project glosses over the land and naval campaigns, and only refers to them in context of the air war. But at the same time I had to be familiar with the entire campaign to be able to argue for the "joint" concepts I proposed, as they were developed at the time. Sometimes it is the lack of evidence that tells the story; the dearth of resources on the interactions between the components was as informative as the official recollections at the time and subsequently. Most primary and secondary sources focus on the land campaigns (Helles, ANZAC, and Suvla) rather than the naval aspects. To date, none have considered in any detail the air component of the Dardanelles and Gallipoli operations; that was the focus of this project.

The Ottoman Turks

The Turkish resources were by far the most difficult to obtain. I was able to rely on graduate students and faculty colleagues in the United States and Turkey for the excellent resources they provided. I did make two trips to Turkey in person: one to visit the battlefields and to perform cursory research in Istanbul, and another to lecture for the centenary of Gallipoli conference. Students and colleagues mined the archives, providing a service that I could not do in person. I do not read Ottoman Arabic script or modern Turkish. Nearly all of the original government documents from the time were in Arabic script; all of the modern accounts are written in Turkish. Students and colleagues with the language skills were able to find and translate important documents and resources for me for the benefit of this book. In the Ottoman Archives (Ankara), the few remaining documents related to the Gallipoli Campaign are found in the listing under "World War: Gallipoli Campaign." They do not have an online guide or search engine, and the catalog system is in dire need of a modern upgrade. The research assistants I was able to find reported that there were only a few documents on the air component of the Turkish defenses, and that finding the resources was extremely difficult. Their help was invaluable. In the secondary material, there were a few books—written in modern Turkish—that proved useful. Cenk Avci, *Canakkale Cephesi'nde Hava Savaslari* (Air Battles at the Canakkale Front) (Ankara, Turkey: Genelkurmay Basimevi, 2009) was invaluable. This short tome offered insight into the German and Turkish pilots and observers at Gallipoli from the Turkish perspective, and was useful in crafting a balanced narrative. Although the Turks relied heavily on the Germans for pilots and machines, it is good to see that there are emerging Turkish scholars writing on the Gallipoli Campaign from their perspective and using Turkish archival materials. There were other books on the land and naval campaigns, to say nothing of the Atatürk hagiographies, but this single volume is a start in the right direction of the analysis of the campaign at the tactical and operational levels of war.

The single best source on the Turkish air component at Gallipoli is located at the Australian War Museum and Archives, cited below. Other works in English include the American historian Edward Erickson's *Ordered to Die; A History of the Ottoman Army in the First World War* (Westport, CT: Greenwood Press, 2001) and *Gallipoli: The Ottoman Campaign* (Barnsley, UK: Pen and Sword, 2010). Another useful source was Kevin Fewster, Vecihi Basarin, and Hatice Basarin, *Gallipoli: The Turkish Story* (Crows Nest, New South Wales, Australia: Allen and Unwin, 2003), which included Turkish sources in an English language secondary work. A number of books were consulted for insight into Mustafa Kemal Atatürk and his role in the Gallipoli Campaign, in hopes of gleaning insight into the air war, but none offered any relevant information. Neither Partick Balfour's biography *Attaturk: A Biography of Mustafa Kemal, Father of Modern Turkey* (London, UK: Quill, 1992) nor Andrew Mango's work *Attaturk* (London, UK: John Murray, 1999), offered much help. Two journals provided the initial interest in the topic, both of which were useful in this story: *Over the Front: The Journal of World War One Aviation* ran a series of articles on the Gallipoli Campaign in volume 9 (1994) and volume 11 (1996) including Richard Layman, "Over the Wine Dark Sea: Aerial Aspects of the Dardanelles/Gallipoli Campaign" (Part 1), 9, no. 1 (1994); "Samson vs. Kemal: Did it Really Happen?" 9, no. 1 (1994); Ian Burns, "Over the Wine Dark Sea: Aerial Aspects of the Dardanelles/Gallipoli Campaigns Part Two: Operations of the HMS *Ben-my-Chree*, June 1915–January 1916," 9, no. 2 (1994); Richard Whistler, "Over the Wine Dark Sea: Aerial Aspects of the Dardanelles/Gallipoli Campaign Part 4: The German Wasserfliegerabteilung," 11, no. 2 (1996); and Richard Whistler "Over the Wine Dark Sea: Aerial Aspects of the Dardanelles/Gallipoli Campaign, Part Five: The Defense of the Bosphorus and the Fokker Staffel," 11, no. 2 (1996). The *Over the Front* articles built on original interest in *Cross and Cockade* (UK) in Brian Flanagan, "The History of the Ottoman Air Force in the Great War, The Reports of Major Erich Serno," 11, no. 2 (1970) and Peter Wright, "Kite Balloon Observer at Gallipoli," 23, no. 3 (1982). These short article pieces sparked this author's initial interest as well as offered insight and resources for additional information.

The Germans

The German records were incomplete, but incredibly useful as well. During World War II, most of the German records were destroyed by Allied bombing. But of the records that remain, I was able to track down some interesting sources in the German archives. After the reunification, the German government reopened the Federal Archives (Bundesarchiv) at an old army post in the Berlin suburbs. At Lichterfeld, I was able to gather Reichsarchiv documents relating to the interaction between the German Empire and the Ottoman Empire before and during World War I. The "R" series documents were especially important; R43 *Alte Reichskanzlerei* records and relations to Turkey (German: *Turkei*), R2 *Deutsche Militär Kimmissionen in Turkei*, R8034 *Militärwesen in Ausland*, and the R901 collection describing the military contributions to the Ottomans during the war were especially helpful. All of these records were free to use, and the German Archives now promote digital photography rather than photocopying. Unfortunately, almost all of the military documents are located in Freiburg im Breisgau, southeast of Stuttgart near the French and Swiss border. The Bundesarchiv Militärarchiv (BA/MA) is the repository for German military records. The BA/MA had excellent resources for the German military mission to Turkey, including records relating to Erich Serno's interactions with the Turks and his influence on Ottoman aviation. The Serno Reports in records group MSG 2 were outstanding and useful. Some, however, could not be photocopied (or photographed) by decision of the archive, and had to be manually transcribed (in true archive fashion: in pencil on supplied paper). This collection was the basis for the bulk of the German records relating to the air war over Gallipoli. True to form, Serno wrote daily reports (most days), monthly synopses, and even provided a post-campaign overview (MSG 2 / 10873). The Liman von Sanders collection in N 907 and PH 30 were useful as an overview, but interesting in that there was very little on the air war. RH 61 included Sander's postwar reports on his military mission to Turkey. The document collection RM 40 / 6 through 19 included daily reports from the pilots in the German/Ottoman squadrons, and was incredibly useful in constructing the operational story from the perspective of the defenders.

In addition to the primary documents, there were a number of important secondary sources on the German perspective of the Gallipoli Campaign.

The first and most significant was Liman von Sander's recollections in *Fünf Jahre Türkei* (Berlin, Germany: A. Scherl, 1920), translated as *Five Years in Turkey* (Nashville, TN: Battery Press, 2000). In his autobiography, he recounts his actions and decisions in the Gallipoli Campaign, working on behalf of the Turks to defend against the Allied attacks. The first part of the book chronicles his travels to Turkey and subsequent command of the defending forces at Gallipoli. Another pair of books were informative: Carl Mühlmann was Sander's aide-de-camp in the campaign, and a history professor before the war. He wrote an overview of the Germans in the Balkans (including Turkey) during the war in *Oberste Heeresleitung und Balkan im Weltkrieg* (Berlin: Wilhelm Limpert, 1942), as well as a volume in the German Official History of the World War (Volume 16), *Der Kampf um die Dardanellen, 1915* (Oldenburg, Germany: Stalling, 1927). He chronicles the war from the German perspective, but like Sanders, offers little insight into the air component of the campaign. Unfortunately, Erich Serno left no other record, and there are no biographies of him. His life and contribution to the history of airpower is an interesting hole in the research that warrants examination in more detail.

The Australians

On an unrelated trip to Canberra, I was fortunate to have a few days in the Australian War Museum and Archives for research on this project. Although there was a vast collection (in the "E" series) on the role of the ANZACs at Gallipoli, there was not much on the air aspects of the campaign. One intrepid archivist found a document that he thought might be of interest, and produced an unpublished manuscript that proved invaluable from record group M550862. It was Ole Nikolajsen and Bülent Yilmazer, *Ottoman Aviation, 1909–1919*. In it, the two chronicle the birth of Ottoman aviation and its use in the Italo-Turkish War and leading into World War I. Although there is not much narrative, the document compiles the list of Turkish/Ottoman aircraft, origins, and pilot's records from the beginning of Ottoman flight through World War I. This in-depth research and statistical analysis provided the core of the German-Ottoman-Turkish story and the basis for this project from the defender's perspective. Cross-referencing from available sources confirmed most of the data that these two authors provided in the unpublished pages. Although lacking in source citations (and photo credits), it was a treasure trove of information on the numbers and types of aircraft available to the defenders in the Gallipoli Campaign. Overall it was a good resource, although it has not been cited elsewhere, and remains hidden in the archive as far as I can tell.

A few ANZAC-focused secondary sources were also consulted for context, including John Robertson, *Anzac and Empire* (Port Melbourne, Australia: Hamlyn Australia, 1990) and John Millar, *The Soul of Anzac: General Sir William Birdwood and the A.I.F., 1914–1918* (North Melbourne, Australia: Vic Australian Scholarly, 2015). These added to the official published record in Charles Bean, *The Official History of Australia in the War of 1914–1918*, especially Volume 2: *The Story of ANZAC* (St. Lucia, Queensland, Australia: University of Queensland Press, 1981). A colleague was concurrently working on a similar project that was published just before this work. His research was confined to the British perspective, whereas this project incorporated more source material from a wider range of archives. Nonetheless, our communication, and his book, is useful: Hugh Dolan, *Gallipoli Air War: the Unknown Story of the Fight for the Skies over Gallipoli* (Sydney, New South Wales, Australia: Pan Macmillan Australia, 2013).

The French

The French Military Archives at the Chateau de Vincennes (Service historique de la Défense) is a wonderful repository of sources. Used by researchers for years, the archives contain a wealth of information on French military history. As most visitors search for Napoleonic and Western Front materials, I was fortunate to have entire collections to myself. There were no other researchers (at the time) looking at the French contributions to the Gallipoli Campaign. Unfortunately, there was not much to find. The archive does contain a few documents related to Gallipoli, but mostly in the naval records as was expected (16 N, 17 N, and 20 N collections in the Great War catalog). As well as the same records consulted for the Oriental Expedition Corps (Corps expeditionnaire d'Orient), the land contribution to the campaign. There were few records pertaining directly to the air component; that information had to be gathered from other sources. The commander of the MF. 98(T) Tenedos squadron, Césari, had a file in the 1P23098 (15), *Dossier Administratif*, Césari, *Antoine* collection, outlining his service records and dates. But there was not much to go on. The rest of the French story was pieced together from a collection of obscure French secondary sources that filled in the numerous holes in the research. As above, interested historians with a passion for finding obscure references should think about a comprehensive analysis of the French at Gallipoli.

After extensive research, a few memoirs emerged that offered great value. Emile Guépratte was the French naval commander in the Mediterranean at the outset of the campaign until October 1915. Twenty years after the ill-fated Gallipoli Campaign he wrote his memoirs of the war, *L'Expédition Des Dardanelles, 1914–1915* (Paris: Payot, 1935). In it he outlined his role, and the disastrous naval attacks, passing blame to the British. He offered little on the air campaign.

From the ground perspective, Elizabeth Greenhalgh, *The French Army and the First World War* (Cambridge, UK: Cambridge University Press, 2014); Pierre Miquel, *Les Poilus d'Orient* (Paris: Fayard, 1998); and George Cassar, *The French and the Dardanelles* (London, UK: George Allen and Unwin, 1971) offer good information on the land component, but like most analyses of Gallipoli leave out the air component. That information came from books on French military aviation, none of which offered much specificity. The French aviation books included Jean-Marc Olivier, ed., *Histoire de L'Armee de L'Air et des Forces Aeriennes Francaise du XVIIIe Siecle a nous jours* (Toulouse, France: Editions Privat, 2014); Rene Martel, *L'Aviation Francaise de Bombardment* (Paris: Paul Hermann, 1939), trans. Allen Suddaby as *French Strategic and Tactical Bombardment Forces in World War I* (Lanham, MD: Scarecrow Press, 2007); and Charles Christienne and Pierre Lissarrague, *The History of French Military Aviation*, trans. Frances Kianka (Washington D.C.: Smithsonian Institution Press, 1986). Each of the aviation books provides some information, but none focus on the role of MF. 98(T) specifically, or the missions of the French in the Near East in general. They are generalist books on French military aviation, with reference to the Gallipoli Campaign. As with Erich Serno, there is no specific work on Captain Césari, either a memoir or a biography. These are additional areas for further exploration and exploitation.

The British

Maybe the history can be written by the losers. By far, the most documentary evidence as well as secondary source material on the Gallipoli Campaign is from the British archives and presses. The efforts to chronicle the events, as well as analyze after the fact, come from British sources. After scouring multiple archives and extensive literature search, this became obvious. The British have produced—by far—the most resources on the Gallipoli Campaign.

Two archives in London hold the bulk of the resources on the campaign. The National Archives UK (formerly Kew Gardens, but still located in Kew, only recently renamed) hold all of the government and nearly all of the military resources pertaining to the Dardanelles and Gallipoli. From the War Office records (WO 161) to the Admiralty records in the ADM series to the RNAS documents in AIR 1 and 20 (and their related guides), the British government kept extensive records during the war on the naval, land, and air operations in the Dardanelles theater and Gallipoli Campaign. Additional resources, specifically the squadron logs of RNAS 3 Squadron/Wing, are held at the Imperial War Museum Downtown London branch, along with an excellent photo archive. Whereas the National Archives is usually full with researchers looking at literally any part of England and British history, the IWM is usually very quiet, with ample staff to help with finding materials. One word of caution: nearly all of the archives (and especially the British) charge a fee for photocopying. But all allow digital photography. The cost of a good digital camera is offset quickly.

In addition to the primary government documents, after the war the British published numerous records for use in research. Some of the best are Cecil Aspinall-Oglander, *History of the Great War*, especially volume 1: Gallipoli Operations (London: Imperial War Museum, 1929); Stephen Roskill, *Documents Relating to the Naval Air Service*, vol. 1 (London: Navy Records Society, 1969); and Walter Raleigh, *The War in the Air*, vol. 1 (London: Hamish Hamilton, 1922). Published memoirs rounded out the personal information for the story. The most informative book was Charles Rumney Samson, *Fights and Flights* (Nashville, TN: Battery Press, 1990). Others included Winston Churchill, *The World Crisis, 1915* (New York: Charles Scribner's Sons, 1929); John Clark-Hall, *Air Marshal Sir Robert Clark-Hall, K.B.E., C.M.G., D.S.O.: Autobiographical and Biographical Reminiscences* (Amberly, New Zealand: The Raven Press, 1995); Ian Hamilton's two books *Gallipoli Diary*, 2 vols. (London: E. Arnold, 1920); and *Sir Ian Hamilton's Despatches from the Dardanelles, etc.* (London: G. Newnes, 1916); Richard Davies, *Sailor in the Air* (Barnsley, UK:

Pen and Sword, 2008); and Frederick Sykes, *From Many Angles* (London: G. G. Harrap, 1943).

There are many overviews of the campaign; I relied on my master's thesis advisor for the most comprehensive account of the Gallipoli Campaign: Tim Travers, *Gallipoli 1915* (Stroud, Gloucestershire, UK: Tempus Publishing, 2003). Dr. Travers first ignited my interest in the topic and very early on provided some essential reading materials and primary documents. Other Dardanelles and Gallipoli campaign studies include Alan Moorehead, *Gallipoli* (New York: Harper and Brothers, 1956); Robin Prior, *Gallipoli* (New Haven, CT: Yale University Press, 2009); William Puleston, *The Dardanelles Expedition* (Annapolis, MD: Naval Institute Press, 1927); and Jeffrey Wallin, *By Ships Alone: Churchill and the Dardanelles* (Durham, NC: Carolina Academic Press, 1981). Books dealing with specific aspects of the campaign are numerous, this project focused on the works that contributed most significantly to the aerial aspects, either in the command and control or the actual recollections of the air operations. These were Eric Ash, *Sir Frederick Sykes and the Air Revolution, 1912–1918* (London: Frank Cass, 1999); David Brown, *The Grand Fleet: Warship Design and Development, 1906–1922* (Annapolis, MD: Naval Institute Press, 1999); Ray Burt, *British Battleships of World War One* (Annapolis, MD: Naval Institute Press, 1986); Thomas Frothingham, *The Naval History of the World War* (Cambridge, MA: Harvard University Press, 1924); Paul Halpern, *The Naval War in the Mediterranean, 1914–1918* (Annapolis, MD: Naval Institute Press, 1987); and Roger Keyes, *The Fight for Gallipoli* (London: Eyre and Spottiswoode, 1941).

***

On aircraft development specifically, several sources helped with the discussion of aircraft capabilities and limitations, John Bruce, *British Aeroplanes, 1914–1918* (London: Putnam, 1957); Tom Crouch, *The Bishop's Boys* (New York: W. W. Norton, 2003); Louis Blériot, *Flight into the XXth Century* (London: Austin Macauley Publishers, 2015), Guillaume De Syon, *Zeppelin! Germany and the Airship, 1900–1939* (Baltimore, MD: Johns Hopkins University Press, 2002); Hugh Driver, *The Birth of Military Aviation: Britain, 1903–1914* (London: Royal Historical Society, 1997); Brian Elliot, *Blériot: Herald of an Age* (Mount Pleasant, SC: Arcadia Publishing, 2000); Richard Layman, *Naval Aviation in the First World War: Its Impact and Influence* (Barnsley, UK: Chatham Publishing Group, 1996); John Morrow, *The*

Great War in the Air: Military Aviation from 1909–1921 (Washington DC: Smithsonian Institution Press, 1993); and the definitive Jane's Encyclopedias, especially *Fighting Aircraft of World War I* (New York, NY: Military Press, 1919, 1990).

Additional resources were consulted, but this is a broad overview by nationality of the depth of research and extensive reading that went into the project. In addition to all of the personal work of the author, numerous archivists and graduate researchers were instrumental in the finished project. A lot of work was done, but more work is needed in several of these areas for a more complete history of the Gallipoli Campaign, and World War I in general. But hopefully, this research will inspire and guide future researchers to greater heights and exciting accounts.

Notes

Chapter One. The Birth of Airpower

1. Napoleon took his newly formed balloon corps on campaign to Egypt. The balloons were destroyed in their shipping containers when the French fleet was sunk at the Battle of Aboukir Bay (1799).
2. Charles Evans, *The War of the Aeronauts: A History of Ballooning During the Civil War* (Mechanicsburg, PA: Stackpole, 2002).
3. Guillaume De Syon, *Zeppelin! Germany and the Airship, 1900–1939* (Baltimore, MD: Johns Hopkins University Press, 2002), 72–74.
4. For an excellent examination of the Wright Brothers' achievements, see Tom Crouch, *The Bishop's Boys* (New York: W. W. Norton, 2003).
5. Ernst Lehmann, *Zeppelin: The Story of Lighter-Than-Air Craft* (Stroud, UK: Fonthill Media, 2015).
6. Otto Lilienthal, *Birdflight as the Basis for Aviation* (Hummelstown, PA: Markowski International Publishers, 2000), translated from the German original, *Der Vogelflug als Grundlage der Fliegekunst* (Berlin: 1889).
7. Louis Blériot, *Flight into the XXth Century* (London: Austin Macauley, 2015).
8. Brian Elliot, *Blériot: Herald of an Age* (Mount Pleasant, SC: Arcadia, 2000).
9. "Paris Flight Show," *Flight* I, no. 40, (2 October 1909), 609–11.
10. Stephen Roskill, *Documents Relating to the Naval Air Service*, vol. I (London: Navy Records Society, 1969), #2, Extracts from the Report of the Aerial Navigation Sub-Committee of the C.I.D., dated 28 January 1909, 7–13.
11. Roskill, *Documents*, 7–13.
12. Stephen Roskill, *Documents Relating to the Naval Air Service*, vol. I (London: Navy Records Society, 1969), #12, Paper by Rear-Admiral E.C.T. Troubridge, Chief of Staff, Admiralty, 'The Development of Naval Aeroplanes and Airships', dated 23 January 1912, 29–33.

13. Jean-Marc Olivier, ed., *Histoire de L'Armée De L'Air et des Forces Aériennes Françaises du XVIIIe Siécle à nous jours* (Toulouse, France: Éditions Privat, 2014).
14. H. G. Wells, *The War in the Air* (London: G. Bell and Sons, 1908).
15. Von Hardesty, "Early Flight in Russia," in Robin Higham, John Greenwood, and Von Hardesty, eds., *Russian Airpower in the Twentieth Century* (London: Routledge, 1998), 18–36.
16. Charles Christienne, and Pierre Lissarrague, *The History of French Military Aviation*, trans. by Frances Kianka (Washington DC: Smithsonian Institution Press, 1986).
17. Hugh Driver, *The Birth of Military Aviation: Britain, 1903–1914* (London: Royal Historical Society, 1997).
18. John Morrow, *The Great War in the Air: Military Aviation from 1909–1921* (Washington DC: Smithsonian Institution Press, 1993).
19. Istanbul was called Constantinople in nearly all of the contemporary (and immediate postwar) British accounts; this author will use the Ottoman Turkish name for the city throughout.
20. Ole Nikolajsen and Bülent Yilmazer, *Ottoman Aviation 1909–1919* (unpublished manuscript), located at the Australian War Museum and Archives (hereafter AWMA), M550862, 9.
21. Yeşilköy, once a separate town, is now a suburb south of Istanbul and the location of the Atatürk International Airport.
22. William Beehler, *The History of the Italian-Turkish War* (Annapolis, MD: Proceedings of the United States Naval Institute, 1913).
23. Rebecca Maksel, "The World's First Warplane," in *The Smithsonian Air and Space Journal*, (October 21, 2011), http://www.airspacemag.com/daily-planet/the-worlds-first-warplane-115175678/?no-ist=.
24. Maksel, "World's First Airplane."
25. Nikolajsen, *Ottoman Aviation*, 14–15.
26. Nikolajsen, *Ottoman Aviation*, 17.
27. Edward Erickson, *Defeat in Detail: The Ottoman Army in the Balkans, 1912–3* (Westport, CT: Praeger, 2003).
28. Nikolajsen, *Ottoman Aviation*, 22–40.
29. Nikolajsen, *Ottoman Aviation*, 27.
30. Nikolajsen, *Ottoman Aviation*, 27–28.

31. Ray Burt and W. P. Trotter, *Battleships of the Grand Fleet* (Annapolis, MD: Naval Institute Press, 1982). The contracted *Rashadieh* was handed over to the Royal Navy and renamed the HMS *Erin*, 58–59, the Brazilian Navy ordered the *Rio de Janeiro* but could not pay, so the Turks paid £2.25 million for the renamed *Sultan Osman 1*. Although already paid for (and nearly bankrupting the Ottoman Empire) the British kept it—and the money—at the outbreak of war. It was renamed the HMS *Agincourt*, 60–61.
32. Liman von Sanders, *Five Years in Turkey* (Nashville, TN: Battery Press, 2000; reprint), 1. See also, Liman von Sanders, *Fünf Jahre Türkei* (Berlin, Germany: A. Scherl, 1920), 1.
33. Service Historique de la Défense, Château de Vincennes (hereafter SHD), *Livret Matricule d'Officier, de Goys de Mèzeyrac* (official military record of Goys de Mèzeyrac), 1P6215-1, 3, 5.
34. SHD, page unnumbered.
35. Sanders, *Five Years*, 1–18.
36. Sanders, *Five Years*, 1–3. See also records from the *Bundesarchiv* (German Federal Archives, Lichterfeld, hereafter BA-L), R2/50245, Fische 2, report 42 and 43 (annex), *Deutsche Militär Kommissionen in Bulgarien, Turkei, und Persien, Reichsfinanzministerium, 17 Nov 1914—10 Marz 1920.*
37. BA-L R2/50245, File 43 (appendix).
38. Brian Flanagan, "The History of the Ottoman Air Force in the Great War, Reports of Major Erich Serno," in *Cross and Cockade Journal* 11, no. 2 (Summer 1970).
39. Richard Whistler, "Over the Wine-Dark Sea: Aerial Aspects of the Dardanelles/Gallipoli Campaign, Part 4: The German Wasserfliegerabteilung," in *Over the Front* 11, no. 2, (1996).
40. Brian Flanagan, "The History of the Ottoman Air Force in the Great War: The Reports of Major Erich Serno," in *Cross and Cockade*, 11, no. 2, (Winter 1970).
41. Bundesarchiv Militärarchiv (Freiburg, hereafter BAMA), MSG 2/10876 Serno's reports titled "*Sammlung Luftwessen vor 1918*," 32.
42. BAMA, Serno's reports, 33. See also Cenk Avci, *Canakkale Cephesi'nde Hava Savaslari*, (Ankara, Turkey: Genelkurmay Basimevi, 2009), 15.

43. BAMA, Serno's Reports, 32.
44. BAMA, Serno's Reports, 35–39. Serno provided reports at the time as well as a comprehensive after action report at the end of the war. Both sets of documents were consulted, for the ease of citations the final report will be used specifically. The Serno files at the BAMA are a treasure trove of information on his service for the Turks in World War I.
45. Cecil Aspinall-Oglander, *Military Operations Gallipoli* (Nashville, TN: Battery Press, 1992), vol. I, 44–57. Kitchener responds well to the planned operation in the Dardanelles, but comments that "not a man [from the Western Front, including the RFC] should be detached to a subsidiary theater," 56.
46. Richard Layman, *Naval Aviation in the First World War: Its Impact and Influence* (Barnsley, UK: Chatham Publishing, 1996), 119–22.
47. Layman, *Naval Aviation*, 141.
48. Layman, *Naval Aviation*, 141.
49. Charles Rumney Samson, *Fights and Flights* (Nashville, TN: Battery Press, 1990), 1–7.
50. British National Archives (Formerly Kew Gardens, UK, hereafter National Archives [UK]), ADM 273/31, Charles Rumney Samson Service Record, 1.
51. National Archives (UK), Samson Service Record, 6–7.
52. National Archives (UK), Samson Service Record, 10 specifically, but also throughout the memoir. Samson later states that he brought the idea to Gallipoli where the RNAS armored car squadron concept was implemented in the front lines against the Turks.
53. National Archives (UK), Samson Service Record, 174–75.
54. National Archives (UK), Samson Service Record, 206–9.
55. National Archives (UK), Samson Service Record, 210.
56. Elizabeth Greenhalgh, *The French Army and the First World War* (Cambridge, UK: Cambridge University Press, 2014), 102–3.
57. Greenhalgh, *French Army*, 102–3.
58. Mentioned in Émile Paul Aimable Guépratte, *L'Expédition Des Dardanelles, 1914–1915* (Paris: Payot, 1935), 28.
59. SHD, 1P23098, Dossier Administratif CESARI, Antoine Marie, 1, 3, and 12, and in notes throughout. Cesari was promoted on 5 May 1915, and dispatched to the Dardanelles to support the campaign with a squadron of planes.

60. Jean-Marc Olivier, ed., *Histoire de L'Armée De L'Air et des Forces Aériennes Françaises du XVIIIe Siécle à nous jours* (Toulouse, France: Éditions Privat, 2014), 63.
61. SHD, 1P 23098, 12–15.
62. According to the incomplete records, compiled from official documents and memoirs. The records are not specific, but chronology and cross-referencing suggest that these were close to the numbers and types for the squadron. Samson (242) mentions eighty hp Maurice Farmans, the HF.20 was the correct plane for the engine cited and the type available at the time. The official record (SHD, Dardanelles Report #2, 16N1205 D2) cites thirteen (or fifteen) aircraft transferred from the Serbian Front to the Turkish front around this date, 10. It is also the correct number (14–18) of an operational French aero squadron of the time.
63. Samson, 242+.

Chapter 2. Preparation for War in the Mediterranean

1. Thomas Frothingham, *The Naval History of the World War* (Cambridge, MA: Harvard University Press, 1924), 68.
2. Archibald Bell, *A History of the Blockade of Germany and the Countries Associated with Her in the Great War: Austria-Hungary, Bulgaria, and Turkey, 1914–1918* (London: HMSO, 1937).
3. Jeffrey Wallin, *By Ships Alone: Churchill and the Dardanelles* (Durham, NC: Carolina Academic Press, 1981), 27–28.
4. Wallin, *By Ships Alone*, 35–38.
5. Churchill was the civilian master of the Royal Navy as the first lord of the admiralty; Sir Jackie Fisher was the military commander of the Royal Navy, the first sea lord.
6. Field Marshal Horatio Herbert Kitchener, secretary of state for war, did not disagree with Churchill's idea, but was unwilling to support the proposed landings with British troops (or RFC squadrons) from the Western Front.
7. Wallin, *By Ships Alone*, 40.
8. Paul Halpern, *The Naval War in the Mediterranean 1914–1918* (Annapolis, MD: Naval Institute Press, 1987), 53.
9. Halpern, *Naval War*, 53.

10. Wallin, *By Ships Alone*, 55.
11. Wallin, *By Ships Alone*, 55–56.
12. Halpern, *Naval War*, 59.
13. Halpern, *Naval War*, 59.
14. Halpern, *Naval War*, 59.
15. Émile Paul Aimable Guépratte, *L'Expédition des Dardanelles, 1914–1915* (Paris: Payot, 1935), 28.
16. Pierre Miquel, *Les Poilus d'Orient* (Paris: Fayard, 1998), 19.
17. Liman von Sanders, *Five Years in Turkey* (Nashville, TN: Battery Press, 2000; reprint), 1–4.
18. Robin Prior, *Gallipoli* (New Haven, CT: Yale University Press, 2009), 35.
19. I will employ the anglicized names throughout. Today, Imbros is a Turkish island named *Gökçeada*, Tenedos is called Bozcaada in Turkish, Tavşan Adası is the modern name for Rabbit Island, also Turkish. Samothrace and Lemnos, regardless of their proximity to Turkey, are Greek islands to this day.
20. The anglicized name is the Gallipoli Peninsula, locally it was called Gelibolu Yarımadası.
21. In modern Turkish: Seddülbahir.
22. Hill 971 was mistakenly named Sari Bair by the Allies and was known as Kocaçimentepe (or Kojatemen Tepe) in Turkish. Its height is 971 feet (296 m), hence the designation.
23. This was not particular to 1915. When I visited in 2010, maps were unavailable in country. The reason still escapes me.
24. The town inspired the English name for the peninsula, known as Gelibolu in Turkish.
25. Kevin Fewster, Vecihi Başarin, and Hatice Başarin, *Gallipoli, The Turkish Story* (Crows Nest, New South Wales, Australia: Allen and Unwin, 2003), 56–59.
26. Tim Travers, *Gallipoli 1915* (Stroud, Gloucestershire, UK: Tempus Publishing, 2003), 45–47.
27. I contend that World War I was the first mechanized industrial war. Previous wars included mechanization (Franco-Prussian War, U.S. Mexican Expedition, etc.) and all wars contain technology, but World War I was the first war to include mechanized industrial warfare at all

levels—strategic, operational, and tactical. The ideas and logic of their use was ill defined and primitive, nonetheless World War I was the birth of mechanized industrial warfare.

28. David Brown, *The Grand Fleet: Warship Design and Development 1906–1922* (Annapolis, MD: Naval Institute Press, 1999), 76–77. Brown argues that the *Ark Royal* was the first purpose-designed seaplane carrier, while the French Defense Ministry state that the French seaplane tender *Foudre* was the first ship to carry seaplanes. While the *Foudre* was converted from its former duties as a torpedo-boat carrier, the *Ark Royal* was purpose-built. The *Foudre* was the first ship to carry seaplanes; the *Ark Royal* was the first built specifically for the purpose. See also National Archives (UK), Air 1/7/6/195, Air Department Memo Regarding Suitable Seaplane Carrying Ship—Gives Seaplane Carrying Ships to Date 1912–1914, undated, no author listed.
29. Henry Jones, *The War in the Air, The Official History of the War* (London: Hamish Hamilton, 1928), vol. II, 9–11. See also *Jane's Fighting Aircraft of World War I* (New York: Military Press, 1919; 1990), and *Jane's Encyclopedia of Aviation* (New York: Military Press, 1989). Richard Layman, "Over the Wine-Dark Sea, Aerial Aspects of the Dardanelles/Gallipoli Campaign," in *Over the Front* 9, no. 1, (Spring 1994), 7–8, gives an account of the types and Admiralty procurement numbers of the planes from the *Ark Royal*.
30. Undated and unsigned letter, reprinted as the "Particulars of the HMS *Ark Royal*" in Stephen Roskill, *Documents Relating to the Naval Air Service* (London: Navy Records Society, 1969), 201–4.
31. Roskill, *Documents Relating*, 205–6. Wing Commander Charles Samson to Commodore Suetter, dated 2 May 1915. Samson complained that he needed more and better aircraft.
32. Peter Wright, "Kite Balloon Observer at Gallipoli," in *Cross and Cockade Journal* 23, no. 3 (Autumn 1982), 268–72.
33. Walter Raleigh, *The War in the Air*, vol. I (London: Hamish Hamilton, 1922), 461.
34. Raleigh, *War in the Air*, vol. I, 460.
35. See specifically Jones, *War in the Air*, vol. II, 22–25.
36. Jones, *War in the Air*, vol. II, 23.
37. Jones, *War in the Air*, vol. II, 26–28; Raleigh, *War in the Air*, vol. I, 166 and 205–6, as well as an extensive discussion of the formation of the

Eastchurch Squadron (3 Squadron RNAS) and Samson's squadron's exploits in France in Charles Samson, *Fights and Flights* (Nashville, TN: Battery Press, 1990).

38. Samson, *Fights and Flights*, 210.
39. Jones, *The War in the Air*, vol. II, 23.
40. Lieutenants Collett, Osmond, Butler, and Bill Samson, Charles Samson's younger brother.
41. No. 50 was important enough to get its own file and citation in the archives, National Archives (UK), Air 1/675/21/13/1245, "Some Notes on B.E.50," undated, no author given.
42. Richard Layman, "Over the Wine-Dark Sea: Aerial Aspects of the Dardanelles/Gallipoli Campaign," (Part 1), in *Over the Front*, 9, no. 1 (Spring 1994).
43. Samson, *Fights and Flights*, 221.
44. Samson, *Fights and Flights*, 221.
45. Samson, *Fights and Flights*, 224. "Old No. 1241 . . . the pride of the squadron. She had already done 120 hours' flying for us in France, and she carried on in the same style at the Dardanelles."
46. Samson, *Fights and Flights*, 404. See also Césari's dossier, located at the SHD, 1P 23098 (15 Pages), 6—orders to Tenedos, 12—promotion and assignment to Tenedos.
47. SHD, File 16N 3135, Dardanelles (Number 1), no page listed.
48. SHD, 1P 23098, 6–7. To paraphrase, operate immediately to reconnoiter the enemy encampments, photographing and mapping, designating enemy strongholds, and spot for naval artillery. In his citation at the end of the campaign, he is credited with "great courage" in completing his orders with no more than twelve machines on station.
49. Samson, *Fights and Flights*, 242–43.
50. Ole Nikolajsen and Bülent Yilmazer, *Ottoman Aviation 1909–1919* (unpublished manuscript), Australian War Museum and Archives, M550862, 49–50.
51. Nikolajsen, *Ottoman Aviation*, 51–55.

Chapter 3. The Dardanelles Naval Campaign

1. See specifically "The Dardanelles Commission Report," found at the National Archives (UK), WO 106/63, 16–19. In addition, in Thomas

Frothingham, *The Naval History of the World War* (Cambridge, MA: Harvard University Press, 1924), 245–48. See also Tim Travers, *Gallipoli 1915* (Stroud, Gloucestershire, UK: Tempus Publishing, 2004), 19–21; and Robin Prior, *Gallipoli* (New Haven, CT: Yale University Press, 2009), 14–15. These are only a few of the numerous accounts.

2. National Archives (UK), WO 106/63, "The Dardanelles Commission Report," 17–18.
3. National Archives (UK), "Dardanelles Commission Report," 17–18.
4. National Archives (UK), "Dardanelles Commission Report," 25–29. See also Frothingham, *Naval History*, 250–52.
5. SHD, Document Z6208, *Consitution de L'aviation*, a report from Mèzeyrac to the Ottoman Minister of Defense on the *Organisation de l'aviation ottomane*. Dated 10 July 1914. Note that according to his report, the Ottomans at the time had four pilots but no planes.
6. Général Louis de Goÿs de Mèzeyrac, writing in the preface to the translation of René Martel's, *L'aviation Française de Bombardement* (Paris: Paul Hartmann, 1939). René Martel, *French Strategic and Tactical Bombardment Forces in World War I* (Lanham, MD: Scarecrow Press, 2007), trans. by Allen Suddaby, xiv–xvi.
7. Martel, *French Strategic*, xvi.
8. Winston Churchill, *The World Crisis, 1915* (New York: Charles Scribner's Sons, 1929), 32–37.
9. Jeffery Wallin, *By Ships Alone: Churchill and the Dardanelles* (Durham, NC: Carolina Academic Press, 1981), especially chap. IV in which Churchill and Sir John French argue over the composition of the Dardanelles forces at the expense of the BEF in France. See also Cecil Aspinall-Oglander, *Military Operations Gallipoli*, from the series *History of the Great War* (London: Imperial War Museum, 1929), vol. 1, 39–62, for the entire discussion of the best methods for attacking the Ottoman Empire.
10. David Brown, *The Grand Fleet: Warship Design and Development 1906–1922* (Annapolis, MD: Naval Institute Press, 1999), 76–77.
11. National Archives (UK), AIR 30/45. See also John Clark-Hall, *Air Marshal Sir Robert Clark-Hall, K.B.E., C.M.G., D.S.O.: Autobiographical and Biographical Reminiscences* (Amberley, New Zealand: The Raven Press, 1995), 57–59.

12. Henry Jones, *The War in the Air, The Official History of the War* (Oxford: Oxford University Press, 1928), vol. II, 9–11. See also, *Jane's Fighting Aircraft of World War I* (London: Random House, 1919; 1990), and *Jane's Encyclopedia of Aviation* (London: Random House, 1989). See also Richard Layman, "Over the Wine-Dark Sea, Aerial Aspects of the Dardanelles/Gallipoli Campaign" in *Over the Front* 9, no. 1 (Spring 1994), where he gives an account of the types and Admiralty procurement numbers of the planes for the *Ark Royal.*
13. National Archives (UK), AIR 1/2099/207/20/7, "Dardanelles Operations, Reports from the H.M.S. Ark Royal," 2. See also John Bruce, *British Aeroplanes 1914–18* (London: Putnam, 1957), 712–13. The only successful flight was a reconnaissance by Flight Lieutenant Bromet and Flight Commander Williamson.
14. Jones, *War in the Air*, 11–12.
15. Flanagan, Brian, "The History of the Ottoman Air Force in the Great War, the Reports of Maj. Erich Serno," in *Cross and Cockade Journal* 11, no. 2 (Summer 1970), 97–114. See also BAMA Serno's Reports.
16. Flanagan, "The History of the Ottoman Air Force."
17. Layman, "Over the Wine Dark Sea."
18. Aspinall-Oglander, *Military Operations Gallipoli*, vol. 1, 77–78.
19. Jones, *War in the Air*, 7.
20. National Archives (UK), "Dardanelles Operations, Reports from the H.M.S. Ark Royal," 2.
21. Jones, *War in the Air*, 12–13. See also National Archives (UK), "Dardanelles Operations, Reports from the H.M.S. Ark Royal," 2–3, 5–7.
22. Jones, *War in the Air*, 13. Also National Archives (UK), "Dardanelles Operations, Report from the H.M.S Ark Royal," 2–3.
23. Aspinall-Oglander, *Military Operations Gallipoli*, vol. 1, 73.
24. See specifically Aspinall-Oglander, *Military Operations Gallipoli*, vol. 1, 66.
25. National Archives (UK), "Dardanelles Operations, Report from the H.M.S Ark Royal," 3.
26. Aspinall-Oglander, *Military Operations Gallipoli*, vol. 1, 78–80.
27. Aspinall-Oglander, *Military Operations Gallipoli*, vol. 2, 83–84. The author writes "Constantinople."

28. National Archives (UK), "Dardanelles Operations, Report from the H.M.S Ark Royal," 3.
29. National Archives (UK), "Dardanelles Operations," 3.
30. National Archives (UK), "Dardanelles Operations," 3–4.
31. National Archives (UK), "Dardanelles Operations," 4. See also Jones, *War in the Air*, 17.
32. National Archives (UK), "Dardanelles Operations, Report from the H.M.S Ark Royal," 4, 9. See also Jones, *War in the Air*, 17–18.
33. National Archives (UK), AIR 1/669/17/122/788, no page numbers listed, telegram from Carden to the Admiralty requesting more planes (dated 25 February 1915) and a response dated the same day that two planes were on the way and, "Further reinforcements will be arranged in almost a fortnight's time."
34. Samson, *Fights and Flights* (Nashville, TN: Battery Press, 1990), 209–10. See also Jones, *War in the Air*, 23–24.
35. SHD, Dossier Administratif, Cesari, Antoine, page not numbered.
36. Jones, *War in the Air*, 18–20.
37. Wallin, *By Ships Alone*, 158–59. Aspinall-Oglander, *Military Operations Gallipoli*, 93–94.
38. See specifically Thomas Frothingham, *The Naval History of the World War*, (Cambridge, UK: Harvard University Press, 1924), 278–80.
39. Carl Mühlmann, *Der Kampf um die Dardanellen, 1915* (Oldenburg, Germany: Stalling, 1927), vol. 16 in the German official history of the World War, 71–72. See also Kevin Fewster, Vecihi Başarin, and Hatice Başarin, *Gallipoli, The Turkish Story* (Crows Nest, New South Wales, Australia: Allen and Unwin, 2003), 49–55.
40. National Archives (UK), "Dardanelles Operations, Report from the H.M.S Ark Royal," 17–18.
41. National Archives (UK), "Dardanelles Operations," 18.
42. Guépratte, *L'Expédition des Dardanelles*, 75–78. See also Frothingham, *Naval History*, 280–81.
43. Frothingham, *Naval History*, 281–82.
44. Flanagan, "The History of the Ottoman Air Force," see also BAMA Serno's Reports.
45. Flanagan, "History."

46. Flanagan, "History." See also Avci, Cenk, *Canakkale Cephesi'nde Hava Savaslari* (Ankara, Turkey: Genelkurmay Basimevi, 2009), 31.
47. Frothingham, "History of the Ottoman Air Force," 283.

Chapter 4. The Landings

1. Thomas Frothingham, *The Naval History of the World War*, vol. 1 (Cambridge, UK: Cambridge University Press, 1924), 283–84.
2. Frothingham, *Naval History*, 283.
3. Liman von Sanders, *Fünf Jahre Türkei* (Berlin: Scherl, 1919), 77. Translated as *Five Years in Turkey* (Nashville, TN: Battery Press, 2000).
4. Sanders, *Five Years in Turkey*, 58.
5. Sanders, *Five Years in Turkey*, 61.
6. Nikolajsen, Ole and Bülent Yilmazer, *Ottoman Aviation, 1909–1919*, 51–53. See also Flanagan, "The History of the Ottoman Air Force in the Great War, Reports of Major Erich Serno," in *Cross and Cockade Journal*, (vol. 11, No. 2, Summer 1970), as well as BAMA Serno Reports.
7. Nikolajsen, *Ottoman Aviation*, 49. Captain Erich Serno was given the rank of major in the Turkish forces. See also Edward Erickson, *Ordered to Die: A History of the Ottoman Army in the First World War* (Westport, CT: Greenwood Press, 2001), 228.
8. Nikolajsen, *Ottoman Aviation*, 51. See also Avci, Cenk, *Canakkale Cephesi'nde Hava Savaslari* (Ankara, Turkey: Genelkurmay Basimevi, 2009), 41. Avci reports four air bases, a land and a seaplane base at Çanakkale, the airplanes at Galata, and a fourth base at Kocacay. The last cannot be confirmed from the German sources.
9. Flanagan, "The History of the Ottoman Air Force," see also BAMA Serno's Reports.
10. Henry Jones, *The War in the Air, The Official History of the War*, vol. 1, (London: Hamish Hamilton, 1928), 28. See also Richard Layman, "Over the Wine-Dark Sea: Aerial Aspects of the Dardanelles/Gallipoli Campaign," (Part 1), in *Over the Front* 9, no. 1 (Spring 1994), 22.
11. Layman, "Over the Wine-Dark Sea," 22. See also Jones, *War in the Air*, 28, who lists the equipment as a "small folding Goertz-Anschutz camera."
12. Jones, *War in the Air*, 29.
13. Samson, *Fights and Flights*, 227.

14. Samson, *Fights and Flights*, 229.
15. Samson, *Fights and Flights*, 229.
16. Samson, *Fights and Flights*, 229.
17. Jones, *War in the Air*, 31.
18. National Archives (UK), AIR 1/2099/207/20/7, *Dardanelles Operations, Reports from the H.M.S. Ark Royal*, 12.
19. National Archives (UK), *Dardanelles Operations*, 25, 26.
20. National Archives (UK), *Dardanelles Operations*, 26.
21. Imperial War Museum Archives (hereafter IWM), Records Group 12080, File 33, Samson, Private Papers, Flying Log, no page number.
22. Samson, *Fights and Flights*, 230.
23. Edward Erickson, *Gallipoli: The Ottoman Campaign* (Barnsley, UK: Pen and Sword, 2010), 32.
24. Erickson, *Gallipoli*, 40.
25. Samson, *Fights and Flights*, 230.
26. John Robertson, *Anzac and Empire* (Port Melbourne, Australia: Hamlyn Australia, 1990), 68–70.
27. National Archives (UK), *Dardanelles Operations, Reports from H.M.S. Ark Royal*, 28.
28. National Archives (UK), *Dardanelles Operations*.
29. Jones, *War in the Air*, 47–48.
30. Jones, *War in the Air*, 36. See also Alan Moorehead, *Gallipoli* (New York: Harper and Brothers, 1956), 140–42 as well as Cecil Aspinall-Oglander, *Military Operations Gallipoli* (Nashville, TN: Battery Press, 1992), vol. I. Originally published in the *History of the Great War* series (London: Imperial War Museum, 1929), 201–56.
31. IWM, Squadron Flying Log, 25 April 1915.
32. Samson, *Fights and Flights*, 231. "I thought the landing would be impossible."
33. Samson, *Fights and Flights*, 233.
34. IWM Squadron Flying Log, 25 April 1915. Samson recalls six squadron flights in his memoirs (237), but the flying log lists seven planes flying that day. Three flights each by Maurice Farman No. 1, Maurice Farman No. 1241, Maurice Farman No. 2, and Henri Farman No. 1. Henri Farman No. 3 flew two flights and the BE2c and Henri Farman No. 2 flew once each. No. 50 (BE2a) did not fly that day.

35. Samson, *Fights and Flights*, 236.
36. Samson, *Fights and Flights*, 237.
37. IWM Squadron Flying Log, 25 April 1915.
38. Jones, *War in the Air*, 36.
39. Jones, *War in the Air*, 36–38.
40. See specifically *Dardanelles Operations, Reports from Ark Royal*, 30, 34, 39; end of month reports for March, April, and May. Clark-Hall reports lack of pilots, awaiting spares and equipment, and requests more aircraft. See also *Letter from Wing Commander C.R. Samson to Commodore Sueter, Dated 2 May 1915* (National Archives [UK], AIR 1/361), reprinted in *Documents Relating to the Naval Air Service*, vol. I, (London: Navy Records Society, 1969), 205–6.
41. *Dardanelles Operations, Reports from Ark Royal*, 28, 37.
42. IWM Squadron Flying Log, 29 April 1915.
43. Samson, *Fights and Flights*, 238.
44. As mentioned in *Dardanelles Operations, Reports from Ark Royal*, 28. Clark-Hall reported on 27 April, "The General signaled that seaplane being up keeps the enemies' gunfire down." Samson in *Fights and Flights* recounted that "the Asiatic [side of the Dardanelles] fire always died down whenever an aeroplane was up" on 240.
45. Samson, *Fights and Flights*, 238. This author visited the site in 2010, and after some searching (there is no marker) found what is at best guess the location.
46. Samson, *Fights and Flights*, 238.
47. As cited in Samson, *Fights and Flights*, 238, as well as seen from the ground—from both sides. From the landing field the location of the wartime Turk emplacement at Achi Baba can be seen clearly; from Achi Baba the location of the airfield is quite clear.
48. Alan Moorehead, *Gallipoli*, (New York: Harper and Brothers, 1956), 233.
49. Probably Flight Lieutenant Thomson and Major Hogg's two-and-a-half-hour reconnaissance and bombing flight in Maurice Farman No. 1241. IWM, Squadron Flying Log, for 30 March 1915.
50. Samson, *Fights and Flights*, 239. The flights most likely included: Samson in No. 50, Flight Commander Collet and Lieutenant Isaac in Maurice Farman No. 1241, Flight Commander Osmund and Midshipman

St. Aubry in BE2c No. 1, and Squadron Commander Davies and Midshipman Sissmore in Maurice Farman No.1. Although Samson says in his memoirs he was on the flight, the flight logs do not support this claim. IWM, Squadron Flying Log, 30 March 1915.

51. Samson, *Fights and Flights*, 239.
52. SHD, Document 1P23098 (15), *Dossier Administratif, Cesari, Antoine*, page not numbered. Date of command was 10 March 1915, the squadron arrived at Tenedos the first week of May.
53. Samson, *Fights and Flights*, 242.
54. Samson, *Fights and Flights*, 243.
55. French Penguin aircraft. The clipped-wing aircraft could taxi and fly to heights of about 50 feet, but were unsuitable as anything but trainers, and known as "birds that could not fly."
56. Nikolajsen, *Ottoman Aviation*, 45.
57. Samson, *Fights and Flights*, 239–40. Samson's memory cannot be confirmed by either the Turkish records or 3 Squadron's flight logs; the incident was not recorded in either of the official records.
58. National Archives (UK), "Dardanelles Operations, Reports from Ark Royal," 29.
59. BAMA Serno's Reports. See also Flanagan, "The History of the Ottoman Air Force."

Chapter 5. Summer over Gallipoli

1. See specifically William Puleston, *The Dardanelles Expedition* (Annapolis, MD: Naval Institute Press, 1927), 98.
2. Puleston, *Dardanelles Expedition*.
3. IWM, Squadron Flying Log, no page numbers, Squadron Flying Log Book for 1–14 May. Of the 124 recorded flights, 69 were for bombing or spotting.
4. Alan Moorehead, *Gallipoli* (New York: Harper and Brothers, 1956), 171.
5. Roy Jenkins, *Churchill, A Biography* (New York: Farrar, Straus, and Giroux, 2001), 282–88.
6. Roger Keyes, *The Fight for Gallipoli* (London: Eyre and Spottiswoode, 1941), 152–53.

7. Paul Halpern, *The Naval War in the Mediterranean, 1914–1918* (Annapolis, MD: Naval Institute Press, 1987), 106.
8. Halpern, *Naval War*, 114.
9. Ole Nikolajsen and Bülent Yilmazer, *Ottoman Aviation 1909–1919*, unpublished, Australian War Museum and Archives, M550862, 60.
10. Peter Shankland and Anthony Hunter, *Dardanelles Patrol, the Incredible Story of the E.11* (London: Granada Press, 1971).
11. Nikolajsen, *Ottoman Aviation*, 60.
12. Samson, Charles Rumney, *Fights and Flights*, (Nashville, TN: Battery Press, 1990), 223–34.
13. SHD, 16N2892 (1), *de Commandant de Goys de Mèzeyrac, Chef du 1er Groupe de Bombardement au Chef du Service Aéronautique*, dated March 1914. In the letter to the GHQ he states that a sustained bombing campaign to be carried out by his squadron could force the Turks to capitulate.
14. IWM, Squadron Flying Log, for 15–17 May 1915.
15. Samson, *Fights and Flights*, 241.
16. Henry Jones, *The War in the Air: The Official History of the War*, vol. 1 (London: Hamish Hamilton, 1928), 50–51.
17. Jones, *War in the Air*.
18. Jones, *War in the Air*, 51.
19. Samson, *Fights and Flights*, 242.
20. Jones, *War in the Air*, 51.
21. Cecil Aspinall-Oglander, *Military Operations Gallipoli*, vol. 1 (Nashville, TN: Battery Press, 1992). Originally published in the *History of the Great War* series, (London: Imperial War Museum, 1929), 37–38.
22. National Archives (UK), AIR 1/2099/207/20/7, "Dardanelles Operations, Reports from H.M.S. Ark Royal," 45.
23. John Clark-Hall, *Air Marshal Sir Robert Clark-Hall, K.B.E., C.M.G., D.S.O.: Autobiographical and Biographical Reminiscences* (Amberley, New Zealand: Raven Press, 1995), 79.
24. Samson, *Fights and Flights*, 243.
25. Samson, *Fights and Flights*, 243–44.
26. IWM, Squadron Flying Log, 29 May 1915. See also Samson, *Fights and Flights*, 245.
27. Samson, *Fights and Flights*, 235–36.

28. Jones, *War in the Air*, 53–54.
29. Samson, *Fights and Flights*, 246.
30. Jones, *War in the Air*, 55; Samson, *Fights and Flights*, 247.
31. Samson, *Fights and Flights*, 248.
32. Samson, *Fights and Flights*, 249.
33. Samson, *Fights and Flights*, 249.
34. Samson, *Fights and Flights*, 249.
35. Samson, *Fights and Flights*, 250.
36. IWM, Squadron Flying Log, 22 June 1915. In his memoirs (*Fights and Flights*, 251) Samson writes the 21st, but the squadron flight log records the 22nd.
37. Samson, *Fights and Flights*, 251.
38. Alternately spelled Dessaussois, mentioned in dispatches at the end of the campaign. In his memoirs, Samson never gives the first name of his favorite mechanic in four citations. In the dispatch he is listed as Chief Petty Officer Edmond Dessaussois (RNAS), O.N. F.1663.
39. Samson, *Fights and Flights*, 251–52.
40. IWM, Squadron Flying Log, 22 June 1915. See also Samson, *Fights and Flights*, 251, Jones, *War in the Air*, 55.
41. IWM, Squadron Flying Log, 4 July 1915.
42. Samson, *Fights and Flights*, 254. Smyrna is modern day Izmir, Turkey.
43. IWM, Squadron Flying Log, see specifically 12–15 July 1915. Barr is recorded in the flying log book, whereas Samson calls him "Ball" in his memoirs, Samson, *Fights and Flights*, 255.
44. See specifically IWM, Squadron Flying Log for 24 July 1915 onward. See also Samson, *Fights and Flights*, 255–58.
45. IWM, Squadron Flying Log, 4 August 1915. The most flights to Imbros were on the 4th, but there were flights back and forth to Tenedos a day before and after the 4th.
46. "On 24 July the Admiralty appointed Sykes . . . with the temporary rank of Colonel, 2nd Commandant, Royal Marines. . . . In order to command RNAS units he was made a Wing Captain in the Royal Navy (O-6) with three years seniority as Captain. He was to assume the position held by Samson, who had been commanding No. 3 Squadron." Eric Ash, *Sir Frederick Sykes and the Air Revolution 1912–1918* (London: Frank Cass, 1999), 78.

47. Ash, *Sir Frederick Sykes*, 77.
48. Ash, *Sir Frederick Sykes*, 77.
49. Ash, *Sir Frederick Sykes*, 77.
50. Samson, *Fights and Flights*, 265.
51. Samson, *Fights and Flights*, 265.
52. Samson, *Fights and Flights*, 265.
53. Samson, *Fights and Flights*, 265.
54. Ash, *Sir Frederick Sykes*, 79–82.
55. Ash, *Sir Frederick Sykes*, 81.

Chapter 6. The Suvla Bay Offensive and the End of the Summer

1. IWM, Number 12080, Squadron Flying Log, in File 33, Samson, Private Papers. No page numbers. See dates 1–5 August 1915.
2. IWM, Number 12080, Squadron Flying Log, Samson. See dates 1–5 August 1915.
3. Tim Travers, *Gallipoli 1915* (Stroud, Gloucestershire, UK: Tempus Publishing, 2003), chaps. 6 ("The Anzac Breakout") and 7 ("Operations at Suvla and the Turkish Reaction").
4. Henry Jones, *The War in the Air: The Official History of the War*, vol. 1, (London: Hamish Hamilton, 1928), 58–59.
5. Jones, *War in the Air*.
6. Jones, *War in the Air*, 59.
7. Jones, *War in the Air*, 59. See also IWM Squadron Flying Log for the 4th and 5th.
8. Jones, *War in the Air*, 59.
9. IWM, Squadron Flying Log, 6 August 1915. See also Jones, *War in the Air*, 59.
10. Richard Davies, *Sailor in the Air* (Barnsley, UK: Pen and Sword, 2008), 126–27.
11. Davies, *Sailor*, 128.
12. Davies, *Sailor*, 129.
13. Travers, *Gallipoli*, 179–98.
14. Edward Erickson, *Gallipoli, the Ottoman Campaign* (Barnsley, UK: Pen and Sword, 2010), 139–83.
15. Erickson, *Gallipoli*. See also Liman von Sanders, *Five Years in Turkey* (Nashville, TN: Battery Press, 2000), 85, as well as the official German

history, Carl Mühlmann, *Der Kampf um die Dardanellen, 1915*, vol. 16 in the German official history of the World War (Oldenburg, Germany: Stalling, 1927), 161.

16. Davies, *Sailor in the Air*, 129.
17. IWM, Squadron Flying Log, 8–9 August 1915.
18. Probably HF.20s. The engine upgrades allowed the planes to fly faster and longer, and carry a small bomb load. Davies, *Sailor*, 129, says 120-horspower engines; Samson, *Fights and Flights*, 258 says 130-horsepower engines.
19. Most likely Nieuport 10s. See specifically Davies, *Sailor*, 129.
20. The Taube was obsolete by the start of the war. However, it was used as a trainer in Germany and sent to peripheral theaters like Gallipoli. It was outclassed by all of the Allied aircraft, but was all that was available.
21. Davies, *Sailor*, 129.
22. Samson, *Fights and Flights*, 258–59.
23. Samson, *Fights and Flights*, 259.
24. Davies, *Sailor*, 125.
25. Samson, *Fights and Flights*, 258.
26. The British Mk IX 14-inch torpedo was designed in 1891 and continued in use with the Royal Navy through the World War. The 14-inch diameter torpedo was 100 inches long (just over 8 feet), with a weight of 722 pounds. It was designed to be released 600–1,000 yards from the target, and ran at 26 knots. It was fitted with a 90-pound (gunpowder) warhead.
27. Jones, *War in the Air*, 64.
28. As cited in Ian Burns, "Over the Wine-Dark Sea: Aerial Aspects of the Dardanelles/Gallipoli Campaign, Part Two, Operations of the *HMS Ben-my-Chree*, June 1915-January 1916," in *Over the Front* 9, no. 2 (Summer 1994).
29. Jones, *War in the Air*, 64–65, see also Burns, "Over the Wine-Dark Sea."
30. Samson, *Fights and Flights*, 259.
31. Samson, *Fights and Flights*, 259–62.
32. Samson, *Fights and Flights*, 262. See also Davies, *Sailor in the Air*, 130. The Albert Medal was a British decoration for heroism in lifesaving; it has been superceded by the George Cross.

33. Ole Nikolajsen and Bülent Yilmazer, *Ottoman Aviation 1909–1919* (unpublished manuscript), Australian War Museum and Archives, M550862, 64. The "large formation" was mostly French aircraft, but included one or two 3 Wing planes.
34. Nikolajsen and Yilmazer, *Ottoman Aviation*, 56. Some of the planes went to Gallipoli, most were kept at Yeşilköy for training and missions there.
35. Nikolajsen and Yilmazer, *Ottoman Aviation*, 55. The Rumpler B.1 flew at a maximum speed of 90 mph. The LVG B.1 was similar to the Rumpler, with the same engine, but slower at only 65 mph. The Albatros C.1 was a substantial upgrade to the previous models, with a Mercedes D.III engine, rated at 160-horsepower and capable of over 80 miles per hour. The significant improvement was a Parabellum MG 14 machine gun in the rear cockpit for the observer, attached to a ring mount that allowed the observer to fire at targets to the rear, above, and below. See also BAMA, Serno's Reports.
36. Nikolajsen and Yilmazer, *Ottoman Aviation*, 73–74. The authors painstakingly record the number of aircraft available to the Turks, as well as their dates of service.
37. IWM, Squadron Flying Log, dates for end of August 1915.
38. This was studied extensively after the war—see specifically the (U.S.) National Advisory Committee for Aeronautics (NACA) reports 103 and 108. At the time there were no scientific studies of the phenomenon, but suffice it to say that the pilots understood that when it got too hot they simply could not fly.
39. The Morane-Saulnier L was pre-war vintage, first flown in August 1913, and completely outclassed by summer 1915 on the Western Front. However, it proved useful in Gallipoli as an observation platform.
40. Samson, *Fights and Flights*, 264.
41. Jones, *War in the Air*, 63.
42. Jones, *War in the Air*, 63.
43. Jones, *War in the Air*, 63–64.
44. Davies, *Sailor*, 133.
45. Davies, *Sailor*, 133.
46. Samson, *Fights and Flights*, 265.
47. Jones, *War in the Air*, 68–69.
48. IWM, Squadron Flying Log, 31 August 1915.

Chapter 7. Autumn over Gallipoli

1. Ole Nikolajsen and Bülent Yilmazer, *Ottoman Aviation 1909–1919*, (unpublished manuscript), Australian War Museum and Archives, M550862, 55, 64. See also BAMA, Serno's Reports, as well as Brian Flanagan, "The History of the Ottoman Air Force in the Great War: The Reports of Major Erich Serno," in *Cross and Cockade* 11, no. 2 (Winter 1970).
2. Nikolajsen and Yilmazer, *Ottoman Aviation*, 56, 64, 74.
3. Nikolajsen and Yilmazer, *Ottoman Aviation*, 73–74.
4. IWM, Squadron Flying Log, dated 5 and 6 September. See also Charles Rumney Samson, *Fights and Flights* (Nashville, TN: Battery Press, 1990), 266.
5. IWM, Squadron Flying Log, 8 September 1915. See also Samson, *Fights and Flights*, 266.
6. IWM, Squadron Flying Log, 18 September 1915. See also Samson, *Fights and Flights*, 267.
7. Samson, *Fights and Flights*, 267.
8. Aspinall-Oglander, Cecil, *Military Operations Gallipoli*, Volume 1 (Nashville, TN: The Battery Press, 1992). Originally published in the "History of the Great War," series (London: Imperial War Museum, 1929), 375–76.
9. IWM, Squadron Flying Log, 21 September 1915.
10. Samson, *Fights and Flights*, 268–70. See also Henry Jones, *The War in the Air: The Official History of the War*, vol. 1 (London: Hamish Hamilton, 1928), 71. It is noteworthy that Richard Layman in his short article "Samson vs. Kemal: Did it really Happen?" in *Over the Front* 9, no. 1 (Spring 1994), 39–40, questions the events. Although Samson's memoirs and Jones recount the event, Patrick Balfour (Lord Kinross) in his biography of Kemal *Attaturk: A Biography of Mustafa Kemal, Father of Modern Turkey* (London: Quill, 1992; reprint) does not mention the event. Layman ends his argument with the statement, "Readers may draw their own conclusions."
11. Nikolajsen and Yilmazer, *Ottoman Aviation*, 65 and IWM, Squadron Flying Log for the month of September.
12. Nikolajsen and Yilmazer, *Ottoman Aviation*, 65.

13. IWM, Squadron Flying Log, September 1915.
14. Nikolajsen and Yilmazer, *Ottoman Aviation*, 65. See also IWM, Squadron Flying Log for 27 September 1915. The Flying Log lists Samson's flight as a "Taube Chase," most likely the plane that contacted the Albatros, and Davies' flight as "Taube Patrol" indicating that it could have been his flight instead. Either way, the Albatros was misidentified as a (Rumpler) Taube.
15. Nikolajsen and Yilmazer, *Ottoman Aviation*, 65.
16. Nikolajsen and Yilmazer, *Ottoman Aviation*, 65.
17. Jones, *War in the Air*, 73. See also George Cassar, *The French and the Dardanelles* (London: George Allen and Unwin, 1971), 203–5.
18. Jones, *War in the Air*, 73.
19. Alan Moorehead, *Gallipoli* (New York: Harper and Brothers, 1956), 303–04.
20. Alan Moorehead, *Gallipoli*, 313.
21. IWM, Squadron Flying Log, October 1915.
22. Samson, *Fights and Flights*, 274.
23. Samson, *Fights and Flights*, 274.
24. IWM, Squadron Flying Log, 10 November 1915.
25. Samson, *Fights and Flights*, 275.
26. Samson, *Fights and Flights*, 275–76.
27. Samson, *Fights and Flights*, 276.
28. IWM, Squadron Flying Log, 13 November 1915. See also Samson, *Fights and Flights*, 275–76.
29. Samson, *Fights and Flights*, 277.
30. Samson, *Fights and Flights*, 278–79.
31. IWM, Squadron Flying Log, 19 November 1915.
32. Richard Davies, *Sailor in the Air* (Barnsley, UK: Pen and Sword, 2008), 134–35.
33. *London Gazette*, 1 January 1916.
34. IWM, Squadron Flying Log, November 1915.
35. Roger Keyes, *The Fight for Gallipoli* (London: Eyre and Spottiswoode, 1941), 294.
36. Keyes, *Fight for Gallipoli*, 294.
37. Samson, *Fights and Flights*, 283.

38. IWM, Squadron Flying Log, 1 December 1915. Samson continually refers to the enemy planes as "Taubes" although the Turks had not been flying that model since March of that year.
39. IWM, Squadron Flying Log, 2 December 1915. See also Samson, *Fights and Flights*, 283.
40. IWM, Squadron Flying Log, 2 December 1915. In the margins is a note that the bombers hit lighters alongside the port facilities.
41. Samson, *Fights and Flights*, 283–84.
42. Samson *Fights and Flights*, 284, records a 100-pound bomb, the IWM, Squadron Flying Log for the day note a 60-pound bomb.
43. Samson, *Fights and Flights*, 284.
44. Tim Travers, *Gallipoli 1915* (Stroud, UK: Tempus Publishing, 2001), 277.

Chapter 8. The Evacuation and the End of the Gallipoli Campaign

1. Charles Bean, "The Story of ANZAC," vol. 2 in *The Official History of Australia in the War of 1914–1918* (St. Lucia, Queensland, Australia: University of Queensland Press, 1981), 867.
2. Bean, "Story of ANZAC," 2:867.
3. BAMA, Serno's Reports; see also Brian Flanagan, "The History of the Ottoman Air Force in the Great War: The Reports of Major Erich Serno," in *Cross and Cockade* 11, no. 2 (Winter 1970).
4. Richard Layman, "Over the Wine-Dark Sea: Aerial Aspects of the Dardanelles/Gallipoli Campaign, Part One," in *Over the Front* 9, no. 1 (Spring 1994), 5–40.
5. Layman, "Over the Wine-Dark Sea," 5–40.
6. Layman, "Over the Wine-Dark Sea," 5–40.
7. Ole Nikolajsen and Bülent Yilmazer, *Ottoman Aviation 1909–1919*, (unpublished manuscript), Australian War Museum and Archives, M550862, 74. The Fokker E.I was the latest aerial weapon in the German inventory, an air superiority fighter with a synchronized machine gun that fired through the propeller arc. It was the first true fighter airplane. See also Richard Whistler, "Over the Wine-Dark Sea: Aerial Aspects of the Dardanelles/Gallipoli Campaign, Part Five, The Defense of the Bosphorus and the *Fokker Staffel*," in *Over the Front* 11, no. 3 (Fall 1996).

8. Nikolajsen and Yilmazer, *Ottoman Aviation*, 74.
9. IWM, Squadron Flying Log, see specifically 9 to 19 December 1915.
10. Tim Travers, *Gallipoli 1915* (Stroud, Gloucestershire, UK: Tempus Publishing, 2003), 279.
11. Charles Rumney Samson, *Fights and Flights*, (Nashville, TN: Battery Press, 1990), 285.
12. IWM, Squadron Flying Log, 16 December 1915. See also Nikolajsen and Yilmazer, *Ottoman Aviation*, 68, 74.
13. Nikolajsen and Yilmazer, *Ottoman Aviation*, 68.
14. Nikolajsen and Yilmazer, *Ottoman Aviation*, 68, as well as IWM, Squadron Flying Log, 16 to 20 December 1915.
15. IWM, Squadron Flying Log, 19 December 1915.
16. IWM, Squadron Flying Log, 20 December 1915.
17. Samson, *Fights and Flights*, 286.
18. Bean, "Story of ANZAC," 2: 905.
19. IWM, Squadron Flying Log, 21 to 29 December 1915.
20. Jones, *War in the Air*, 75.
21. Jones, *War in the Air*, 75. See also Nikolajsen, *Ottoman Aviation*, 74.
22. Nikolajsen and Yilmazer, *Ottoman Aviation*, 74.
23. Keyes, Roger, *The Fight for Gallipoli* (London, UK: Eyre and Spottiswoode, 1941), 340.
24. Layman, "Over the Wine-Dark Sea."
25. Jones, *The War in the Air*, 75. See also Nikolajsen and Yilmazer, *Ottoman Aviation*, 74.
26. See Nikolajsen and Yilmazer, *Ottoman Aviation*, 74; see also Jones, *War in the Air*, 75.
27. Jones, *War in the Air*, 75.
28. Samson, *Fights and Flights*, 292–93.
29. Richard Layman, *Naval Aviation in the First World War: Its Impact and Influence* (Barnsley, UK: Chatham Publishing Group, 1996), 153–54.
30. Layman, *Naval Aviation*, 155.
31. Nikolajsen and Yilmazer, *Ottoman Aviation*, 177.
32. Liman von Sanders, *Five Years in Turkey* (Nashville, TN: Battery Press, 2000), 321–25.
33. See for example the excellent biographies from Patrick Balfour (Lord Kinross), *Attaturk: A Biography of Mustafa Kemal, Father of Modern*

Turkey (London: Quill, 1992), and Andrew Mango, *Attatürk* (London: John Murray, 1999).

34. Jones, *War in the Air*, 75.
35. Samson, *Fights and Flights*, 286.

Chapter 9. Campaign Evaluations and Lessons Learned

1. The very few Turkish documents were located in the Ottoman State Archives in Istanbul and the Republic of Turkey State Archives in Ankara.
2. The Imperial German political and economic records were accessed at the Bundesarchiv Berlin-Lichterfeld, especially the names and numbers associated with the German military mission to the Ottoman Empire. The military records of the mission were found at the Bundesarchiv Militärarchiv, BA/MA, in Freiburg, including the two invaluable Erich Serno Reports. Interestingly, they were closed until 1968 and this researcher was still (in 2018) not able to photograph them.
3. BA/MA (Freiburg) *Kriegtagesbücher Dardanellen* (Daily War Reports—Dardanelles), in the RM 40/6 to /19 collection, recounted the daily reports from the front.
4. BA/MA (Freiburg) MSG 2/10876 and MSG 2/10873. Serno's Reports of his time in the Dardanelles. One written during, one written after the war.
5. BA/MA (Freiburg) MSG 2/10873, Erich Serno, *Sammlung Luftwesen vor 1918*.
6. Carl Mühlmann, *Schlachten des Weltkrieges* (Battles of the World War), vol. 16 in the official history, *Der Kampf um die Dardanellen* (The Fight for the Dardanelles), (Berlin: Oldenburg, 1927).
7. Admiral Émile Paul Amable Guépratte, *L'Expédition des Dardanelles, 1914–1915*, Paris: Payot, 1935.
8. *Service Historique de la Défense, Château de Vincennes*, Paris. Includes two collections in files 16N2135 (82 pp.) and 16N1205D2 (55 pp.) labelled Dardanelles 1 and 2.
9. David Méchin, "Escadrille MF. 98T" accessed in 2018, http://albindenis.free.fr/Site_escadrille/escadrille524.htm.

10. National Archives (UK) (formerly Kew Gardens), AIR 1 files, "*Ark Royal* flying logs" (AIR 1/726/137/2).
11. National Archives (UK), AIR 1/665/17/122/714 and AIR 1/726/137/2.
12. Imperial War Museum in Record Group 12080, File 33, titled "Samson, Private Papers, Flying Log."
13. National Archives (UK), AIR 1/669/17/122/788, Sykes Report.
14. Charles Rumney Samson, *Fights and Flights* (London: Benn, 1930; reprint Nashville, TN: Battery Press, 1990).
15. National Archives (UK), First Report of the Dardanelles Commission, CAB 19/1, 12 February 1917.
16. National Archives (UK), Final Report of the Dardanelles Commission, CAB 19/1, 4 December 1917.
17. National Archives (UK), Final Report, 4 December 1917.
18. Walter Raleigh, *The War in the Air* (London: Hamish Hamilton, 1922); Henry Jones, *The War in the Air, Volume 2* (London: Hamish Hamilton, 1928).
19. Cecil Aspinall-Oglander, *Military Operations Gallipoli*, vol. I (London: Imperial War Museum, 1929).

Bibliography

Archives

Australian War Museum and Archives (AWMA)
Bundesarchiv Lichterfelde (BA-L) Berlin, Germany
Bundesarchiv Militärarchiv (BAMA) Freiburg im Breisgau, Germany
The Imperial War Museum Archives (IWM) London
The National Archives (Kew Gardens), London
Service Historique de la Défense, Château de Vincennes (SHD), Paris

Unpublished Sources

Nikolajsen, Ole, and Bülent Yilmazer. "Ottoman Aviation 1909–1919." Unpublished manuscript, M550862. Australian War Museum and Archives.

Primary Sources

Aspinall-Oglander, Cecil. *Military Operations Gallipoli*. Vol. I. Nashville, TN: Battery Press, 1992. Originally published in the *History of the Great War.* London: Imperial War Museum, 1929.

Bean, Charles. "The Story of ANZAC." In *The Official History of Australia in the War of 1914–1918*. Vol. 2. St. Lucia, Queensland, Australia: University of Queensland Press, 1981.

Jones, Henry. *The War in the Air, The Official History of the War*. 2 vols. London: Hamish Hamilton, 1928.

Mühlmann, Carl. *Der Kampf um die Dardanellen, 1915*. Vol. 16 in *Schlachten des Weltkrieges*, (the German official history of the World War). Oldenburg, Germany: Stalling, 1927.

Raleigh, Walter. *The War in the Air*. Vol. I. London: Hamish Hamilton, 1922.

Roskill, Stephen. *Documents Relating to the Naval Air Service*. Vol. I. London: Navy Records Society, 1969.

Secondary Sources

Ash, Eric. *Sir Frederick Sykes and the Air Revolution 1912–1918*. London: Frank Cass, 1999.

Avci, Cenk. *Canakkale Cephesi'nde Hava Savaslari*. Ankara, Turkey: Genelkurmay Basimevi, 2009.

Balfour, Patrick, Lord Kinross. *Attaturk: A Biography of Mustafa Kemal, Father of Modern Turkey*. London: Quill, 1992. Reprint.

Beehler, W. H. *The History of the Italian-Turkish War*. Annapolis: Proceedings of the United States Naval Institute, 1913.

Bell, Archibald. *A History of the Blockade of Germany and the Countries Associated with Her in the Great War: Austria-Hungary, Bulgaria, and Turkey, 1914–1918*. London: HMSO, 1937.

Best, Geoffrey. *Churchill: A Study in Greatness*. Oxford, UK: Oxford University Press, 2003.

Birdwood, William Riddell. *In My Time: Recollections and Anecdotes*. London: Skeffington, 1946; 1948.

———. *Khaki and Gown: An Autobiography*. New York: Robert Speller & Sons, 1941; 1957.

Blériot, Louis. *Flight into the XXth Century*. London: Austin Macauley, 2015.

Brown, David. *The Grand Fleet: Warship Design and Development 1906–1922*. Annapolis, MD: Naval Institute Press, 1999.

Bruce, John. *British Aeroplanes 1914–18*. London: Putnam, 1957.

Burt, Ray, and W. P. Trotter. *Battleships of the Grand Fleet*. Annapolis, MD: Naval Institute Press, 1982.

Cassar, George. *The French and the Dardanelles*. London: George Allen and Unwin, 1971.

Christienne, Charles, and Pierre Lissarrague. *The History of French Military Aviation*. Translated by Frances Kianka. Washington, DC: Smithsonian Institution Press, 1986.

Churchill, Winston. *The World Crisis, 1915*. New York: Charles Scribner's Sons, 1929.

Clark-Hall, John. *Air Marshal Sir Robert Clark-Hall, K.B.E., C.M.G., D.S.O.: Autobiographical and Biographical Reminiscences*. Amberley, New Zealand: Raven Press, 1995.

Crouch, Tom. *The Bishop's Boys*. New York: W. W. Norton, 2003.

Crowley, Patrick. *Loyal to Empire: The Life of General Sir Charles Munro, 1860–1929*. Stroud, UK: History Press, 2016.

Davies, Richard. *Sailor in the Air*. Barnsley, UK: Pen and Sword, 2008.

De Syon, Guillaume. *Zeppelin! Germany and the Airship, 1900–1939*. Baltimore: Johns Hopkins University Press, 2002.

Driver, Hugh. *The Birth of Military Aviation: Britain, 1903–1914*. London: Royal Historical Society, 1997.

Elliot, Brian. *Blériot: Herald of an Age*. Mount Pleasant, SC: Arcadia, 2000.

Erickson, Edward. *Gallipoli: The Ottoman Campaign*. Barnsley, UK: Pen and Sword, 2010.

———. *Ordered to Die: A History of the Ottoman Army in the First World War*. Westport, CT: Greenwood Press, 2001.

Evans, Charles. *The War of the Aeronauts: A History of Ballooning During the Civil War*. Mechanicsburg, PA: Stackpole, 2002.

Fewster, Kevin, with Vecihi Başarin and Hatice Başarin. *Gallipoli, The Turkish Story*. Crows Nest, New South Wales, Australia: Allen and Unwin, 2003.

Frothingham, Thomas. *The Naval History of the World War*. Cambridge, MA: Harvard University Press, 1924.

Greenhalgh, Elizabeth. *The French Army and the First World War*. Cambridge, UK: Cambridge University Press, 2014.

Guépratte, Paul Emile. *L'Expédition des Dardanelles, 1914–1915*. Paris: Payot, 1935.

Halpern, Paul. *The Naval War in the Mediterranean 1914–1918*. Annapolis, MD: Naval Institute Press, 1987.

Hamilton, Ian. *Gallipoli Diary*. London: E. Arnold, 1920. 2 vols.

———. *Sir Ian Hamilton's Despatches from the Dardanelles, etc.* London: G. Newnes, 1916.

Higham, Robin, John Greenwood, and Von Hardesty, eds. *Russian Airpower in the Twentieth Century*. London: Routledge, 1998.

Jane's Encyclopedia of Aviation. New York: Military Press, 1989.

Jane's Fighting Aircraft of World War I. New York: Military Press, 1919; 1990.

Jenkins, Roy. *Churchill, A Biography*. New York: Farrar, Straus, and Giroux, 2001.

Keyes, Roger. *The Fight for Gallipoli*. London: Eyre and Spottiswoode, 1941.

Layman, Richard. *Naval Aviation in the First World War: Its Impact and Influence*. Barnsley, UK: Chatham, 1996.

Lee, John. *A Soldier's Life: General Sir Ian Hamilton, 1853–1947*. London: Pan, 2001.

Lehmann, Ernst. *Zeppelin: The Story of Lighter-Than-Air Craft*. Stroud, UK: Fonthill, 2015.

Lilienthal, Otto. *Birdflight as the Basis for Aviation*. Hummelstown, PA: Markowski, 2000. Translated from the German original, *Der Vogelflug als Grundlage der Fliegekunst*. Berlin: 1889.

Mango, Andrew. *Attatürk*. London: John Murray, 1999.

Martel, René. *L'Aviation Française de Bombardement*. Paris: Paul Hermann, 1939.

———. *French Strategic and Tactical Bombardment Forces in World War I*. Translated by Allen Suddaby. Lanham, MD: Scarecrow Press, 2007.

Millar, John. *The Soul of Anzac: General Sir William Birdwood and the A.I.F., 1914–1918*. North Melbourne, Australia: Vic Australian Scholarly, 2015.

Miquel, Pierre. *Les Poilus d'Orient*. Paris: Fayard, 1998.

Moorehead, Alan. *Gallipoli*. New York: Harper & Brothers, 1956.

Morrow, John. *The Great War in the Air: Military Aviation from 1909–1921*. Washington, DC: Smithsonian Institution Press, 1993.

Mühlmann, Carl. *Oberste Heeresleitung und Balkan im Weltkrieg*. Berlin: Wilhelm Limpert, 1942.

Olivier, Jean-Marc, ed. *Histoire de L'Armée de L'Air et des Forces Aériennes Françaises du XVIIIe Siécle à nous jours*. Toulouse, France: Éditions Privat, 2014.

Prior, Robin. *Gallipoli*. New Haven, CT: Yale University Press, 2009.

Puleston, William. *The Dardanelles Expedition*. Annapolis, MD: Naval Institute Press, 1927.

Robertson, John. *Anzac and Empire*. Port Melbourne, Australia: Hamlyn Australia, 1990.

Samson, Charles Rumney. *Fights and Flights*. Nashville, TN: Battery Press, 1990.

Sanders, Liman von. *Five Years in Turkey*. Nashville, TN: Battery Press, 2000. Reprint. Translated from Liman von Sanders. *Fünf Jahre Türkei*. Berlin: A. Scherl, 1920.

Shankland, Peter, and Anthony Hunter. *Dardanelles Patrol, the Incredible Story of the E.11*. London: Granada Press, 1971.

Sykes, Frederick. *From Many Angles*. London: G. G. Harrap, 1943.

Travers, Tim. *Gallipoli 1915*. Stroud, UK: Tempus, 2003.

Wallin, Jeffrey. *By Ships Alone: Churchill and the Dardanelles*. Durham, NC: Carolina Academic Press, 1981.

Wells, H. G. *The War in the Air*. London: G. Bell and Sons, 1908.

Journal Articles

Burns, Ian. "Over the Wine-Dark Sea: Aerial Aspects of the Dardanelles/Gallipoli Campaign, Part Two, Operations of the *HMS Ben-my-Chree*, June 1915–January 1916." *Over the Front* 9, no. 2 (Summer 1994).

Flanagan, Brian. "The History of the Ottoman Air Force in the Great War, Reports of Major Erich Serno." *Cross and Cockade* 11, no. 2 (Summer 1970).

Layman, Richard. "Over the Wine-Dark Sea: Aerial Aspects of the Dardanelles/Gallipoli Campaign, Part 1." *Over the Front*. 9, no. 1 (Spring 1994).

———. "Samson vs. Kemal: Did It Really Happen?" *Over the Front* 9, no. 1 (Spring 1994).

Maksel, Rebecca. "The World's First Warplane." *Smithsonian Air and Space Journal* (21 October 2011). http://www.airspacemag.com/daily-planet/the-worlds-first-warplane-115175678/?no-ist=.

"Paris Flight Show." *Flight* I, no. 40 (2 October 1909).

Whistler, Richard. "Over the Wine-Dark Sea: Aerial Aspects of the Dardanelles/Gallipoli Campaign, Part 4: The German Wasserfliegerabteilung." *Over the Front* 11, no. 2 (1996).

———. "Over the Wine-Dark Sea: Aerial Aspects of the Dardanelles/Gallipoli Campaign, Part Five, The Defense of the Bosphorus and the *Fokker Staffel*." *Over the Front*. 11, no. 3 (Fall 1996).

Wright, Peter. "Kite Balloon Observer at Gallipoli." *Cross and Cockade* 23, no. 3 (Autumn 1982).

Index

About the Author

Sterling Michael Pavelec is a professor of airpower history at the Air Command and Staff College, Maxwell AFB, Alabama. He is the author of four books and a number of articles and book chapters on airpower, technology, space, and cyber. When not writing or teaching he is out on his motorcycle exploring.

The Naval Institute Press is the book-publishing arm of the U.S. Naval Institute, a private, nonprofit, membership society for sea service professionals and others who share an interest in naval and maritime affairs. Established in 1873 at the U.S. Naval Academy in Annapolis, Maryland, where its offices remain today, the Naval Institute has members worldwide.

Members of the Naval Institute support the education programs of the society and receive the influential monthly magazine *Proceedings* or the colorful bimonthly magazine *Naval History* and discounts on fine nautical prints and on ship and aircraft photos. They also have access to the transcripts of the Institute's Oral History Program and get discounted admission to any of the Institute-sponsored seminars offered around the country.

The Naval Institute's book-publishing program, begun in 1898 with basic guides to naval practices, has broadened its scope to include books of more general interest. Now the Naval Institute Press publishes about seventy titles each year, ranging from how-to books on boating and navigation to battle histories, biographies, ship and aircraft guides, and novels. Institute members receive significant discounts on the Press' more than eight hundred books in print.

Full-time students are eligible for special half-price membership rates. Life memberships are also available.

For a free catalog describing Naval Institute Press books currently available, and for further information about joining the U.S. Naval Institute, please write to:

Member Services
U.S. Naval Institute
291 Wood Road
Annapolis, MD 21402-5034
Telephone: (800) 233-8764
Fax: (410) 571-1703
Web address: www.usni.org